Building on Bion: Roots

The International Library of Group Analysis
Edited by Malcolm Pines, Institute of Group Analysis, London
The aim of this series is to represent innovative work in group psychotherapy, particularly but not exclusively, group analysis. Group analysis, taught and practised widely in Europe, derives from the work of SH Foulkes.

other titles in the series

Building on Bion: Branches
Contemporary Developments and Applications of Bion's Contributions to Theory and Practice
Edited by Robert Lipgar and Malcolm Pines
ISBN 1 84310 711 2
International Library of Group Analysis 21

Dreams in Group Psychotherapy
Theory and Technique
Edited by Claudio Neri, Malcolm Pines and Robi Friedman
ISBN 1 85302 923 8
International Library of Group Analysis 18

Bion and Group Psychotherapy
Edited by Malcolm Pines
ISBN 1 85302 924 6
International Library of Group Analysis 15

Rediscovering Groups
A Psychoanalyst's Journey Beyond Individual Psychology
Marshall Edelson and David N. Berg
ISBN 1 85302 726 X pb
ISBN 1 85302 725 1 hb
International Library of Group Analysis 9

Group
Claudio Neri
ISBN 1 85302 416 3
International Library of Group Analysis 8

Self Experiences in Group
Intersubjective and Self-Psychological Pathways to Human Understanding
Edited by Irene N.H. Harwood and Malcolm Pines
ISBN 1 85302 587 6 pb
ISBN 1 85302 596 8 hb
International Library of Group Analysis 4

Group Psychotherapy of the Psychoses
Concepts, Interventions and Contexts
Edited by Victor L. Schermer and Malcolm Pines
ISBN 1 85302 584 4 pb
ISBN 1 85302 583 6 hb
International Library of Group Analysis 2

Circular Reflections
Selected Papers on Group Analysis and Psychoanalysis
Malcolm Pines
ISBN 1 85302 492 9 pb
ISBN 1 85302 493 7 hb
International Library of Group Analysis 1

INTERNATIONAL LIBRARY OF GROUP ANALYSIS 20

Building on Bion: Roots

Origins and Context of Bion's Contributions to Theory and Practice

Edited by Robert M. Lipgar and Malcolm Pines

Jessica Kingsley Publishers
London and New York

The right of the contributors to be identified as authors of this work has been asserted by them in accordance with the Copyright, Designs and Patents Act 1988.

First published in the United Kingdom in 2003
by Jessica Kingsley Publishers Ltd
116 Pentonville Road
London N1 9JB, England
and
29 West 35th Street, 10th fl.
New York, NY 10001-2299

www.jkp.com

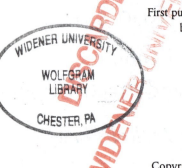

Copyright ©2003 Jessica Kingsley Publishers

Library of Congress Cataloging-in-Publication Data
Building on Bion—roots : origins and context of Bion's contributions to theory and practice / edited by Robert M. Lipgar and Malcolm Pines.
 p. cm. -- (International library of group analysis ; 20)
Includes bibliographical references and index.
ISBN 1-84310-710-4 (pbk. :alk. paper)
 1. Psychoanalysis. 2. Group psychoanalysis. 3. Bion, Wilfred R. (Wilfred Ruprecht), 1897-1979. I. Lipgar, Robert, M., 1928- II. Pines, Malcolm. III. Series.

BF173.B8775 2002
150.19'092--dc21   2002073972

British Library Cataloguing in Publication Data
A CIP catalogue record for this book is available from the British Library

ISBN 1 84310 710 4

Printed and Bound in Great Britain by
Athenaeum Press, Gateshead, Tyne and Wear

Contents

Part II: Bion's Context: Contemporaries and Refinements

Preface

In composing these two volumes, *Building on Bion: Roots* and *Building on Bion: Branches*, we wanted to bring you, the reader, closer to the extraordinary depth and breadth of Wilfred Bion's thought and influence. Our interest in advancing the exploration of the full range of human concerns that preoccupied him was particularly stimulated in Turin, Italy, during the International Centennial Conference on the Work and Life of Wilfred Bion, July 1997. We were impressed there with the relevance and quality of new work being done that extended and enlivened themes Bion had spent a lifetime developing. It was clear that his life and work was having far-reaching influence. Since so many contemporary analysts, theorists, and teachers in different disciplines are working with his insights, we wanted to further the examination of the roots of his genius as well as the many branches of his legacy.

Our plan was to bring together some of the best visions and re-visions building on Bion's writings. With the benefit of the Internet as well as our ability to participate in a number of international gatherings of psychoanalysts, group analysts, psychologists and organizational consultants, we are able now to present new work by authors from Italy, France, Argentina, Brazil, the United States, as well as Great Britain. Collecting these papers seemed to take on a life of its own, perhaps in Bion's spirit, and these volumes found their own shapes. Quite literally, Bion's work was international, and consistent with this we wanted to advance diverse dialogues international in scope. In both volumes, readers will meet clinicians and theorists, individual and group analysts, psychiatrists, psychologists and other social scientists from different countries – men and women with different intellectual and professional backgrounds sharing their encounters with Bion and his work, offering us insights into Bion's vision as well as their own discoveries and re-visions. We believe you will find in these volumes Bion's own passion for learning and profound commitment to psychoanalysis and its pertinence to human survival and development.

Volume I, *Building on Bion: Roots,* explores formative influences affecting Bion's emotional and intellectual development – the roots of his brilliance in the spring of his career. Battlefield experiences in World War I, as well as influences of Kant, Trotter, Freud and Klein are discussed. In these chapters, there is a particular focus on his early work studying groups and how this exploration relates to the work of other psychoanalysts, particularly Foulkes. Bion's experiences with groups are re-examined so that the spirit and shape of his inquiry can be discovered by those not familiar with his writings and revisited, perhaps rediscovered, by those who feel well acquainted with Bion. In examining the context of Bion's work and especially its relation to Foulkes' theory and practice of group-analysis, we are given a deeper appreciation of both pioneers and a much fuller understanding of both psychoanalysis and group psychology.

The second volume, *Building on Bion: Branches,* as the title suggests, explores the growing influence of Bion's work as it is being applied well beyond group psychology and individual psychoanalysis. These chapters show the reach and further development of his theoretical and clinical explorations. Specifically, there are applications in areas of leadership, organizational consultation, experiential learning as well as psychoanalysis. Also in Volume II there are chapters relating Bion's work to that of other geniuses such as the pianist Glenn Gould and the psychologist/research methodologist William Stephenson. The authors of these chapters bring us Bion's originality and passion as he sought the distinctive essence of psychoanalytic learning and how such a pursuit and such learning can be shared and advanced. We meet a spiritual Bion, a scientific Bion, and Bion apprehending Beauty. We encounter Bion's formative personal and intellectual journeys in Volume I; the branches (and blossoms) of his insights and interests are in Volume II: Part 1 Working with Groups; Part 2 Application – Putting Bion's Ideas to Work; Part 3 Bion as Pioneer in Thinking, Learning and Transmitting Knowledge.

Robert M. Lipgar and Malcolm Pines

Introduction

Early Bion[1]

James S. Grotstein

The remarkable double life of Bion

Wilfred R. Bion's reputation as a profound thinker and analytic contributor continues to grow posthumously. An autodidact and polymath extraordinaire, one who spoke from so many points of view (or 'vertices', as he would idiosyncratically say), such as mathematics, science, poetry (particularly Ovid and Milton), art, philosophy, religion, mysticism, logic, history, etc., he has left us with twin legacies that have never until now, in these two volumes, been brought into a unified synthesis: that of his contributions to the theory of groups and that of his contributions to psychoanalysis. I remember when he first came to Los Angeles in the nineteen-sixties, many group therapists consulted him unaware that he was a psychoanalyst, and psychoanalysts approached him unaware that he had been connected with groups.

Bion, a general psychiatrist before he became a psychoanalyst, had been deeply interested in groups since he was a medical student. His collegial relationship with his former analyst, John Rickman, proved to be foundational for his ideas about groups; not least amongst such ideas was the hope of extending the benefits of psychiatry and psychotherapy to the general public. Thus, Bion was a 'social psychiatrist' prior to becoming a psychoanalyst.

Much has been written about his subsequent alleged 'desertion' of group relations work for individual psychoanalysis because of Melanie Klein's urging. Whether or not that is true, we do not know, but we do know, as many of the contributors to this volume attest, that his views of group relations were

fundamentally enhanced by his new-found understanding of Klein's conceptions of splitting, projective identification, the activities of the paranoid–schizoid and depressive positions, the function of unconscious
phantasy, the manic defenses, the death instinct, and the operations of greed
and envy. What was less well known, at least amongst psychoanalysts, was
that his interest in group psychology continued, albeit as a minor chord, in his
psychoanalytic thinking and resurfaced as a major chord in *Attention and Interpretation* (1970).

Bion, who was so keen on studying lines of authority in his group
relations work, was himself quite a contrast in his professional life. He always
questioned authority – ever since his ambivalent relationship to 'Arf Arfer' (his
infantile name for God) and especially as a tank commander in World War I, in
which he felt so disappointed in the failure of his commanders back at head-
quarters to comprehend the battle situation (Bion, 1982. See Sandler, Chapter
2 in Volume 1 for an in-depth study of Bion's war experiences.) In fact, when
Bion came to Los Angeles, he refused to supervise analysts who came to him
for that purpose. He stated that he did not believe in supervision and would
cite his experiences in the war. He agreed only to offer a 'second opinion.'[2]
Actually he was treated badly by 'command' in World War II as well. Bion
apparently had the 'Nelson touch'.[3]

His experiences in World War I were formative for his personality and for
his later ideas about group psychology and psychoanalysis. Dr Paulo Sandler
(this volume) discusses the impact of Bion's war experiences on his later
thinking and makes many correlations between those experiences and
specific psychoanalytic ideas he espoused. One idea in particular is noteworthy, the respect for truth. Truth was later to become part of his metatheory
for psychoanalysis as 'Absolute Truth' and the 'truth instinct,' concepts that
are arguably profounder than Freud's in regard to unconscious mental life.

Bion had become interested in group psychology early on in medical
school largely because of the influence upon him of a surgeon, Wilfred
Trotter. Nuno Torres (Chapter 3 in Volume 1) presents an account of their
relationship and convincingly details how important Trotter's ideas were in
Bion's later thinking, particularly the notion of 'gregariousness.' Torres raises
interesting questions about why Bion may not have cited him more often.
Bion's formal venture into group work seems really to have begun when he
worked on the problem of officer selection while he was attached to the
Scottish Command of the British Army.[4,5] The backdrop of military duty is
very important in understanding Bion's future work with groups, particularly

at Northfield Hospital, where the task was to 're-moralize' troops who had become demoralized in combat.[6] His experiences in the army served as a backdrop for his later work with group relations. His Northfield experience seems to have been unsuccessful (Harrison, 2000), however, and one of the contributors to this present work, Dennis Brown (Chapter 6 in this volume), in speculating on that issue, broadly discusses and compares Bion with Foulkes, who also served at Northfield.

It was clear that his immersion in psychoanalytic training and his training analysis with Klein was to become pivotal for his later thinking about groups. Klein had conceived of a developmental state of mind in the infant that she termed the 'infantile psychosis,'[7] included in which were such categories as regression, projective identification, splitting, and the reversion to the use of omnipotence, amongst others. Bion seems to have instantly grasped the applicability of these ideas for understanding group psychology and revised his earlier conceptions about groups in light of them, i.e., basic assumption groups formed because of persecutory anxiety in the group and their formation was due to splitting and projective identification. Soon enough afterwards, thanks to his work with Klein and his analyses of psychotic patients, he was able to conceive of deeper and more extensive parallels between individual and group psychology and was able to redefine the group as being basically an integral work group that includes members who are both individuals *and* identified with the group. In fact, he began to conceive of the individual self and the group self as being overlapping characteristics of everyone. Individual psychology and group psychology thus became intertwined in his thinking, and eventually 'basic assumptions' sub-groups seemed destined to emerge that would present unconscious resistances to the progress of the work group. He called these basic assumption groups 'pairing,' 'fight–flight,' and 'dependency.' They corresponded to resistances to progress in individual analysis, e.g., pairing corresponds to the erotization of normal dependency; fight–flight corresponds to the sado-masochistic, hostile, or passive–aggressive stance; and dependency (pathological, not healthy) suggests an omnipotent dependency that projects responsibility for growth on others. It must be remembered, however, that these basic assumption designations, even when applied to the individual, retain their group character. Sanfuentes (Chapter 4 in Volume 1) researches the differences between Bion's original publication of *Group Dynamics: A Review* (1952) and his altered version of it (1955) and reveals how much the latter version reflects how much Bion had come to respect Klein's thinking and its applicability to groups.

When one thinks about individual psychoanalysis, one thinks of 'thinking,' but when one thinks about groups, one often thinks of 'group processes' as behaviour. Robert Hinshelwood (Chapter 7 in Volume 1) addresses this issue frontally by suggesting that the group, the work-group in particular, constitutes a group mind that thinks in order to achieve meaning. He goes on to apply Bion's elaborate psychoanalytic epistemology to group thinking processes. Victor Schermer (Chapter 9 in Volume 1) also reviews Bion's psychoanalytic epistemology and applies it to group processes. Hanna Biran (Volume 2) similarly discusses Bion's concepts about thinking and anti-thinking, i.e., alpha function and attacks on linking, and applies them to group psychology.

Another feature of group work that was clarified by Bion was the nature of anxiety in groups. Following Klein, he conceived of these primitive anxieties as being psychotic in nature, and he also conceived that the formation of the basic assumption sub-groups was due to 'proto-mental states' of anxiety, which became the forerunner of his now famous concept of 'beta elements' (Bion, 1962). Lipgar (Volume 1, Chapter 1) cites two other subsequently conceived basic-assumption functions, (a) 'oneness,' as proposed by Pierre Turquet (1974), and (b) "me-ness," as proposed by W. Gordon Lawrence, Alastair Bain, and Laurence Gould (1996). Hopper (Chapter 8 in Volume 1) takes up a thread of an idea left by Bion that there may be yet another basic-assumption process, one which he calls 'incohesion: aggregation/massification,' which occurs after the group has been subjected to trauma.

The group identity of the individual and the individual identity of the group: Bion's 'binocular vision'

What many analysts failed to realize was that Bion was far more invested in the importance of the idea of the group or society than they had thought. In fact, Bion makes society or culture at large, beginning with the infant and its mother and the family as the first group, a basic dimension of normal mental life. His discovery of the normal interpersonal role of projective identification between infant and mother (Bion, 1959) and his notion of container/contained (Bion, 1962) are prime expressions of this line of thought. 'Man always needs someone other than himself,' he would say (personal communication). Bion goes farther, however, as he propounds the dialectic of 'narcissism and socialism,' which Gordon Lawrence discusses in Volume 2. He seems to be stating that individual psychoanalysis (at least Kleinian) leaves out the importance of the group dimension of the individual. As an individual the person is one thing, but as a member of group (s)he is another. In other words, each human being is defined by his/her personal individual identity and by his/her group identity – in parallel with the fact that each group can be thought of as a single whole and as a group composed of individuals. This idea of reciprocity and balancing characterizes one of Bion's most profound ideas, that of *binocular vision*,[8] an idea that seems to have emerged from his formulation of 'reversible perspectives' (Bion, 1962), which he had originally attributed to an aspect of resistance on the part of some psychotic patients but later realized that it was also an important aspect of normal reflective thinking.

Put another way, Bion created a paradigm change by adding this complementary dimension to the individual, one which can be summarized as follows: the individual is both the responsible agent for the initiation of his own will and at the same time is the unconscious medium through which the will of others passes and unconsciously affects him so that his subsequent behavior is comprehensible only by the consideration that he is behaving as if his will is now identical to the will of the group or a division within the group.[9,10] Bion's idea of groups was always balanced between the individual and the group itself. Others, like Dalal (1998), emphasize the group over the individual.

Bion (personal communication) often stated that man is born a dependent creature and needs others for emotional support. The group idea was implicit in these statements. The kind of dependency he had in mind was not just that which Klein had propounded, i.e., the infant's dependency on the breast. What he clearly had in mind was what Joseph Lichtenberg (1989) terms the need for 'affiliation,' i.e., a need to belong to a group.

Bion has often been compared and contrasted with another prominent groupist, Michael Foulkes. Some of the contrasts seem to center around Bion's Spartan starkness, propriety, negativity, and discipline as opposed to the allegedly more human and relating aspects of Foulkes. Dennis Brown (Chapter 6 in Volume 1) undertakes the task of contrasting these men and their ideas about groups and seeks to integrate them. Lipgar (Chapter 1 in Volume 1) does something similar but takes another approach, that of deconstructing the myth of Bion's starkness and remoteness. We begin to surmise from both their contributions that Bion was more strictly 'analytic' and

Foulkes more 'relational.' It is almost as if Bion could be compared with Klein and Foulkes with Winnicott.

Claudio Neri (Chapter 5 in Volume 1) takes a view similar to Brown's, i.e., that Bion was too much into thought and not into affect-sharing as a function of work groups. Yet Lipgar's chapter (Chapter 1, this volume) leads us to consider that these characterizations of Bion as too intellectual may be too pat. He discusses Bion's experiences in groups in detail and summarizes well Bion's attitude toward the importance of groups, and of relating within group life in a subsection in his contribution: 'Relationship to one's group as intrinsic to the full life of the individual.'

The mysterious 'third' in Bion's theory of groups

Bion's description of group phenomenology is vivid and is suggestive of what might be called ESP (extrasensory perception) elements. He states that there is such a thing as the psychology of the group but that the origins of this psychology lie solely with the individuals comprising the group, but he also seems to believe that the potential group-relating aspect within the individual is activated by the group; i.e., the existence of the group *evokes* what we call 'group psychology.' How does this happen? Bion describes how individuals become unconsciously caught up in different strands of the group process as if they were puppets being controlled and manipulated by an invisible puppeteer. Yet Bion did not believe that the group itself had an independent agency. Agency in the group, consequently, became prime cause but remained ineffable and inscrutable – as a mysterious, potentiating, synergistic summation and transformation of the combined agencies of the individuals in the group.

Recently, Ogden (1994, 1997) helped clarify the mystery of the 'agency-at-large' phenomenon in his formulation of the 'analytic third subject' and particularly one aspect of it that he calls the 'subjugating third subject,' the former of which designates the subjectivity of the relationship between the analysand and the analyst, and the latter denoting a mysterious 'virtual' object that inhabits the potential space between the analysand and analyst and represents a combination of the projective identifications of each. This subjugating object thereafter seems to 'subjugate' the wills of the analysand (as transference) *and* the analyst (as countertransference) and often results in enactments.

My own version of this idea of a mysterious third designates the 'dramaturge' aspect of the 'dreamer who dreams the dream,' a subjective presence in the unconscious who 'knows' what is on the agenda of the 'dailies' of the analysis and mysteriously directs each participant to play out his role so that the unconscious theme can become explicated (Grotstein, 1981). However, I believe that there is more to the idea of the 'third,' or, to be more general, to the inescapable tendency for subgroups to form within a group. Abelin (1980, 1981) conceives of an early triangulation in infant development that occurs prior to the Oedipal triangulation during Mahler's stage of rapprochement. This particular triangulation involves infant–sibling–mother, whether the sibling is actual or phantasied. My own extension of Abelin's idea is that this earlier triangulation forms the basis for a 'sibling family' within the parental family. One particularly observes this phenomenon in large families and especially in dysfunctional families where an older sister or brother is looked up to for guidance by the younger siblings in lieu of the parents. Ultimately, this 'sibling' family becomes the model for the 'gang' organizations where an older brother becomes the head of the younger family. My point here is that Abelin may offer us yet another model for the formation of a subgroup within a group, in this case, a sibling or peer subgroup that is in dialectical opposition to the work group analogized to the parental family.

Yet another model for thirdness comes from Stein Bråten (1993), the Norwegian sociologist who believes that the infant is born with an inherent expectation of interaction with the other. He states:

> The infant is born with a virtual other in mind who invites and permits fulfilment by actual others in felt immediacy. Thus, the normal developing learning mind recreates and transforms itself as a self-organizing dyad (i) in self-engagement with the virtual other, as well as (ii) in engagement with actual others who fill and affect the companion space of the virtual other and, hence, are directly felt in presentational immediacy. (Bråten 1993, p.26)

I understand Bråten to be saying that the infant is born with a 'group instinct' whereby it is especially preconditioned to anticipate engagements with others by having an inherent 'reserved space' dedicated to interactions with them (before they happen). This idea would help to confirm Bion's thesis about the inherent tropisms of 'narcissism and socialism.'

Oedipus and the sphinx

Another idea of Bion's that has applicability to the psychologies of both the individual and the group is his notions of the Oedipus complex and the sphinx – in conjunction with the myths of the Garden of Eden and the Tower of Babel. Bion's version of the Oedipal story is that it involves Oedipus' hubris in trying to discover the truth that underlay the pollutions of Thebes. He then calls attention to the riddle of the sphinx in which the sphinx kills those who encounter her and fail to divine her riddle, but perishes when Oedipus successfully answers it. In the Garden of Eden myth God forbids Adam and Eve to taste of the fruit of the Tree of Knowledge about good and evil (presumably sexuality), and in the Tower of Babel myth man is punished for trying to arrogate God's language, by being scattered asunder speaking different tongues. Bion assigns the god-like withholding of knowledge to the sphinx. Oedipus' ability to answer her riddle was tantamount to Prometheus's stealing fire (knowledge) from the gods.

What I believe links the above themes is Freud's (1915) notion of *primal repression*. It is as if the infant is born with the infant wealth of knowledge that can only be known by the 'godhead' (the unconscious). This 'knowledge' is not yet dangerous because the corpus callosum (the bridge in the brain between the two cerebral hemispheres) does not myelinate (and therefore function) until four to five months of age (when the depressive position comes on line). The importance of this last factor is that the beginning integration of the two hemispheres, along with the shortly later acquisition of verbal language and symbolic function, initiates the onset of the function of *significance*. Knowledge is harmless until the significance of the knowledge becomes realized. Primal repression seems to place a massive barrier on the 'godhead knowledge' and the significance that could possibly be attached to it. At the same time, however, the infant is early on dominated in a pre-reflective state by right hemispheric imagery[11] (Jaynes, 1976; Shlain, 1998). This image domination lends a sphinx-like atmosphere to the little mind of the toddler in whom images may become animated into monsters (like sphinxes). The onset of verbalization, which occurs along with the capacity for significance, rings the death knell for the dominance of the animated, pre-reflective imagistic world, which then goes underground (into the unconscious). 'Sexual knowledge' is attributed by Klein to the newborn infant. My thesis is, following Freud, that, if this is so, it enters into primal repression in the first few months of life because the infant, though able to tolerate the *facts* about it, allegedly cannot yet tolerate the *significance* of it –

because the infant needs for a long while, *I* suggest, to believe in its own omnipotent, autochthonous birth from itself in order to establish its own sense of agency before being able to acknowledge the *significance* of the fact that its birth was due to parental (Adam's and Eve's) sexual intercourse (Grotstein, 2000).

The application of the above ideas to the group would be that the members of the group project their 'godhead' font of unconscious knowledge into the group leader, who thereupon becomes the 'sphinx who knows but will not tell – but who will, in his omniscience, omnipotently care for them and their welfare. Yet another factor in the attribution of omniscience to the sphinx is that primitive thinking is pre-reflective in nature. That is, it is concrete, absolute, Cyclopean ('monocular').

Splitting and projective identification in groups

An important aspect in the formation of this mysterious third subject and agent in groups is the employment of the mechanisms of *splitting* and *projective identification*. Bion's whole concept of basic assumption groups predicated splitting on a fundamental level, but it was the projective identification that followed in the wake of splitting that was to become so meaningful in understanding group transformations. Interestingly, Freud (1921) himself understood this mechanism, although he never used it by name, when he suggested that in the formation of groups each group member projects his ego ideal into the group leader. Later, Bion (1959, 1961) was to make fundamental revisions and extensions of the Kleinian theory of projective identification, but in the meantime he was able to apply it to the psychology of the group in many ways. First of all, each member of the group is subject to projective identifications from virtually every other member; second, the group leader or director becomes the focus of countless projections from all the members. Whereas Freud mentioned only the projection of each member's ego ideal onto the leader, Bion was able to detect the projective identification of the members' expectations and anxieties.[12]

Although Bion did not stipulate further about the contents of the members' projective identification in one another and into the leader or director, one can now speculate that the contents include: (a) unprocessed anxiety, i.e., beta elements, (b) agency and role expectations, i.e., love, salvation, aggression towards the 'enemy,' sanctuary, etc., (c) omnipotence, and (d) omniscience. While Bion's ideas about groups certainly apply to individual psychology as well, there is no significant literature to support this.

My own view is that his three basic-assumption groups, when combined with the three others posited by his followers (mentioned above), all apply to the structure of the pathological organizations (psychic retreats – Steiner, 1993) or endopsychic structure (Fairbairn, 1944) of the individual.

Second thoughts: Bion's experiences treating psychotics

Note: I have decided to choose select portions of Bion's works throughout these two Introductions in order to give a representative idea of his thinking. I shall add my annotations of them as I do so.

Bion launched his psychoanalytic career with a series of works on the results and findings in treating psychotic and borderline patients. Most of these experiences were collected and published in his now famous *Second Thoughts* (Bion, 1967). The papers were presented between 1950 and 1962, and he presented a retrospective reflection about them in 1967. They collectively represent Bion as he was acquiring his stride as one of the second-generation leaders of Kleinian psychoanalysis and in close colleagueship with Herbert Rosenfeld and Hanna Segal, who were also psychoanalysing psychotics.

The first paper in the collection was 'The imaginary twin,' in which the psychotic analysand could not tolerate separation or the experience of objects which differed from him, thus, he conjured up 'twins' who were like him. This observation was to be one of many that was to create such a unique contribution to the understanding of psychotics. In 'Notes on the theory of schizophrenia' Bion observed the uniqueness of their language and their object relations and stated that the most important aspects of their thinking could only be adduced from the analyst's countertransference. He states: 'It must mean that without phantasies and without dreams you have not the means with which to think out your problem' (Bion 1967, p.25) – and

> The severe splitting in the schizophrenic makes it difficult for him to achieve the use of symbols and subsequently of substantives and verbs... The capacity to form symbols is dependent on: (1) the ability to grasp whole objects (2) the abandonment of the paranoid–schizoid position with its attendant splitting (3) the bringing together of splits and the ushering in of the depressive position. (Bion 1967, p.26)

With these formulations Bion was establishing the groundwork for his ultimate theory of thinking. One could apply some of these ideas to the understanding of groups in the following way: the group must have its own dreams (by day and by night) in order to cohere as a group and to process cata-strophic changes. While the group's dependence on the leader may typify the psychology of the paranoid–schizoid position, there must also be some attainment of the depressive position, i.e., ambivalence rather than idealiza-tion of the leader in order for the work group to flourish.

Later in the same work he states:

> The experiences I have described...compel me to conclude that at the onset of the infantile depressive position, elements of verbal thought increase in intensity and depth. In consequence the pains of psychic reality are exacer-bated by it and the patient who regresses to the paranoid–schizoid position will, as he does so, turn destructively on his embryonic capacity for verbal thought as one of the elements which have led to his pain. (Bion 1967, p35)

In other words, the attainment of the depressive position comes at the expense of defencelessness, which may cause in its wake a cataclysmic regression to the paranoid-schizoid position, but with such a violence that a traumatic state ensues. This also typifies the situation of groups in crisis.

In his next paper, 'Development of schizophrenic thought,' he continues his exploration of schizophrenic thinking. He states:

> First is a preponderance of destructive impulses so great that even the impulses to love are suffused by them and turned to sadism. Second is a hatred of reality which...is extended to all aspects of the psyche that make for awareness of it... Third, derived from these two, is an unremitting dread of imminent annihilation. Fourth is a precipitate and premature formation of object relations, foremost amongst which is the transference, whose thinness is in marked contrast to the tenacity with which it is maintained. (Bion 1967, p.37)

He then went on to describe the divergence of the psychotic from the non-psychotic personalities in the schizophrenic and the formation of 'bizarre objects.' He also put forth the idea that the schizophrenic employs projective identification of his mental pain *and* his mind that perceives the pain instead of employing repression. He extends his ideas about these themes in his next work, 'Differentiation of the psychotic from the non-psychotic personalities,' where he makes the interesting points (a) that the schizophrenic's ego is never wholly withdrawn from reality, and (b) '...that the withdrawal from reality is an illusion, not a fact, and arises from deployment of projective identification against the mental apparatus...' (Bion 1967, p.46).

One can readily see how much of these initial formulations apply to his theory of groups and why he conceived of group psychology as being at times 'psychotic.' One can also see the beginnings of Bion the epistemologist. In his next work, 'On hallucination,' he remarks, 'The attempt to rid himself of his perceptual system leads to compensatory hypertrophy of sense impressions…' (Bion 1967, p.85), thus, the appearance of hallucinations. The ultimate significance of his succeeding papers, 'On arrogance' and 'Attacks on linking,' was his formulation that psychotic patients employ excessive projective identification currently because in their infancy and childhood they had been deprived of its successful use with their mothers. This was the beginning of his radical revision of the concept of projective identification. First, he normalized it as a function in infantile mental life. Second, he conceived of it as *the* normal means of communication between infant and mother. Third, he conceived of projective identification, consequently, as an interpersonal or intersubjective encounter in which mother, at first, and the analyst, later, are to be 'containers' for the infant's proto-mental experiences, i.e., beta elements. Although Bion did not employ the term 'empathy' for his concepts of reverie and containment, empathy is certainly what he meant by those processes. The mother, like the analyst, must obligatorily attain a state of profound empathy in order to 'sense' the pain of her client, the infant. Pines (Chapter 10 in Volume 1) discusses empathy as a necessary 'sensitive responsiveness' to the analysand on the part of the analyst. One can see how these ideas readily apply to the group's dependency on the leader and on their expectation that the leader will accept, tolerate, detoxify, and rectify their projective identifications into him.

In his 'Theory of thinking,' which represents the summation of his studies on schizophrenic thinking, Bion states the following:

> It is convenient to regard thinking as dependent on the successful outcome of two main mental developments. The first is the development of thoughts. They require an apparatus to cope with them. The second development, therefore, is of this apparatus I shall provisionally call thinking. I repeat – thinking has to be called into existence to cope with thoughts. (Bion 1967, pp.110–111)

> 'Thoughts' may be classified, according to the nature of their developmental history, as pre-conceptions, conceptions or thoughts, and finally concepts… The conception is initiated by the conjunction of a pre-conception with a realization. The pre-conception may be regarded as the analogue in psycho-analysis of Kant's concept of 'empty thoughts'. (Bion 1967, p.111)

This model will serve for the theory that every junction of a pre-conception with its realization produces a conception. Conceptions therefore will be expected to be constantly conjoined with an emotional experience of satisfaction. (Bion 1967, p.111)

I shall limit the term 'thought' to the mating of a preconception with a frustration…with a realization of no breast available for satisfaction. This mating is experienced as a no-breast. Or 'absent' breast inside. The next step depends on the infant's capacity for frustration: in particular it depends on whether the decision is to evade frustration or to modify it. (Bion 1967, pp.111–112)

…[T]he failure to establish, between infant and mother, a relationship in which normal projective identification is possible precludes the development of an alpha-function and therefore of a differentiation of elements into conscious and unconscious. (Bion 1967, p.115)

…[J]ust as sense-data have to be modified and worked on by alpha-function to make them available for dream thoughts etc., so the thoughts have to be worked on to make them available for translation into action… Translation into action involves publication, communication, and commonsense…and correlation. (Bion 1967, pp.117–118)

In this final chapter in his book Bion has consolidated his experiences with psychotics and has evolved the rudiments of the most far-reaching and innovative theory of thinking to date. He is probably the first person in western civilization to have separated *thoughts* from the *thinking* of thoughts and to have given priority in time of emergence to the former. From schizophrenics he learned that the ability to think one's thoughts depends on the ability to tolerate frustrating thought-feelings. His theory of thoughts themselves is that they are fundamentally involved with emotions. He develops an epigenesis for the development of thoughts from pre-conception to conception to concept, and for thinking as evolving from publication to communication to commonsense and correlation. In terms of group theory one could speculate that 'thoughts without a thinker' are equivalent to Freud's concept of the irruption of the instinctual drives, but in this case, from the collective group membership. It is the task of the group leader, consequently, to become the thinker who then thinks them, but Bion also helps us see that this is also a function of leadership within a group and that this work is optimally taken up by different members at different times.

In his 'Commentary' at the end of the book he discusses many retrospective responses to his publications, one of which was his regret that he was unable to use artistic techniques in order to reproduce his experiences with patients more accurately for the reader. He then discusses his soon-to-be-famous grid as a categorical contrivance that could sort out the elements of a session with some scientific accuracy, account for their transformations, and allow for their being placed into convenient categories. I shall discuss the grid later in my introduction to Volume 2.

As one reads through *Second Thoughts*, one gets intimations of Bion's trajectory. One also gets an idea of how he thinks, not just *what* he thinks. He thinks diligently, creatively, imaginatively, idiosyncratically and independently. He respects Freudian and Kleinian theories but is also able to use them as stepping stones for newer ideas. He stands ideas on their heads and observes them from different angles, which he is later to call 'vertices.' His style of language is noteworthy. The language is measured, thoughtful, balanced, and objective. He is seldom *ex*plicit – mainly *im*plicit. He speaks in 'poetics,' i.e, the language of evocation and conjury. One can readily tell that he was schooled in Latin. The genius/messiah in him is about to burst forth.

References

Abelin, E. L. (1980) 'Triangulation, the role of the father and the origin of coregender identity during the rapprochement subphase.' In R. F. Lax, S. Bach and J. A. Burland (eds.) *Rapprochement*. New York: Jason Aronson.

Abelin, E. L. (1981) 'Triangulation.' In R. Lax *et al.* (eds.) *Rapprochement*. New York: Jason Aronson.

Bion, W. R. (1952) 'Group dynamics: A review.' *International Journal of Psycho-Analysis 33*, 225–247.

Bion, W. R. (1955) 'Group dynamics: A review.' In Melanie Klein, Paula Heimann and Roger Money-Kyrle (eds.) *New Directions in Psycho-Analysis: The Significance of Infant Conflict in the Pattern of Adult Behaviour*. London: Tavistock Publications.

Bion, W. R. (1958) 'On hallucination.' In *Second Thoughts: Selected Papers on Psycho-Analysis*. New York: Jason Aronson, 1967.

Bion, W. R. (1959) 'Attacks on linking.' In *Second Thoughts*. London: Heinemann, 1967.

Bion, W. R. (1961) 'A psycho-analytic theory of thinking.' *International Journal of Psycho-Analysis 43* 306–310.

Bion, W. R. (1962) *Learning From Experience*. London: Heinemann.

Bion, W. R. (1967) *Second Thoughts*. London: Heinemann.

Bion, W. R. (1982) 'The Long Week-End 1897–1919.' In F. Bion (ed) *Life*, London: Karnac Books.

Bléandonu, G. (1993) *Wilfred R. Bion: His Life and Works. 1897–1979*. (Trans. C. Pajaczkowska.) London: Free Association Press.

Borges, J. L. (1989) 'The Aleph.' In *Jorge Luis Borges: Collected Fictions*. (Trans. A. Hurley.) New York: Viking, 1998.

Bråten, S. (1993) 'Infant attachment and self-organization in light of the thesis: Born with the other in mind.' In I. L. Gomnaes and E. Osborne (eds) *Making Links: How Children Learn.* Oslo: Yrkeslitteratur.

Dalal, F. (1998) *Taking the Group Seriously: Towards a Post-Foulkesian Group Analytic Theory.* London and Philadelphia: Jessica Kingsley Publishers.

Fairbairn, W.R.D. (1944) 'Endopsychic structure considered in terms of object-relationships.' In *Psychoanalytic Studies of the Personality.* London: Tavistock, 1952.

Freud, S. (1915) 'Repression.' *Standard Edition 14,* 141–158. London: Hogarth Press, 1957.

Freud, S. (1921) 'Group psychology and the analysis of the ego.' *Standard Edition 18,* 67–144. London: Hogarth, 1955.

Grinberg, L., Sor, D. and Tabak de Bianchedi, E. (1977) *Introduction to the Work of Bion.* New York: Jason Aronson.

Grotstein, J. (1978) 'Inner space: Its dimensions and its coordinates.' *International Journal of Psychoanalysis 59,* 55–61.

Grotstein, J. (1981) 'The ineffable nature of the dreamer.' In Grotstein (2000) *Who Is the Dreamer Who Dreams the Dream? A Study of Psychic Presences.* Hillsdale, NJ: Analytic Press, 1–36.

Harrison, T. (2000) *Bion, Rickman, Foulkes and the Northfield Experiments: Advancing on a Different Front.* London: Jessica Kingsley Publishers.

Jaynes, J. (1976) *The Origins of Consciousness in the Breakdown of the Bicameral Mind.* Boston: Houghton Mifflin.

Lacau, J. (1966) Ecrits 1949–1960. (Trans. A. Sheridan.) New York: WW.

Lawrence, W. G., Bain, A. and Gould, L. (1996) 'The fifth basic assumption.' *Free Associations 6,* 37, 28–55.

Lichtenberg, J. (1989) *Psychoanalysis and Motivation.* Hillsdale, NJ: Analytic Press.

Ogden, T. (1994) 'The analytic third: Working with intersubjective clinical facts.' *International Journal of Psycho-Analysis 75,* 3–20.

Ogden, T. (1997) *Reverie and Interpretation: Sensing Something Human.* Northvale, NJ and London: Jason Aronson.

Shlain, L. (1998) *The Alphabet and the Goddess: The Conflict between Words and Images.* New York: Penguin/Arcana.

Steiner, J. (1993) *Psychic Retreats: Pathological Organisations in Psychotic Common Neurotic and Borderline Patients.* London: Routledge.

Symington, J. & Symington, N. (1996) *The Clinical Thinking of Wilfred Bion.* London: Routledge.

Endnotes

1. Although I do not cite them directly, much of what I write here has been informed by the following authors who have written on Bion: Bléandonu 1993; Symington, J. and Symington, N. 1996; and Grinberg, Sor and Tabak de Bianchedi. 1977.

2. Bion often decried the existence of psychoanalytic institutes but would then hasten to add, 'but think of the alternative.'

3. At the battle of Copenhagen *Vice-Admiral* Horatio Nelson was signaled by his superior, Admiral Lord Barham, to withdraw. Nelson held his telescope up to his blind eye, sailed straight for the Danish fleet, won the battle of Copenhagen and became *Admiral Lord Nelson.*

4. There is where he met Fairbairn.

5. Bion hit on the idea of bringing the potential candidates together to observe how they behaved individually and with each other. In effect, the candidates unconsciously 'chose' who were to be the officers. Here Bion was creating a situation which was to facilitate a group process in which the participants would unconsciously (or unwittingly) select their own leaders.

6. I recall a dream I had shortly after my analysis with Bion was over and during a time of deep distress for me. In the dream Bion was garbed in his British officer's uniform and was mock-marching across the stage as if to show me how to behave – courageously and with discipline.

7. The concept of 'infantile psychosis' is still well regarded by current Kleinians. My own view is that the term is an inaccurate hyperbole. What she describes under the rubric of the infantile psychosis would be better described as the first, primitive 'infantile neurosis,' one that anticipates a 'childhood neurosis' (Oedipus complex), which I believe Freud erroneously termed the 'infantile neurosis.' The point is that what Klein described was *primitive*, not psychotic (which Kleinians seem to confuse with 'omnipotent'). Ironically, it was Bion himself (1958) who proffered the truest qualification for psychosis, *bizarreness*, as in 'bizarre objects.'

8. Shortly after my own personal analysis with Bion had been terminated, I published a contribution in which I coined the 'dual-track hypothesis' (Grotstein, 1978). Because of having been in analysis with him, I had refrained from reading his work and had therefore been unaware of his concept of 'binocular thinking.' I can only conclude that I must have been subtly influenced and impressed by how he employed binocular thinking in his analysis of me.

9. This dual idea in regard to psychic responsibility is implicit in his notion of container/contained which he discovered in the background of schizophrenic patients where they were allegedly deprived of the experience of the normal use of protective identification (into mother as container).

10. This latter idea resembles in many ways Lacan's (1966) notion that the Other, his term for the unconscious, originates in the linguistic cultural template of a society; i.e., we are 'born into the symbolic order of language in the name of the father...' 'As the ego speaks, it is being spoken by the Other,' in other words, a *social unconscious*, which differed both from Freud's and Klein's individual or personal unconscious and from Jung's collective unconscious.

11. I am indebted to Professor Ross Skelton (personal communication, 1999) for reminding me of Borges' (1989) haunting imagistic story, *The Aleph*, in which he movingly captures both the essence of Bion's O and Matte-Blanco's concept of infinity and total

symmetry in the first letter of the Hebrew alphabet and a point in space that syncretistically contains an infinity of points.

12. Bion's theory of groups and recommendations on how they should be conducted became the 'Tavistock Method' and has been legendary in its effects here in the States on psychiatric residents, amongst others, who participate in the 'Tavistock' in their training. I have heard several residents say that if they didn't believe in the unconscious before, they certainly do now.

Part I

Roots and Early Developments

1

Re-discovering Bion's
Experiences in Groups
Notes and Commentary on Theory and Practice

Robert M. Lipgar

Introduction

For the past four decades or more, books on group psychotherapy with few exceptions make reference to Bion's work. His *Experiences in Groups* (1961) is a seminal work in group psychology. This collection of papers, mostly written in the late forties, contains a sketch of a group theory, insights and examples of his way of working with groups. He uses an essentially psychoanalytic method to investigate group life much as Freud and others investigated the psychological life of individuals. Despite his prominence and broad influence, or perhaps because of it, Bion's work is often misconstrued and misapplied (Lipgar, 1993b).

By providing a series of quotations from Bion's book together with commentary, I hope to give readers an opportunity to discover or rediscover Bion and his experiences in groups for themselves and to take for themselves what they will that is useful. In this way, I have chosen to have Bion speak for himself and for readers to think for themselves. My intention is to put each reader in a good position to make his or her own constructions of Bion's work and make applications relevant to one's own contemporary practice in psychotherapeutic groups and in other situations of leadership.

To make it as easy as possible to access Bion's observations and opinions and to skip and browse without losing one's sense of the whole, I have placed

Bion's words under several key topic headings. This is one way to make Bion's experiences in groups alive again and relevant to those of us with an active interest in how groups work and how we might participate more effectively as leaders and followers. I hope you find this way of engaging with Bion's work on groups interesting as well as useful.

At the start, Malcolm Pines' comment on reading Bion may be helpful: the reader will be struck by Bion's 'striking originality, the complexity of thought and density of context, the calm assumption that his own responses to the situation he describes are simultaneously noteworthy yet trivial' (Pines 1985, p.xi). This last characteristic of his writing, at once intriguing and baffling, sets the tone for so much about Bion's intellectual and personal leadership that inspires and frustrates, capable of both empowering and humbling us.

Experiences in Groups revisited

The task: It takes a task to make a group

> I had, it was true, had experience of trying to persuade groups composed of patients to make the study of their tensions a group task. (Bion 1961, p.29)

It is important to bear in mind that in Bion's view, a group requires a task and that he made 'the study of their [patients'] tensions' the group's task. Bion conducted such study groups after World War II at the Tavistock Clinic with patients, executives, and clinic staff. These have been remembered as very powerful experiences (Pines (ed.) 1985; Bléandonu, 1994). Bion reported his thoughts, feelings, observations and insights in a series of papers in *Human Relations* (1948–52), published as *Experiences in Groups* in 1961. He gave examples of how he conducted himself in his role as 'taker of groups,' sharing his thoughts on technique and extrapolating from his experiences theoretical insights for a general psychology of group behavior.

Sutherland (in Pines (ed.) 1985) reports that in conducting groups at the Tavistock Clinic, in practice, Bion made little distinction between psychotherapy groups and study groups. Bion and Rickman, however, open the *Experiences in Groups* (1961 p.11, in the section called 'Pre-view, intra-group tensions in therapy: their study as the task of the group') by drawing a distinction between two meanings of the term 'group therapy' – 'treatment of a number of individuals assembled for special therapeutic sessions' vs. 'a planned endeavor to develop ... the forces that lead to smoothly running co-operative activity.' It seems to me quite clear that Bion's attention was on both – the treatment of individuals within the group context, and treatment of the group itself. (I will for now allow the words treatment and analysis to work together and not discuss here possible distinctions.) This dual interest, I believe, has left much room for construing and misconstruing how these two interests are interrelated in Bion's work but also in life.

Confusion between consultative and/or therapeutic interventions designed to 'develop the forces that lead to smoothly running co-operative activity' and/or to advance the work of dealing with 'the psychological diffi-culties of its members' is understandable but not without resolution. In their touchstone book *Psychotherapy Through the Group Process*, Whitaker and Lieberman (1964) make a very systematic effort to synthesize this apparent duality. Chapters in Volume II, *Building on Bion: Branches*, by Ettin and Wilke also explore related issues of leadership in depth. The responsibility, it seems to me, for finding ways to balance therapeutic or personal developmental goals and group development, rests very much with each of us as practitioners and leaders.

Many who have followed Bion, not only in conducting therapy groups at the Tavistock Clinic and elsewhere, but also in conducting small and large study groups in the context of group relations conference work, often do so with insufficient understanding, rigor and discipline, and find themselves neglecting one or another aspect of the complexities of work in groups. Carefully understood and conducted, small and large study groups in the context of 'working conferences' in the A. K. Rice/Tavistock tradition do not have the task 'to deal with the psychological difficulties of its members,' to use Bion's phrase (op. cit. p.64). Rather their task is to 'the study of the group's life as it occurs in the here and now' (cf. brochures from Tavistock/Leicester and AKRI conferences), a rather different focus. But in neither case is it possible to ignore the level of cooperation among its members on behalf of either task. When and how one chooses to intervene so that work proceeds are of course questions which we will explore here with Bion.

In order to build soundly on Bion's work, indeed, we need to understand more not only about group psychology, but also about how different group tasks (those that are stated, explicit and contracted, or those that are only apparent in practice) influence leadership roles and functions and vice versa. Different leadership roles and functions evolve and are appropriate to different groups with different objectives in different organizational, institu-tional, and culture settings. We will seek here to understand the complex interrelatedness of leadership competence, group task, and process of group development.

There has been much controversy about the outcomes of conducting either therapy groups or experiential study groups within a Bionian model. Yalom (1995, first, second and third editions), Malan *et al.* (1976), and Lieberman (1990) among others have found reason to question the wisdom of taking what has become known as the Bion/Tavistock model to either therapy groups or small study groups. Yalom (1995, p.186) saw Bion (and Ezriel) as allowing the therapist only a very limited role, one that was cold and distant, limited to providing interpretations of group-as-a-whole process. Gustafson and Cooper (1979) argue for revisions in the consultant's role in small study groups along similar lines. In re-reading Bion's classic work, it will be useful to consider how his experiences, insights, and behavior in role may require revision and adaptation according to the particular circumstances of oneself, one's own work and circumstances.

The basic assumptions: Mental activity in groups (not a kind of group in-and-of itself)

> The basic assumption is that people come together for purposes of preserving the group. (Bion 1961, p.63)

> The basic assumption of the group conflicts very sharply with the idea of a group met together to do a creative job, especially with the idea of a group met together to deal with the psychological difficulties of its members.[1] (*ibid.* p.64)

The concept of 'basic assumptions,' distinctively associated with Bion's work in groups, is one that is easily misapplied. It has become an easy shorthand for people to refer to a group as though it were in and of itself a 'basic assumption group' or a 'work group,' rather than take the care to consider the complexity of the coexistence and interplay of these aspects of group life as distinct qualities of mental activity experienced directly and subjectively, as well as those inferred from observable behaviors.

> ...but in the group it takes some time before individuals cease to be dominated by the feeling that adherence to the group is an end in itself. (*ibid.* p.63)

These quotations refer to an insight of central importance in Bion's approach to groups: the ongoing tension between *task* (work) and *affiliation* (maintenance of cohesiveness through shared fantasies). As 'group animals' we struggle with our need for individuality and the exercise of individual responsibility and our need for belonging. This challenge is coupled with an awareness of relentless tension between work requirements (the psychological work of 'learning from experience') and valency for the 'basic assumptions' (a kind of tropism toward togetherness, fight/flight, and pairing). As members struggle to deal, or avoid dealing, with the requirements of acting and interacting with reality constraints and demands and learning from experience, group life shifts easily from one basic assumption to another. Conflict and tension occur in Bion's view between the 'basic assumptions' and 'work', not between one and another of the basic assumptions.

Bion observed and described three particular types of 'basic assumptions', three clusters of emotions and desires, shaping attitudes and beliefs.[2] These are identified as 'fight/flight', 'pairing', and 'dependency'. All three are considered to serve as defenses, protections from psychotic anxiety (fragmentation and terror) and serve to preserve the group *qua* group, (regardless of task and adaptive relevance of the group's activity). Such a naive belief in and bonding to the group, however pervasive, was, in Bion's view, regressive.

> From the basic assumption about groups there springs a number of subsidiary assumptions, some of immediate importance. The individual feels that in a group the welfare of the individual is a matter of secondary consideration – the group comes first, in flight the individual is abandoned; the paramount need is for the group to survive – not the individual. (*ibid.* p.64)

When groups are dominated by basic assumption activity, particularly the basic assumption fight/flight (baF/F), the group functions as though individuals and their individual needs, potentialities and responsibilities are of little importance. When groups are heavily under the sway of basic assumption mental activity, certain reactions, resistances, and expectations of leaders will occur as phenomena particular to one basic assumption.

> There will be the feelings that the welfare of the individual does not matter so long as the group continues, and there will be a feeling that any method of dealing with neurosis that is neither fighting neurosis nor running away from the owner of it is either non-existent or directly opposed to the good of the group; a method like my own is not recognized as proper to either of the basic techniques of the group. (*ibid.* p.64)

Bion at this point reflects on and interprets some of his reactions experienced in role as 'taker of groups.'

It is, therefore, not surprising that critics of my attempts to use groups feel that it must be either unkind to the individual or a method of escape from his problems. It is assumed that if the human being as a gregarious animal chooses a group he does so to fight or run away from something.

The existence of such a basic assumption helps to explain why groups show that I, who am felt to be pre-eminent as the leader of the group, am also felt to be shirking the job. The kind of leadership that is recognized as appropriate is the leadership of the man who mobilizes the group to attack somebody, or alternatively to lead it in flight... We learned that leaders who neither fight nor run away are not easily understood. (*ibid.* p.65)

We can turn now more directly to matters of exercising leadership and choosing interventions. As he encounters, inevitably, resistance and conflict with the basic assumptions, Bion engages us in exploring his experience of providing psychological 'work' leadership. Throughout his explorations, we will be asked to attend to affects both in the group-as-a-whole and in ourselves.

...the thing that knocked holes in my theories was not words used, but the emotion accompanying them. I shall, therefore, resort to an avowedly subjective account. (*ibid.* p.61)

Interventions and leadership: Psychological work and group management

We will consider in detail that sequence of interventions reported by Bion in Chapter 1 in *Experiences in Groups*. These reflections of his role behaviors as a 'taker of groups' at the Tavistock Clinic have become the basis for much commentary and are probably as much responsible for characterizations of the Tavistock model as the final chapter, which is more a theoretical review. For instance, Gustafson and Cooper have been particularly critical of Bion's legacy to the group relations conference work and characterized these interventions as 'merciless' and as the 'same interpretation made ten times' (Gustafson and Cooper 1978, pp.144–45).

Let's review these nine or ten interventions as Bion reports them and consider their implications. How would you characterize them? Does Bion's account seem prescriptive? What shall we take from these reports for his legacy?

> 1. It becomes clear to me that I am, in some sense, the focus of attention in the group. Furthermore I am aware of feeling uneasily that I am expected to do something. At this point I confide my anxieties to the group, remarking that, however mistaken my attitude might be, I feel just this. (Bion 1961, p.30)

Unlike the legendary image of Bion as distant and withholding, to me he appears to be intervening in a way which might be classified as sharing his own experience in the here and now – offering data of his own feelings and encouraging them, by example, to take their own feelings seriously and to gain self-awareness. In this light, it can be taken as a contribution which would provide members with opportunities and data for reality testing. If taken as exemplary, this intervention can be construed, ironically perhaps, in light of the mythic 'Bionic' stance as oracular, as modeling 'transparency' which Yalom (1995, third and fourth editions) carefully describes and recommends.

Such behavior by the consultant/therapist would be consistent with what Rice would call the 'primary task' Bion has set for the group – to engage the group in the study of the intra-group tensions. Hence, this and the following interventions may be evaluated as examples of his participating in the psychological work of the group – providing leadership by doing that kind of psychological work which advances learning from experience and counters the dominance of basic assumption activity.[3]

> 2. ...that clearly the group cannot be getting from me what they feel they are entitled to expect. I wonder what these expectations are, and what has aroused them. (*ibid.* p.30)

Rather than 'merciless,' this may be regarded as an empathic comment made to all members present, to the group-as-a-whole, as well as an invitation to members to examine their own individual experiences of the relationship, their bases in reality. Such an intervention implies a recognition of the importance of subjective perceptions in the process of learning from experience. Bion further develops these implications later in the book and even more in later writings.

> 3. When I draw attention to the fact that these ideas seem to me to be based on hearsay, there seems to be a feeling that I am attempting to deny my eminence as a 'taker' of groups. (*ibid.* p.30)

This may seem to be a premature appeal to logic or rationality and might stir feelings of envy and/or inadequacy, and some members might experience such an intervention as a narcissistic injury. By drawing attention early in the group's meetings to the difference between members' present feeling-state, consisting of confusion, uncertainty, or unconnectedness, and the manifested clear-headedness of the consultant/therapist, he may increase members' level of anxiety. Nonetheless, it may also have the effect of mobilizing members' leadership and their capacity for work. This intervention, as well as others, can be used by us as a focal point for useful discussion about therapeutic technique and the timing of interventions, about how to address the dynamics from the perspective of the collective or from the perspective of the individual in relation to it. Bion gives some indications in his report about how he responded to the situation as it unfolded, how he responded to what followed his previous interventions.

> 4. I feel, and say, that it is evident that the group had certain good expecta-
> tions and beliefs about myself, and are sadly disappointed to find they are
> not true. (*ibid.* p.30)

Gustafson and Cooper (1979) have construed these interventions as an example of 'abandonment' of leadership. It seems to me plausible to construe this sequence as an example of empathic understanding of the situation in which the members find themselves, especially vis-à-vis their relationship to leadership and authority. I do not see Bion as continuing 'to abdicate' and 'to intrude' (*ibid.*). Nor does it seem to me that he is being 'authoritarian' (Eisold 1993, p.11).

> 5. I point out that it is hard for the group to admit that this could be my way
> of taking groups, or even that I should be allowed to take them in such a way.
> (Bion 1961, p.30)

This intervention seems empathic toward the group as a whole, a kind of 'mir-roring', if you will, of the group's attitude toward him at the moment. Does not such an intervention enable members to acknowledge their frustrations under the circumstances and to express their anger? Isn't this an example of Bion's preparedness to serve the group in a 'containing' function?

> 6. He therefore asks me directly what my object is, and why I cannot give a
> straightforward explanation of my behavior. I can only apologize, and say
> that, beyond feeling that the statement that I want to study group tensions is
> probably a very inadequate description of my motives, I can throw no light
> on his problem;... (*ibid.* p.32)

This is hardly an 'impersonal, mass group interpretation' (Yalom 1985, p.195), a characterization of Bion's approach common in the group literature.

To me it seems the contrary – forthcoming, frank and personal, a direct response to an individual member.

> 7. Without quite knowing why, I suggest that what the group really wants to know is my motives for being present, and, since these have not been discovered, they are not satisfied with any substitute. (Bion 1961, p.33)

Depending in some measure, perhaps, on the ego-strengths of the members of the group, it may be argued that Bion's stance, unfamiliar and unconventional, could incite frustrations beyond levels compatible with learning. Such a conclusion, however, would not be fair without knowing more about the whole situation, members' expectations and capacities, and perhaps most important, the on-going relationship and presence, interpretations and attentions of the 'taker of groups' – therapist/conductor/study group consultant.

> 8. In the tense atmosphere prevailing my own thoughts are not wholly reassuring. For one thing, I have recent memories of a group in which my exclusion had been openly advocated; for another, it is quite common for me to experience a situation in which the group, while saying nothing, simply ignores my presence, and excludes me from the discussion quite as effectively as if I were not there. (*ibid.* p.34)

Bion's stance here is one of self-awareness, showing access to his own feelings in the moment – although it may also be construed as an example of his determinedly independent, even heroic commitment to engage us in encounters profound and dangerous: 'plung[ing us] as deeply as he can into the depths of the mind. Truth and falsehood, sanity and madness are the matters that concern him and which will not let him go and few who have read him will be free of his concerns thereafter' (Pines 1985, p.xii).

> 9. I point out that the group now appears to me to be coaxing me to mend my ways and fall in with their wish that my behavior should conform more to what is expected or familiar to them in other fields. (Bion 1961, p.35)

I take his comment here as neutral if not warmly empathic, responding to the mood of those in the group at that moment.

> 10. I also remark that the group has, in essence, ignored what was said by Mr. Q. (*ibid.* p.36)

Here again may be a surprising example of Bion attending to an individual, albeit in relation to the group process. Can we take this as an example of the wide range of behaviors which Bion would include as compatible with working on task, or simply regard this as a mis-step which should be overlooked? In caricatures as well as in thoughtful descriptions, Bion and the Tavistock model are commonly represented as addressing only group-as-a-whole, never the individual.

> 11. ...I say that I think my interpretations are disturbing the group. (*ibid.* p.36)

Such an observation of the group's attitude toward him and of his impact on the group may be received as empathic and 'containing' rather than as 'intrusive' and 'abandoning.' Such observations are rather low-level interpretations and over a period of time would demonstrate role consistency and commitment to the task. This model of leadership would make room, even require individual members to experience the consequences of offering their own interpretations and viewpoints to the others and exercise their own leadership.

> 12. I remind the group, it was quite clear that in the beginning the group was most unwilling to entertain any idea that they had not properly satisfied themselves of the accuracy of hearsay reports about myself. In my view, therefore, those who felt that they had been misled by others, and now wished to withdraw, ought seriously to consider why they resisted so strongly any statements that seemed to question the validity of their belief in the value of my contribution to a group. (*ibid.* p.37)

Once again, Bion, by example, would seem to invite us to use our feelings and perceptions, reflect upon these and their underlying assumptions and share experiences in the moment and continue to learn. Such a reading of this series of interventions does not support the stereotypes of Bion's work.

Guidelines and technique: Toward what end?

> It would be satisfying if I could now give a logical account of my technique – the technique the Professional Committee, it will be remembered, wished me to employ – but I am persuaded that it would also be very inaccurate and misleading. ... I will, however, emphasize one aspect of my interpretations of group behavior which appears to the group, and probably to the reader, to be merely incidental to my personality, but which is, in fact, quite deliberate – the fact that the interpretations would seem to be concerned with matters of no importance to anyone but myself. (*ibid.* p.40)

This paragraph concludes with this most interesting and provocative statement, open to much misunderstanding. Is Bion saying that he does not care whether he is understood or that the feelings of others are of no matter to him? I doubt it. Such a reading would fly in the face of everything else Bion stood for and accomplished personally, in his group work and subsequent professional career. Rather, it seems more reasonable to take this statement to be Bion's way of emphasizing the importance of holding to the stance of participant/explorer or participant/analyst – the stance of one who is alive in the moment, responsive and responsible, seeking to symbolize and communicate one's unique comprehension of the experience of one's own membership in the group, including one's awareness of role, feelings, attitudes, behaviors, fantasies. Bion is, I believe, stating role priorities and acting his values as he conducts himself in this leadership role. I take it to be a frank statement of recognition of one's limitations and a caution against presuming to exercise control, authority and power over others, authority and power that has not (as yet) been thoughtfully negotiated and contracted.

> In making interpretations to the group I avoid terms such as group mentality; the terms used should be as simple and precise as possible. (*ibid.* p.60)

> ...the psychiatrist must decide what description best clarifies the situation for him, and then in what terms he should describe it for the group. (*ibid.*)

These statements open the way for the therapist/conductor to be deliberate in choosing words and selecting terms for his/her interpretations, interventions, or consultations according to his/her view of the group's membership and development phase. This is not permission to 'shoot from the hip,' to interpret everything that moves as soon as it moves you. Nor do these sentences convey an indifference to being understood, nor insensitivity to the feelings and needs of others.

> ...the situation should be described in concrete terms and the information given as fully and precisely as possible, without mention of the theoretical concepts on which the psychiatrist's own views have been based. (*ibid.* p.61)

This seems to be a recommendation for simple, direct language and data-based interventions, rather the opposite of the legendary obtuse or 'oracular' ones often attributed to the Tavistock tradition.

> The psychiatrist must see the reverse as well as the obverse of every situation, if he can. He must employ a kind of psychological shift best illustrated by the analogy of this well-known diagram [figure/ground illustration of the

> solid/empty cube drawing]. ... Similarly, in a group, the total of what is
> taking place remains the same, but a change of perspective can bring out
> quite different phenomena. The psychiatrist must not always wait for
> changes in the group before he describes what he sees...for example (to take
> the case of an individual), a patient had complained of considerable anxiety
> about 'fainting off'. Sometimes he had described the same phenomenon as
> 'becoming unconscious'. At a later group he was somewhat boastfully
> saying that, when things happened in the group which he did not like, he
> simply ignored them. It was possible to show him that he was describing
> exactly the same situation, this time in a mood of confidence, as he had on
> another occasion described with anxiety as 'fainting off'. His attitude to
> events in the group had altered with an alteration in the basic assumption of
> the group. (*ibid.* p.87)

Here he gives an example of an intervention linking an individual's behavior
in the group with that individual's reported behavior outside the group.
Although it also draws attention to the influences of group processes on the
individual, this intervention is hardly an impersonal, mass group interpretation. It also serves as an example of 'binocular vision,' a concept which Bion
describes in these papers and was to develop further in subsequent papers and
lectures.

> I interpret only that aspect of the individual's contribution which shows that
> the individual, in attempting, say, to get help for his problems, is leading the
> group to establish the **baD** or, alternatively, to shift to **baP** or **baF**. (*ibid.*
> p.117)

Since each *basic assumption* in Bion's view has its own characteristic anxieties,
and each individual his own *valency*, then this statement reports Bion's
strategy here to be one of interpreting an individual's defenses, i.e., the individual's involvement in shared (group-wide) security operations or
defense-maintenance functions. As such it is quite different from the common
stereotype of the Bion/Tavistock approach, often characterized as being
'intrusive,' prematurely exposing the instincts and primary process (in what is
said to be the 'Kleinian' manner), or attentive only to group-as-a-whole
processes. In this statement, it would seem that Bion has included attention to
the individual, consistent with and possibly prior to Ezriel's (1950) contributions to technique at the Tavistock Clinic.

   This statement may also be used to allow for interpretive activity which
could be considered to be ego-supportive, since clarifying ways in which we
are in the thrall of the basic assumptions can serve to strengthen our hand in

managing their influence. Basic assumptions for Bion are always to be part of a group's culture and are necessary defenses against psychotic anxiety. The 'sophisticated group' would seek to manage and engage basic assumption mentality on behalf of its work in reality adaptation independent of its wish to survive for its own sake. Bion's interpreting and making public that which is known but not yet expressed would be enabling and supportive. (For further discussion of covert processes, cf. the section on group mentality later in this chapter.) Anonymous contributions, unless made public, contribute to the dominance of *basic assumption* activity over *work* activity. Silence is non-participation, non-work that colludes with basic assumption activity. Bion will discuss anonymous contributions and how silence gives consent later in these papers.

> At first, in an attempt to counteract what I thought was some sort of resistance which patients were achieving through use of the group, I used to be beguiled into giving individual interpretations as in psychoanalysis. In doing this I was doing what patients often do – trying to get to individual treatment. True, I was trying to get to it as a doctor, but in fact this can be stated in terms of an attempt to get rid of the 'badness' of the group and, for the doctor, the 'badness' of the group is its apparent unsuitability as a thera-peutic instrument – which is, as we have already seen, the complaint also of the patient. Ignoring those inherent qualities of the group which appear to give substance to the complaint, and choosing instead to regard this unsuit-ability as a function of the failure of the doctor or patient to use the group in a therapeutic way, we can see that the failure, at the moment when the analyst gives in to his impulse to make individual interpretations, lies in being influenced by **baD** instead of interpreting it, for, as soon as I start to give supposedly psycho-analytic interpretations to an individual, I reinforce the assumption that the group consists of patients dependent on the doctor, which is the **baD**.[4] (*ibid.* pp.115–116)

In his reflections above, Bion explores the group-as-a-whole and uses the group as both the context and instrument for personal growth and learning. In this way, Bion, like Foulkes and few others at the time, was making a bold departure from what had been the more common approach to psychotherapy in group settings. It was more common for the doctor to engage patients one at a time, with other group members present as audience. Bion's commitment is to the task stated at the start: to engage members in the study of intra-group tensions, consistent with his belief that such work would challenge and enable members more fully to develop as individuals. In sharing his experiences as a 'taker of groups,' Bion shows his awareness of being subject to covert group processes and the need to recognize and interpret such experiences.[5]

Bion's interventions are aimed toward promoting 'learning from experience' in the context of the group experience. Here his work is fundamentally psychotherapeutic, taking psychotherapy as that enterprise which is directed toward individuation and self-definition, interdependency and capacity for intimacy.[6]

Bion's work here is that of the analyst/consultant/therapist who serves as a container for group members' projections. Working with these projections in the resonating, complex and emotion-laden context of a group requires profound awareness of self and others, as well as a profound commitment to learning in the 'here and now.' Often, the term 'container' itself, so identified with Bion, does not connote the kind of active participation and interaction, the processing and modifying of the projected part-objects which he shows is required of leaders who would contribute to developmental psychological work in groups. The term is often taken in a more static sense, not conveying a sense of the kind of subjective activity, the stressful experiences entailed in working creatively with internalizations and projective identifications.

Now we will consider in greater depth 'learning from experience' in the context of the group and the part Bion plays in this learning.

Relationship to one's group as intrinsic to the full life of the individual

> Aristotle said man is a political animal, and in so far as I understand his *Politics*, I gather that he means by this that for a man to lead a full life the group is essential. I hold no brief for...[this] extremely dreary work, but I think that his statement is one that psychiatrists cannot forget without danger of achieving an unbalanced view of their subject...the group is essential to the fulfillment of a man's mental life. (*ibid.* p.53)

> ...I consider that group mental life is essential to the full life of the individual, quite apart from any temporary or specific need, and that satisfaction of this need has to be sought through membership of a group. (*ibid.* p.54)

Given this profound assertion that group mental life is essential to the full life of the individual, it follows that Bion might in practice, as J. Sutherland recalls (Pines [ed] 1985, pp.47–86), make little distinction between psychotherapeutic task groups and staff self-study groups. Such a distinction, however, is, I believe, of critical importance. The socio–economic political context, psychosocial situation, as well as the contractual responsibilities, are different for each, and exploring and understanding these matters requires extending his insights, building on Bion's work. But for Bion, the overarching concern was for growth and development.

> ...anyone who has any contact with reality is always consciously or unconsciously forming an estimate of the attitude of his group toward himself. (*ibid.* p.43)

> ...the way in which a man assesses the group attitude to himself is, in fact, an important object of study even if it leads us to nothing else. (*ibid.* p.43)

Here Bion shares his existential view of the human condition and reasserts his commitment to searching for insight and truth. For Bion, at this time, seeking truth included *forming an estimate of the attitude of one's group toward oneself.* In the process of assessing the group's attitude toward oneself, interpretations emerged for Bion as primary to his contributions. From many of his examples and selected quotations here, it is clear that he means to link interpretations immediately to personal and emotional experience. They are not to be mystical, abstract formulations or pronouncements from a presumed superior authority, but rather expressions of sophisticated participation, full engagement in the here and now.

> Many people dispute the accuracy of these interpretations... This objection to the accuracy of the interpretations must be accepted, even if we modify it by claiming that accuracy is a matter of degree; for it is a sign of awareness that one element in the individual's automatic assessment of the attitude of the group towards himself is doubt. If an individual claims he has no doubt at all, one would really like to know why not... Or is the individual unable to tolerate ignorance about a matter in which it is essential to be accurate if his behaviour in a society is to be wise? In a sense, I would say that the individual in a group is profiting by his experience if at one and the same time he becomes more accurate in his appreciation of his position in the emotional field, and more capable of accepting it as a fact that even his increased accuracy falls lamentably short of his needs. [*Compare with note from Bion 1961 p.91 reprinted below.*]

> It may be thought that my admission destroys the foundations of any technique relying on this kind of interpretation; but it does not. The nature of the emotional experience of interpretation is clarified but its inevitability as part of human mental life is unaltered, and so is its primacy as a method. (*ibid.* p.45)

Courage is required to bring a group 'to task' and into the 'here and now'. Skill is required to reflect on, and share one's emotional experience in ways which bring others to reflect on theirs. More critically, interpretation is emphatically affirmed as having 'primacy as a method.' It is this process of 'sense-making' and 'hypothesis-building' that are given special importance in Bion's view of the psychological work leader. Although this is said to be primary, I do not find that he models interpretive activity exclusively, nor that he omits or argues against other interventions.

> One of the problems of group therapy, then, lies in the fact that the group is often used to achieve a sense of vitality by total submergence in the group, or a sense of individual independence by total repudiation of the group, and that part of the individual's mental life, which is being incessantly stimulated and activated by his group, is his inalienable inheritance as a group animal.
>
> It is this feature of group membership that gives rise to a feeling in the individual that he can never catch up with a course of events to which he is always, at any given moment, already committed. (*ibid.* p.91)

Bion's appreciation of the human dilemma, of the inevitability of having to take risks (of having to act without full knowledge of the consequences), of being unprepared, vulnerable and subject to feelings of shame and fragmentation, is almost palpable. His modesty and humor, as well as his wisdom and independence show clearly.

> In any event, as I hope to be able to show, the group reactions are infinitely more complex than the foregoing theories, even in this full deployment, suggest. (*ibid.* p.131)

Contrast this with Yalom's statement that Bion's theory leads people to believe they have an 'all-inclusive system [which] satisfies one's need for closure...a citadel of such impregnability...' (Yalom 1995 (2nd. edition) p.181). In this way, I believe Yalom finds the teacher guilty, so to speak, for the students' shortcomings. In this next excerpt, Bion builds on Freud but separates as well.

> In his *Group Psychology and the Analysis of the Ego*, Freud opens his discussion by pointing out that individual and group psychology cannot be absolutely differentiated because the psychology of the individual is itself a function of the individual's relationship to another person or object. He objects (p.3) that it is difficult to attribute to the factor of number a significance so great as to make it capable by itself of moving in over mental life a new instinct that is otherwise not brought into play. In my view no new instinct is

brought into play…it is always in play. The only point about collecting a group of people is that it enables us to see just how the 'political' characteristics of the human body operate… The individual is a group animal at war, not simply with the group, but with himself for being a group animal and with those aspects of his personality that constitute his 'groupishness'. (*ibid.* p.131)

Group mentality: a pool of anonymous contributions

[Group mentality is]…the unanimous expression of the will of the group, an expression of will to which individuals contribute anonymously. (*ibid.* p.59)

In this simple sentence, Bion makes one of his most profound observations of 'how the political characteristics of the human body operate.' I find this image of us unwittingly engaged in contributing to a pool of anonymous contributions, striking and illuminating. After some discussion of how he sees a picture of 'hard-working individuals striving to solve their psychological problems' (*ibid.* p.48), his focus shifts and he sees a picture of 'a group mobilized to express its hostility and contempt for neurotic patients'. He reflects on this mental activity as analogous to shifting focus as one does when looking through a microscope. He builds his picture by noticing one member's '*supercilious tone*' as another 'examines her fingernails with an air of faint distaste.' (*ibid.* p.49) He sees these as 'followers' of two absent members who serve as 'leaders' of that part of the group that feels there are better ways of spending their time.

It can be seen that what the individual says or does in a group illumines both his own personality and his view of the group; sometimes his contribution illumines one more than the other. Some contributions he is prepared to make as coming unmistakably from himself, but there are others which he would wish to make anonymously. If the group can provide means by which contributions can be made anonymously, then the foundations are laid for a successful system of evasion and denial, and in the first examples I gave it was possibly because the hostility of the individuals was being contributed to the group anonymously that each member could quite sincerely deny that he felt hostile. We shall have to examine the mental life of the group closely to see how the group provides a means for making these anonymous contributions. I shall postulate a group mentality as the pool to which the anonymous contributions are made, and through which the impulses and desires implicit in these contributions are gratified. (*ibid.* p.50)

Here Bion sets the stage for introducing the concept of projective identification as a key mechanism for understanding human behavior and group life. Knowing that we seek and find others willing to receive our exportation of what is toxic and indigestible to ourselves, he brings us face to face with the irrevocability of interdependency – in the most intimate and profound ways.

> …in group mentality the individual finds a means of expressing contributions which he wishes to make anonymously, and, at the same time his greatest obstacle to the fulfillment of the aims he wishes to achieve by membership of the group. (*ibid.* pp.52–53)

It is clear that the first thing they are aware of is a sense of frustration produced by the presence of the group of which they are members. It may be argued that it is quite inevitable that a group must satisfy some desires and frustrate others, but I am inclined to think that difficulties that are inherent in a group situation, such, for example, as a lack of privacy which must follow from the fact that a group provides you with company, produce quite a different sort of problem from the kind of problem produced by the group mentality. (*ibid* p.53)

> …it is the nature of a group to deny some desires in satisfying others, but I suspect that most resentment is caused through the expression in a group of impulses which individuals wish to satisfy anonymously, and the frustration produced in the individual by the consequences to himself that follow from this satisfaction… The situation will be perceived to be paradoxical and contradictory… (*ibid.* p.54)

> Group mentality is the unanimous expression of the will of the group, contributed to by the individual in ways of which he is unaware, influencing him disagreeably whenever he thinks or behaves in a manner at variance with the basic assumption. It is thus a machinery of intercommunication that is designed to ensure that group life is in accordance with the basic assumptions. (*ibid.* p.65)

It is this 'machinery of intercommunication' that must be lived and worked with in ways that enable development of individuality even as we struggle as 'group animals.' Development of individuality – subjective integrity and the capability for responsible choice – is required for the survival of the species, and both the individual and the species are required to undertake that kind of psychological work in group settings that Bion has been describing. Such work is not accomplished 'leaderless' but requires psychological work leaders. The study of intra-group tensions, however, does not imply or require the survival of that particular group as it is composed or organized in its particularity. It is the process and quality of the psychological work that transcends the commitment or attachment to a particular composite of persons.

Group culture: Outcome of conflicting interests

Group culture is understood as '...those aspects of the behaviour of the group which seemed to be born of the conflict between group mentality and the desires of the individual' (Bion 1961, pp.59–60).

> I shall assume that the group is potentially capable of providing the individual with the gratification of a number of needs of his mental life which can only be provided by a group. I am excluding, obviously, the satisfactions of his mental life which can be obtained in solitude, and, less obviously, the satisfaction which can be obtained within his family. The group meets this challenge by the elaboration of a characteristic culture of the group... I include in it ('culture of the group') the structure which the group achieves at any given moment, the occupations it pursues, and the organization it adopts. (*ibid.* pp.54–55)

This discussion of group psychology needs to be examined further in conjunction with Bion's statement in the final chapter, 'Group dynamics': the 'belief that a group exists, as distinct from an aggregate of individuals, is an essential part of this regression...' (*ibid.* p.142). Bion's statement is puzzling and would appear to contradict the basic premise of the preceding work. This apparent but important contradiction has not received sufficient attention. In my view, it expresses Bion's 'binocular vision' in the sense that studying groups and endeavoring to understand one's relations within the context of groups is essential to the full life of an individual and essential to the understanding of human psychology. Much of Bion's experiences in groups contains or anticipates what he would learn and elaborate later in his study of psychotic thought processes. For instance, his observations about a 'hatred of learning' is a precursor to his later work on the 'attacks on linking.'

> ...in the scheme I am now putting forward the group can be regarded as an interplay between individual needs, group mentality, and culture. (*ibid.* p.55)

> I was then able to suggest that the group had adopted a cultural pattern analogous to that of the playground, and that while this must be presumed to be coping fairly adequately with some of the difficulties of the group – I meant coping with the group mentality but did not say so – it was a culture

which only permitted of the broaching of the kind of problem one might well expect a school-child to help with. (*ibid.* p.57)

These examples, I hope, give some idea of what I mean by culture, and also some idea of what I consider to be the need to attempt to elucidate, if possible, two of the three components in the triad (of group mentality, group culture, and individual needs). (*ibid.* p.57)

...operations of what I have called the group mentality, or of the group culture, only occasionally emerge in any strikingly clear way. Furthermore, the fact that one is involved in the emotional situation oneself makes clear-headedness difficult. (*ibid* p.57)

Practising group therapists and others who wish to have positive influence as group leaders or group members may acknowledge that 'clear-headedness' is difficult, particularly at time of turmoil and conflict. And so Bion's recognition of one's emotional involvement may seem disarmingly simple, even trivial. The difficult challenge, however, is not in the recognition so much as in the performance. Being aware that one may be taken up in the projections of others, the 'emotional situation,' and being able to discern and interpret the basic assumption activity which may be impeding rather than supporting work, is unendingly complex and difficult. It requires self-awareness, empathy, courage and commitment to others and the task.

...silence, it is said, gives consent. Nobody is very happy about insisting on collective responsibility in this way, but I shall assume, nevertheless, that unless a group actively disavows its leader it is, in fact, following him. In short, I shall insist that I am quite justified in saying that the group feels such and such when, in fact, perhaps only one or two people would seem to provide by their behavior warrant for such a statement, if, at the time of behaving like this, the group show no outward sign of repudiating the lead they are given. I dare say it will be possible to base belief in the complicity of the group on something more convincing than negative evidence, but for the time being I regard negative evidence as good enough. (*ibid.* p.58)

This was written not long after the defeat of Hitler and the Nazis. Finger-pointing, as well as on-going analysis of, and reflection on, the guilt of all the Germans and the guilt of many other sectors, governments, groups, and agencies had just gotten underway. Although throughout the course of the twentieth century, we have witnessed horrors which for many national, racial, and ethnic sub-groups can deservedly rival the catastrophes of World War II and the Holocaust for the Jews, no serious scholar of our times can confidently say that we have learned our lessons from the horrors throughout the globe, but especially in Europe in the twentieth century. Bion's personal career both in World War I and World War II would make one wonder how he managed the calm, modest and restrained perspective to say simply that 'Nobody is very happy about insisting on collective responsibility in this way…' Rather an understatement I would say, but an observation which for Bion leads, I believe, to rather profound analysis and insight. And he goes on to say that 'unless a group actively disavows its leader it is, in fact following him' (ibid. p.58).

> Group culture is a function of the conflict between the individual's desires and the group mentality.
>   It will follow that the group culture will always show evidence of the underlying basic assumptions. To the two basic assumptions I have already described (fight/flight and pairing) it is necessary to add one more. It is the basic assumption that the group has met together to obtain security from one individual on whom they depend. (ibid. p.66)

> It requires the authority conferred by my position as psychiatrist to keep me in the picture at all when the basic assumption (in this example, the fight/flight b.a.) implies that a person whose primary concern is with the welfare of the individual is out of place. (ibid. p.70)

Once again, we see that Bion commits himself to disrupting the dominance of 'basic assumption' activity and that his leadership is focused on the 'welfare of the individual.' In view of this, it is somewhat puzzling that his reputation in the group literature is that his method was to conduct leaderless groups, that his leadership was passive rather than active and that his focus was on the group as a whole rather than supportive of the individual. To explain this puzzle, one is hard pressed not to refer back to his own formulations about the basic assumptions and the profound resistance he found to meeting the demands of development – resistance so profound as to be viewed by Bion as 'hatred of a process of development' (ibid. p.89).

> But the group designed to perpetuate the state of dependence means for the individual that he is being greedy in demanding more than his fair term of parental care. There is, therefore, a quite sharp clash in the group between the basic assumption and the needs of the individual as an adult. In the other two group cultures the clash is between the basic assumption of what is required of the individual as an adult, and what the individual, as an adult, feels prepared to give. (ibid. p.74)

> It seems so rational that we should think of it as a therapeutic group, that we should assume that the psychiatrist is the leader, and that we should talk

only about neurotic ailments, that it may not be observed that by thinking in this way, and behaving, appropriately, we are attempting to peg the group to a mode of behavior that will prevent the obtrusion of kinds of group that are feared. (*ibid.* p.75)

In the group the patient feels he must try to co-operate. He discovers that his capacity for co-operation is emotionally most vital in the basic group, and that, in the pursuit of objectives that do not easily lend themselves to the techniques of the basic group, his ability to co-operate is dependent on a kind of give and take that is achieved with great difficulty compared with the swift emotional response that comes of acquiescence in the emotions of the basic group. In the group the individual becomes aware of capacities that are only potential so long as he is in comparative isolation. The group, therefore, is more than the aggregate of individuals, because an individual in a group is more than individual in isolation. (*ibid.* p.90)

This last sentence again bears further discussion in relation to Bion's statements quoted above from pp.54–55 and p.142 of *Experiences in Groups.* In the review chapter, titled 'Group dynamics,' Bion remarks that a belief that the group is more than an aggregate of individuals is a regressive notion. Once again, Bion shifts the frame, requiring that we do further work, empowering us to be 'sense-makers.'

Now all this, and more like it, really boils down to the hatred of a process of development. (*ibid.* p.89)

In the group it becomes very clear that this longed-for alternative to the group procedure is really something like arriving fully equipped as an adult fitted by instinct to know without training or development exactly how to live and move and have his being in a group. (ibid. p.89)

…the whole group-therapeutic experience shows that the group and the individuals in it are hopelessly committed to a developmental procedure, no matter what might have been the case with our remote ancestors. (*ibid.* pp.89–90)

It might have been thought that the group makes a common assumption and that all else, including the emotional state associated with it, springs from this. This does not reflect my belief. On the contrary, I consider the emotional state to be in existence and the basic assumption to be deducible from it. As far as the group is concerned the basic assumption is essentially a tacit assumption…the assumption is not overtly expressed even when it is being acted on… We thus have a situation in which the individuals behave as if they were conscious, as individuals, of the basic assumption, but unconscious of it as members of the group. This is as it should be: the group has not a conscious: and it is not articulate: it is left to the individual to be both. (*ibid.* p.94)

Here Bion presents us with an apparent paradox: individuals in and of the group are the group's intelligence, yet without individual responsibility and intelligence, the group is dumb! The primitive resistances to our learning from experience, to change and development are powerful. Without the individual's vigorous struggle to learn and develop, the group to which s/he belongs, or rather, in which s/he participates, may falter, and without working actively on one's relatedness to the group, one's growth, learning and fullness of life is thwarted. Belief in the group seems both necessary and regressive. Truly, Bion's 'man' is at war with his 'groupishness.'

The sophisticated work group: A higher level of functioning

I propose from now on to reserve the word 'co-operation' for conscious or unconscious working with the rest of the group in work, whereas for the capacity for spontaneous instinctive co-operation in the basic assumption ...I shall use the word 'valency'. (*ibid.* p.116)

there is no way in which the individual can, in a group, 'do nothing' – not even by doing nothing... all members of a group are responsible for the behaviour of the group [see *ibid.* p.58]. (*ibid.* p.118)

Silence gives consent! (cf. p.48 in this chapter and Bion 1961, p.58)

The reciprocal sub-group is composed of those ostensibly supporting the new idea and this sub-group sets out to achieve the same end as the first sub-group, but in a rather different manner; it becomes so exacting in its demands that it ceases to recruit itself. In this way there is none of the painful bringing together of initiated and uninitiated, primitive and sophisticated, that is the essence of the developmental conflict... To exaggerate for the sake of clarity, I would say that the one sub-group has large numbers of primitive unsophisticated individuals who constantly add to their number, but who do not develop; the other sub-group develops, but on such a narrow front and with such few recruits that it also avoids the painful bringing together of the new ideas and the primitive state. (*ibid.* p.128)

This brief use of the concept of sub-groups must be considered in relation to Bion's ideas about 'aberrant forms of change from one basic assumption to another' and 'the specialized work group' (cf. Bion 1961, pp.155–158). Bion sketches ideas about the function of schisms within groups and the reforming of groups in relation to their social context. The flexibility of his thinking and the powerful reach of these conceptualizations are impressive. He opens for us a consideration of how failure to deal with the problems and challenges of what is now generally discussed as 'diversity' results in ossification or regression. When group boundaries become too rigid or too loose, growth and development will fail.

There follows the introduction of an interesting view of the relationship of the 'work group' and the '**ba** group', one that is often overlooked in discussions and applications of Bion's views:

> When Freud criticizes McDougall's views on the highly organized group, he points out that McDougall considers that the conditions of reorganization remove 'the psychological disadvantages of group formation'. This comes very near to my view of the specialized work group as having as its function the manipulation of the basic assumption to prevent its obstruction of the work group. (*ibid.* p.135)

Bear in mind that for Bion, the 'work group' makes use of the **ba's** and manages them, mobilizing or managing one **ba** to protect the work from one of the other **ba's**. His view did not stop with the notion that the 'work group' merely suppresses or avoids the basic assumptions. In this way he leaves open for study, exploration and further discovery a limitless range of possible arrangements between *work* and **ba** and how development of different cultures occurs, of how the conflicts between 'group mentality' and individual desires can be resolved.

> He [Freud] postulates an individual outside the primitive group, who possessed his own continuity, his self-consciousness, his traditions and customs, his own particular functions and position. He says that owing to his entry into an 'unorganized' group, the individual had lost his distinctiveness for a time. In my view the struggle of the individual to preserve his distinctiveness assumes different characteristics according to the state of mind of the group at any given moment. Group organization should give stability and permanence to the work group, which is felt to be much more easily submerged by the basic assumptions if the group is unorganized; individual distinctiveness is not part of the life in a group acting on the basic assumptions. Organization and structure are weapons of the work group. They are the product of co-operation between members of the group, and their effect once established in the group is to demand still further co-operation from the individuals in the group. ... Action inevitably means contact with reality, and contact with reality compels regard for truth and therefore imposes

scientific method, and hence, the evocation of the work group. (*ibid.* pp.135–136)

Here Bion, more explicitly than Freud, puts the individual in a social systems context. Bion places himself and us deep in the context of a group-as-a-whole, and in so doing would not seem to support the model of a distant, authoritarian group analyst so often attributed to him.

'Proto-mental' phenomena: A meta-psychological construct

> ...there were no observations at present available to the psychiatrist to explain why emotions associated with a basic assumption were held in combination with each other with such tenacity and exclusiveness. In order to explain this linkage and at the same time to explain the fate of the inoperative basic assumptions, I propose to postulate the existence of 'proto-mental' phenomena... Starting, then, at the level of proto-mental events we may say that the group develops until its emotions become expressible in psychological terms. (*ibid.* pp.100–101)

In this way Bion leaves unanswered, wisely so, it seems to me, the question of whether the observations presented in these papers as 'basic assumptions' represent 'instinctual drives' or learned response-patterns. He does attempt further to formulate the relationship between '**ba**' and 'work', between the basic group and the sophisticated group. In doing so, he comes to the idea of 'proto-mental' phenomena, positing events and/or a domain of activity which are observable only upon the accomplishment of developmental group work. In introducing this concept, he uses the phrase 'expressible in psychological terms' which characteristically, I believe, leaves open the question of whether the 'psychological terms' are observable behaviors or subjectively known experiences. Here and throughout his subsequent work, it seems to me, Bion attempts to reconcile the requirements of psychoanalytic study and knowledge with the scientific methods of his time. He honors both empirical, objective reality and subjectivity, experiential knowledge and 'common sense.'

> The emotional state associated with each basic assumption excludes the emotional states proper to the other two basic assumptions, but it does not exclude the emotions proper to the sophisticated group. ...there is, however, a conflict between the group that is formed through co-operation between individuals at a sophisticated level – the sophisticated group – and the basic group, and in this respect the relationship between sophisticated and basic

group differs from the relationship that obtains between the emotional states associated with the three basic assumptions. There is no direct conflict between basic assumptions, but only changes from one state or another, which are either smooth transitions or brought about through intervention of the sophisticated group. They do not conflict, they alternate; conflict rises only at the junction between the basic group and the sophisticated group. (*ibid.* p.96)

Although Yalom (1995, 3rd edition) as well as Rutan and Stone (1984) represent Bion's theory as stating that the 'work group' alternates with one of the 'basic assumption groups', it seems clear here that Bion conceptualized the matter quite differently. Bion's view is of group dynamics in which the group's work efforts are saturated or colored with differing amounts of one of the 'basic assumption' clusters of emotions, attitudes and beliefs. Tensions and conflicts are not between groups dominated by different 'basic assumptions', but rather between the 'work' group (dominant in the 'sophisticated' group) and the 'group mentality' (which is given expression through the mental activity of one of the 'basic assumptions').

> The interventions of the sophisticated group are diverse, but they all have this in common: they are expressions of a recognition for the need to develop rather than to rely upon the efficacy of magic; they are intended to cope with the basic assumptions, and they mobilized the emotions of one basic assumption in the attempt to cope with the emotions and phenomena of another basic assumption. (*ibid.* pp.97–98)

Bion is clearly interested in putting his theoretical insights to empirical test, on the scale of large social systems. *Experiences in Groups* includes evidence of the broad scope of his interests, curiosity and ambition. He opens the possibility of applying his learning from his study of groups to questions of the relationship between cultural characteristics and occurrence of certain illnesses.

> Tuberculosis is known to be very sensitive to developments in the psychology of a group, numbers fluctuating in what appears to be some kind of sympathy with the changes in mentality of the group. … The existence of these facts has led often, before a tubercular lesion was demonstrated, to suggestion that the patient was malingering (Wittkower, 1949), or to use my terminology, that **baD** is the teleological cause of the patient's disorder, but for reasons I have given I cannot regard **baD** as a cause of any kind; it is the mental state with which tuberculosis is affiliated, and is therefore neither cause nor effect. (*ibid.* p.107)

I am not aware of references to these ideas in other reviews of Bion's work. Given the many contemporary social problems and illnesses, e.g., domestic and school violence, homelessness, AIDS, and chemical dependence, Bion's inquiry into the relation of culture and illness deserves serious attention. As suggested by Steven Brown (cf. Chapter 6 in this volume), it may well be that William Stephenson's Q-methodology is the empirical tool that will make further exploration and development of this aspect of Bion's vision possible.

Further reflections

In his biography of Bion, Gérard Bléandonu (1994) provides us with an excellent understanding of Bion's intellectual development and clinical contributions. At the end of a section describing Bion's work with groups, Bléandonu represents, I believe, a core characteristic of Bion's leadership, relentlessly reaching but reluctantly assertive, politically and interpersonally.

> In other words, Freud's idea that the family group is the basic prototype of all groups seemed to him to have some basic validity, but it seemed inadequate in that it left obscure the origins of some of the most powerful emotional forces in a group.
>
> The more stable the group, the more it reflects the Freudian view. The more disturbed the group, the closer it approaches the mechanisms and primitive phantasies described by Melanie Klein. Freud considered group psychology from the starting point of whole-object relations and neurotic defences, whereas Bion considered the group in terms of part-objects and more psychotic defences. It seems that although he wanted to liberate himself from being constrained by existing theories, Bion was hesitant to begin a Copernican revolution in which family life and psychonanalysis would be specific examples of a more generalized group dynamic. (Bléandonu 1994, p.94)

In his address as Chair of the Medical Section of the British Psychological Society early in 1947 Bion (1948) proposed a critical and broad agenda for psychiatrists, his group of colleagues. In this address he outlined the need to accept the challenge of developing methods for 'dealing with the underlying emotional tensions in human relationships' [and] it is precisely these primitive unconscious tensions which present the fundamental problem in all human relationships (Bion 1948, p.83). Bion makes it clear that he would take psychiatry beyond the dyadic doctor–patient relationship. He sets his sights on studying the dynamics and interpreting the needs of groups and society: 'I consider nothing but Western Civilization' (*ibid.* p.82).

In 1947, in his opening address as chair to the British Psychological Society, Bion sets forth a vision and a mission:

> There is no corpus of knowledge that does for the study of the group what psycho-analysis does for the study of the individual. The material which is relevant for our study is embedded in the information amassed by several at present widely separated disciplines... In the field of emotional and intellectual development, the situation is very different [from that of the scientific field of acquiring of technical skills of the mechanical type]; mimesis is of no value and, indeed, is a great danger, for it produces a spurious appearance of growth; no method of communication of emotional development has yet been found which is not hopelessly limited in its field of influence... Hope...must depend on the development of a technique of emotional development, and, one would imagine, that is precisely what we in this society are concerned to provide. (Bion 1948, p.84)

Bion went first, often alone, to the edges of new knowledge. Later in his career, perhaps, as Bléandonu says, Bion was reluctant to declare the revolution, and reluctant even more perhaps, to mark himself as the flag-bearer, target in battle. Nevertheless, he moved the frontiers forward for colleagues, students, analysands, and for us. Bion has staked out new territories of knowledge for us to explore, settle, and develop though our own efforts and individual experiences.

References

Bion, W. R. (1948) 'Psychiatry in a time of crisis.' *British Journal of Medical Psychology 21*, 2, 81–89.

Bion, W. R. (1961) *Experiences in Groups*. New York: Basic Books, Inc.

Bion, W. R. (1962) *Learning from Experience*. New York: Basic Books, Inc.

Bléandonu, G. (1994) *Wilfred Bion: His Life and Works 1897–1979*. London: Free Association Books. New York: Guilford Press.

Eisold, K. (1985) 'Recovering Bion's contributions to group analysis.' In A. D. Colman and M. H. Gelder (eds) *Group Relations Reader 3*. Jupiter, FL: A. K. Rice Institute.

Eisold, K. (1993) 'Changing group relations: Some problems and symptoms.' In T. W. Hugg, N. M. Carson & R. M. Lipgar (eds) *Changing Group Relations: The Next Twenty-five Years in America*. Proceedings of the ninth scientific meeting of the A. K. Rice Institute. Jupiter, FL: A. K. Rice Institute.

Ezriel, H. (1950) 'A psychoanalytic approach to group treatment.' *British Journal of Medical Psychology 23*, 93–100.

Gustafson, J. P. and Cooper, L. (1979). 'Collaboration in small groups: Theory and technique for the study of small group process.' *Human Relations 31*, 155–171.

Lawrence, W. G., Bain, A. and Gould, L. (1996) 'The fifth basic assumption.' *Free Associations 6*, 37, 28–55.

Lieberman, M. A. (1990) Personal communication.

Lipgar, R. M. (1993b) 'Bion's work with groups: Construed and misconstrued.' In S. Cytrynbaum, and S. A. Lee, (eds) *Transformations in Global and Organizational Systems: Changing Boundaries in the 90s,* 98–106. Proceedings of the Tenth Scientific Meeting of the A. K. Rice Institute. Jupiter FL, A. K. Rice Institute.

Malan, D. H., Balfour, F. H. G., Hood, V. G., and Shooter, F. H. G. (1976) 'A long-term follow-up study of group psychotherapy.' *Archive of General Psychiatry 33,* 1303–15.

Pines, M. (ed) (1985) *Bion and Group Psychotherapy.* London: Routledge & Kegan Paul.

Rutan, J. S. & Stone, W. N. (1984) *Psychodynamic Group Psychotherapy.* New York: Macmillan, Inc.

Sutherland, J. D. (1985) 'Bion revisited: Group dynamics and group psychotherapy.' In M. Pines (ed) *Bion and Group Psychotherapy.* London: Routledge and Kegan Paul.

Turquet, P. (1974) 'Leadership: The individual and the group.' In G. Gibbard (ed) *Analysis of Groups.* San Francisco: Jossey-Bass.

Yalom, I. D. (1995) *Theory and Practice of Group Psychotherapy.* (4th ed., 1995; 3rd ed., 1985; 2nd ed., 1975) New York: Basic Books.

Whitaker, D. S. & Lieberman, M. A. (1964) *Psychotherapy Through the Group Process.* New York: Atherton.

Suggested reading

Edelson, M. & Berg, D. N. (1999) *Rediscovering Groups: A Psychoanalyst's Journey Beyond Individual Psychology.* London: Jessica Kingsley Publishers.

Grinberg, L., Sor, D. and Tabak de Blanchedi, E. (1977) *Introduction to the Work of Bion.* New York: Jason Aronson, Inc.

Grotstein, J. A. (ed) (1981) *Do I Dare Disturb the Universe?* Beverly Hill, CA: Caesura.

Lipgar, R. M. (1992) 'A programme of group relations research: Emphasis on inquiry and the trial of techniques.' *Group Analysis 25,* 365–375.

Lipgar, R. M. (1993a) 'Views of the consultant's role: A Q-methodology study.' In T. W. Hugg, N. M. Carlson and R. M. Lipgar (eds), *Changing Group Relations: The Next Twenty-Five Years in America,* 57–70. Proceedings of the Ninth Scientific Meeting of the A. K. Rice Institute. Jupiter, FL: A. K. Rice Institute.

Meltzer, D. (1978) *The Kleinian Development.* Clunie Press for the Roland Harris Trust Library. Reading, Great Britain: Radavian Press.

Rice, A. K. (1965) *Learning for Leadership.* London: Tavistock Publications, Ltd.

Rioch, M. J. (1975) 'The work of Wilfred Bion on groups.' In A. D. Colman and W. H. Bexton (eds) *Group Relations Reader 1.* Jupiter, FL: A. K. Rice Institute.

Thelen, H. A. (1984) 'Research with Bion's concepts.' In Pines, M. (ed) *Bion and Group Psychotherapy.* London: Routledge & Kegan Paul.

Endnotes

1. Since Bion acknowledges that dealing 'with the psychological difficulties of its members' is at least one of many work group tasks, it is appropriate to examine his experiences and thoughts as they may apply to how we conduct psychotherapy treatment groups, as well as providing insight into general laws of group life.

2. Pierre Turquet (1974) has identified 'oneness' as a fourth basic assumption. W. Gordon Lawrence, Alastair Bain, and Laurence Gould (1996) have argued for a fifth basic assumption which they call 'me-ness.' Earl Hopper, Chapter 8 of this volume, identifies another basic assumption.

3. Bion offers this description of his method of conducting groups in 'Group dynamics,' the final paper in *Experiences in Groups*: 'There are times when I think that the group has an attitude to me, and that I can state in words what the attitude is; there are times when another individual acts as if he also thought the group had an attitude to him, and I believe I can deduce what his belief is; there are times when I think that the group has an attitude to an individual, and that I can say what it is.' (Bion 1961, pp.142–143)

4. When Bion reflects on defensive uses of the doctor role, we can better see the relevance and meaning of his earlier rather unexpected statement that his comments are 'matters of no importance to anyone but myself.' He wisely points out here (pp.114–15) how important it is to resist the temptation to avoid the complexities of the group situation by recreating a kind of individual psychotherapy or psychoanalytic relationship within the group.

5. Although Eisold (1985, p.39) among others has puzzled over Bion's statement in 'Group dynamics,' the final chapter of *Experiences in Groups*, that belief in the group is regressive, there seems to be little doubt here that Bion believed the face-to-face group situation allowed the examination of human behavior not otherwise available for study in dyadic circumstances. In this sense the group is something other than, if not more than, a collection of individuals. For further discussion of this chapter, see M. Sanfuetes' Chapter 4 in this book.

6. This reading of his aims is, I believe, in contrast to the goals attributed to Bion's method by Rutan and Stone (op. cit.). They describe his approach as one which would result in increasing the individual's capacity for good 'peer relations' as though the aim of the Bion/Tavistock group were the enhancement of one's ability to form or join cohesive groups. It seems to me that Bion's aim is much broader and that a thoughtful employment of his model would require an understanding of his concern for human growth and development, psychological achievements much broader than improved 'peer relations.' Bion aims to enhance members' capacities to articulate group tasks, appreciate and manage task and other boundary issues, and to engage creatively with interpersonal and inner experiences of deepest human consequence and import.

2

Bion's War Memoirs:
A Psychoanalytical Commentary[1]

Living Experiences and Learning from them:
Some Early Roots of Bion's Contributions
to Psychoanalysis

Paulo Cesar Sandler

Judgements and mindlessness[2]

> That evening I went to see *The Boy*... There were lots of lights, brilliant
> scenes, nice banging music, loud-voiced and shrieking actors...ridiculous
> old men sat about and laughed at silly jokes. Electric light and noise – that
> was all there was, as far as London was concerned. That London show was a
> nightmare, and France was a nightmare – but the latter was positively
> healthy in comparison. [About a theatre show to which his mother had
> insisted on taking him during two days' leave from the front; Bion 1917-19,
> p.153]

War Memoirs may be regarded as the autobiographical counterpart of *Cogitations* (1992) in the sense that both contain preparatory notes – a laboratory? –
for books that were written later but published at an earlier date. *Cogitations*
contains the foundations and musings that led to *Learning from Experience*,
Elements of Psycho-Analysis and *Transformations* (1962b, 1963, 1965). That is,
in *Cogitations*, one has the experiences and thoughts that allowed Bion to
formulate verbally a mental function that 'de-sensefies' external and internal
stimuli (which he called beta-elements, felt as things-in-themselves) that are

apprehended by the sensory apparatus, in order to transform those stimuli into elementary 'elements' (he called them alpha-elements). Those 'alpha-elements' are useful to think, to dream, to store in the form of memories. Bion's daughter Parthenope once[3] compared alpha-elements to Lego blocks, and the human mind has the same playing – I would say, free associative – capacity as a child's mind. It also has the foundations of Bion's search of the processes of knowing, seen as one of the human links, born from instinctual needs. He described three links, indistinguishable from emotional experiences, initially between baby and breast: the L link (standing for Love), an expression of the life instincts; the H link (standing for Hate) an expression of the death instincts; and the K link (standing for Knowledge), an expression of the epistemophilic instincts. Those are links of the mind with itself and between human beings. Also, some discriminations between dream and hallucination, apprehension of reality and falsehood and special characteristics of the mother–baby relationship form the core of his book *Learning from Experience* (1962b). The two other books quoted above (*Elements of Psycho-Analysis* and *Transformations*) further the epistemological investigation of psycho-analytic theory, of the reliability (and lack of it) and bearings of the analyst's interpretations that try to apprehend psychic facts *as they are*. Bion assembles a special 'epistemological gauging device' to train the analyst's intuition and to evaluate the epistemological status of any statement uttered in a session, which he called 'the Grid'.

The Grid, which was further developed in *Transformations* (1965), *Attention and Interpretation* (1970) and *The Grid and Caesura* (1977c), is a still underrated, not widely used and much misunderstood device especially by those who see it as an attempt to mathematize psycho-analysis – which it is not. It is also not a periodic table such as the one used in chemistry – another common misunderstanding based on a superficial formal resemblance between the two. Bion was not wholly satisfied with it and continuously tried to improve its usage[4]. It is a two-dimensional highly dynamic, functional tool made with the constant conjunction of two perpendicular axes drawn visually into a Euclidian plane, which is construed from Hume's, Locke's, Freud's and Klein's contributions. Both axes have a developmental ethos. Or, in other words, they represent a possibility of development within some patterned spectrums. The horizontal axis represents graphically, by numbers (from 1 to 6) Freud's functions of the ego, and the spectrum of those functions is augmented by two functions devised by Bion. One of them, Level 1, is deeply embedded with a Kantian ethos, linked to innate preconceptions; he calls them 'definitory hypothesis', simply the assessment of a starting point from which thought may spring. The vertical axis is genetic and its levels are represented by letters (A to H). It posits a spectrum ranging from cruder phases or states of development of thoughts to the most sophisticated. The cruder phases (level A) are pure sensory stimuli, yet with no obtrusion of thought processes. Bion called them 'beta-elements', apprehended by the individual as things-in-themselves, felt as sensations of having grasped absolute truth; from them may evolve level B, which Bion called 'alpha-elements', 'de-sense-fied' elements which are useful to think, to dream and to store as memories. One should say, those are building blocks that allow for thought processes, duly detoxified of their sensory-based, concrete materialness. From them evolves level C, dream processes, preconceptions, concepts, reaching scientific deductive systems and algebraic calculus. Bion leaves space for future developments of thought processes yet unknown, unnamed (Sandler 1990).

Any specific level of this vertical, genetic axis must function constantly conjoined with any specific level of the horizontal axis. Level C interests us here in a very special way, for it contains a hitherto unavailable, deepening study on the function of dream work (always following Freud) and myths as tools that uncover and give further knowledge of the human mind. As Bion observes in the paper *Tower of Babel* (1960) and dwells on in the theme of *Elements of Psycho-Analysis* (1963), Freud, as a scientist investigating a problem, was confronted with the search for a solution to it that required the application of the old Greek myth Oedipus. In doing so, he did not discover the Oedipus complex – it was already discovered by the ancient Greeks. From his search resulted the discovery of psychoanalysis. It remains to be discovered, through a practical work, by any single psychoanalyst who is fully involved in emotional experience, being and thinking. The most effective way to accomplish this task is a personal analysis. How to do it through the publication of verbal written formulations? Perhaps it is doomed to failure, in many degrees. But those observations allow for a hypothesis: is the whole autobiographical cycle written by Bion a gigantic effort to formulate verbally a universal human myth conjoined with a specific individual's experiencing of it, a parable around the pain and growth involved in realizing mindlessness, bestiality, phantasies of superiority, arrogance and all manifestations of death instincts, especially lies and lying? In Freud's terms, 'insight'. In Klein's terms, the working through of the depressive position. In Bion's terms, *War Memoirs* may be regarded as an exercise in the C category of the Grid – 'the function of the narrative form is to enable the individual and the race to observe and to maintain this constant conjuction' (Bion, circa 1960, p.226). Musically speaking: an 'Impromptu in C'.

It is also interesting here how Bion made verbal formulations trying to describe some types of transformations that reality undergoes when knowing attempts to take place: rigid transformations, corresponding to the classical concept of transference; projective transformations, corresponding to the concept of projective identification; transformations in hallucinosis, which seem to compose the bulk of social life, transformations in 'K' (talk about something, understanding) and transformations in 'O' (the symbol that Bion uses to depict Kant's noumenic realm), which correspond to *becoming* and *being* – the realm of insight, of contact with 'all sins remembered' or a free movement towards the depressive position as observed by Melanie Klein. Bion uses many epistemological definitions such as selected fact (borrowed from Poincaré) and constant conjunction (borrowed from Hume). From these definitions he proceeds and aptly uses, for the first time in human science, Dirac's epistemological concept of invariances and transformations (Dirac 1930; Sandler 2002), narcissism and social-ism, tropisms, among others; and some quasi-mathematical symbols such as PS$\leftrightarrow$D and $\male\female$. The former depicts Melanie Klein's model of the developing mind, the tandem, transient, dynamic, to-and-fro movements from paranoid–schizoid to depressive positions and the latter, that which he called container/contained relation-ship, one of the elements of psychoanalysis, whose paradigm is breast/mouth and whose counterpart in adult life is vagina and penis, expressing the basic, elementary creative couple. *Cogitations (1992)* sets out his 'laboratory' to develop all of this and much more and the papers display the compacted final form of the experiences. The verbal and symbolic devices are drawn from classical psychoanalytic theory, from philosophy and from science (Sandler 1997a).

War Memoirs, Bion 1997, in its turn, embodies experiential material and dialogic verbal formulations that are similar to those of *A Memoir of the Future* (1975a, 1977a, 1979a; Sandler 1988) and *The Long Week-End* (1982). He abandons resorting to more conventional, scientific verbal formulations and – we now know – returns to a commonsensical colloquial mode to attempt communication. Hardly surprising, for Bion, together with Winnicott but in a much more explicit way, did for the psychoanalytic movement the same that Wordsworth did for poetry and Bertrand Russell for philosophy, namely, he replaced the pompous, rarefied 'jargonized' phraseology with real life speech. In *War Memoirs* and in *Cogitations* the notes make for a useful synthesis in the sense that they contain the seeds of the subsequent works. Descriptions of psychotic states, and the use that the psychotic part of the personality makes of the neurotic part, states of shared hallucinosis (suggested in the quotation that heads this paper; see subsection on 'Splitting, denial and absolute truth' p.75; see also Bion 1919. pp.40–51, 54, 61, 94, 103, 106, 200, 216), as well as profound and living human experiences and obstacles to them indicated in *The Long Week-End* and in the *A Memoir of the Future* trilogy seem to me more marked and in a certain sense less elaborated in *War Memoirs.*[5]

Not counting Francesca Bion's introduction and Parthenope Bion Talamo's postface, there are three parts in *War Memoirs*. Even the first one, young Captain Bion's report, is more than a 'war report'. It is the description of a real life, of a real analysis, of Hamlet's 'ocean of difficulties'. It is also a profound study of human groups. Does human life as it is differ from the descriptions of an army captain and his tank?

The book starts with an account by a young man, who seems to be in the grip of a psychotic bout. He joined millions of Europeans, in one single week, in the main capitals of the Old Continent. Other people experienced this event quite differently. I refer to people who not only willingly engaged in war, but were in the same places, so had the opportunity of the same experiences. Three of them, who in the future would be a psychoanalyst, a soldier and a politician and would be known as Dr Bion, Field Marshall Montgomery and the Führer Hitler were in the very same Flanders fields, the Somme mud, in the same days. Adolf Hitler's accounts glorified those experiences, that seemed to be containers for his inner hate, contempt of life and disregard of truth he stated that this time of his life was 'pure happiness' (Fest 1963; Bracher 1968; Bullock 1997). Field Marshall Montgomery's also offers a good comparison. The so-called apolitical or perhaps the non-medical minded soldier displays an interest in inanimate objects rather than in animated beings (Law, 1958). Bion's description is closer to Siegfried Sassoon's, Robert Graves's, and in a certain sense, Rupert Brooke's, Winston Churchill's and Ernst Jünger's. Why did the mud of France feel 'positively healthy' to the young Captain Bion? Perhaps because it bore witness in its depths to the undisguised cruelty of which human beings are capable, with 'London' as a hallucinated environment; social hypocrisy, a feature much emphasized by Freud (for example, when he comments on money and sex) plays a predominant role here. Perhaps it was an early manifestation of a concern for truth and life, which Bion would later expand (e.g. in 'Compassion and Truth', circa 1960, in *Cogitations*, p.125; and 'Metatheory', op. cit, specially pp.246 and 249) – and soon he was revealing his love of truth. It seems that he was doomed to have to face the issue again, as described in *Attention and Interpretation* (specially 'The mystic and the group'; see also Oliver Lyth's obituary on Bion, 1980).

One is prone to regard that fateful European 'week of joining'[6] in the restrictive social sense, namely the military meaning of the word. Perhaps the psychoanalytic view made possible by Bion's extensions of Freud's observations on malignant narcissism and Klein's observations on the paranoid–schizoid position features, specially those contained in 'A Theory of Thinking' (Freud 1911, 1914; Klein 1946; Bion 1962a, pp.116 and 119) enables us to perceive it as a joining of value judgements constantly conjoined with feelings of possessing what can be called 'the absolute truth'. This led to enlisting 'for the only truth', 'against evil'. Bion was unable to write to his parents – one may infer from the writings, especially to his mother – during the time he spent at the front. The diary was intended as a compensation for this telling failure. Telling of what? Of the envious hate of the breast, and difficulties in capacity to love, and concern for truth, as he would write later (Bion circa 1960), difficulties in attaining the depressive position. Years later – many years later – he would choose a Shakespeare line ('…all my sins be remembered') to depict the same compulsively repeated fact of lack of compassion and immobilized clinging to the paranoid–schizoid position. It presented itself in a seemingly new form; in fact it was the persistence of a hallucination, ever-repeating, reproducing, as a transference phenomenon, what Melanie Klein was able to enlighten as hate toward the nourishing breast. This time, his first wife and his first daughter would be the concretised goals, as a 'past presented', of this still unresolved hate (Bion 1975, p.70). He stated that he neglected his first wife Betty, and that he was responsible for her dying during the delivery of his first daughter, who was also object of the same lack of compassion he had towards his mother. He displayed a distinct preference to stay with his past analyst and now friend, Rickman, to dedicate himself more fully to their experiences at the Northfield hospital with mentally disabled servicemen, according to himself, and thus derived from the darkness of unconscious drives an awful, ineffable pain for the rest of his life. The real encounter with a real woman was postponed during that difficult time between 1917 and 1950; and he seemed to be a man with a rare capacity to learn from experience (to the point of writing a book on it), for his second marriage was marked by an interruption of the patterned behaviour. To Bion, as perhaps with any human being, 'war', or in Freud's notation, the manifestation of death instincts, would prove not to be restricted to external, extra-psychic facts.

Does the practising analyst need to make use of the Kantian tradition of critique?[7] Elsewhere I try to show that Freud used it regarding outward, external appearances, and in doing so he discovered and practised psychoanalysis (Sandler 1997b). Perhaps coming from another source of influence, often defined as the Jewish scholarly tradition, he added to this philosophical and scientific criticism a criticism directed at himself. This tradition of criticism enabled Freud to develop psychoanalysis: he abandoned his theories at least three times. *War Memoirs*, as I see it, enlightens as a specific contribution stemming from psychoanalytical practice, an unnoticed use that transforms scientific criticism and self-criticism into something destructive: it shows that any criticism, under the aegis of the death instinct, is manifested as hetero-criticism.[8] Under the aegis of the life instinct it transforms itself into self-criticism. This is the origin of one of Bion's legacies that seem to me exceptionally useful to the practising analyst: the 'sense of truth' (Bion 1962a, p.119). A sense of truth arises when one makes a constant conjunction of two views on the object. The constant conjunction of two opposite experiences allows for the achievement of a special correlation; the object is loved and the object is hated. Those passions usually cloud the fact that the object is the same – an integration that according to Klein appertains to the working through of depressive position but can take many years to attain some stability in the self. As Oscar Wilde puts it in the introduction of *The Picture of Dorian Gray*: people initially think that dad and mom are the greatest people on earth, later on they despise and hate them and still later on, they pardon them. Deprived of this sense of truth, we may lose contact with reality ('O'-truth). This implies lack of discrimination between false and true; it usually leads to value judgements of 'right' or 'wrong', which tend to replace, respectively, 'true' and 'false'. This is a special and very common case of *splitting*, which usually passes for normal. Bion made it explicit in 'A theory of thinking (1962a). It emerges when omniscience seems to be a replacement for the discrimination between truth and falsity, or reality and hallucination. One achieves the 'sense of truth', out of the perception that the loved object and the hated object are the same and only object, which is the same as saying that there is an important counterpart of the integration of the whole object observed by Klein in the area of thinking. Psychoanalytically speaking, one may state that judgemental values (Bion, 1962a, p.114) are an attempt to compensate for the lack of capacity to appreciate and apprehend truth and lie.

It is doomed to failure. Judgemental values (right or wrong instead of true or false) are linked to what Bion would make explicit in later years as the psychic facts he grouped within the semantic field of verbal formulations such as 'hyperbole' (*Transformations*, 1965) and 'violence of emotions' ('Metatheory', c. 1960, in *Cogitations*, 1992). The young Bion *judged* (splitting), while adding contempt and denial to judgement. He assessed everything and everyone according to criteria of certainty, of absolute truth. Judging and despising, as inanimate manifestations of the death instinct, can be found on pages 6–8, 65 and 71 of *War Memoirs*. The importance of the discrimination between judgement and appreciation (or assessment) cannot be overstressed when it comes to a real psychoanalyst's intra-session work. To present the real self to someone else, or to introduce one to oneself, or to propitiate conditions to a psychoanalytical insight precludes judgement and values.

Projective identification, hetero-criticism and self-criticism

War Memoirs provides practical lessons of what Melanie Klein called 'projective identification', i.e. the omnipotent fantasy of the capacity of splitting, denial and expulsion of undesired aspects of the mind, and, eventually, often as a consequence, of the mind itself and of the whole personality (Klein 1946), followed by the fantasy of having inoculated those painful and undesired aspects – including personal authority and responsibility – into the mind of other people. Let us take Bion's early descriptions of Major de Freine, of the officers Aitches, Clifford, Homfray, and Bargate, as reproduced in the Diary (see *War Memoirs*). He endows them with many characteristics he hates in himself, including what he saw as cowardice and physical evasion during action, or refusal to go into battle. It does not mean that those people did not possess such characteristics: the question for the practising psychoanalyst is their *use*, as 'deposits' or 'containers'. Conversely, when the young Bion saw something in someone else that, his own criteria, possessed a positive quality, he would nullify and deny it. The embryo of the depressive position still coupled with self-envy would make him deny it when it appeared in himself as well as in other people. Bion speaks of certain attitudes worthy of an officer; one can see that he emulated his Major. This can be found, for instance, in the 'not speaking too much' attitude. The Major had it, but it took many years for Bion to recognize that he was inspired by him; the first report suggests that this posture was parthenogenetic, born from himself, and thus it would be not an emulation, as it was fact. This posture countered the widespread tendency of the combatants to display and advertise self-eulogic triumphalism, over-exaggerating non-existent victories and denying failures and defeat. The same occurred with an excess of jokes and banality, connected with a flight from reality, as if there was no war and heavy killing. Later all of this could be understood as propaganda, which Bion would later synthesize in the fourth chapter of *Transformations* (1970). Freud had already pointed out the 'awful truth' that could underlie the banalization of facts through jokes, that denies reality as it is – in fact this was one of the roots of psychoanalysis. Let us examine this point with the aid of Bion's text:

> Hauser and I talked over all those matters and resolved to counteract these tendencies as best we could by pretending, in future, to enjoy action and to discourage in mess and elsewhere all talk of 'wind up' and that kind of thing. We had seen already where casual joking in that way led to…looking back on it all now, I can see how the standard rose as a result. It was no longer funny to talk of 'wind up' and 'beating it' and so on…people discovered that such talk was not expected of an officer. But this all took time. There was little chance for improvement till bad seniors like Clifford & Co. were cleared out. Later, as we gained in position, things became easier. I really believe this was the start of a better fighting spirit in the battalion. I don't mean to suggest that *we* were responsible for courage or anything in others. But I do think that we gave good officers who came to our company a chance to show their mettle. They did not immediately have their spirit undermined by foolish and beastly talk. (Bion 1970, p.89; author's italics)

Despite all his limitations of perception, it is remarkable how this 20-year-old man[9] seems to have a fine perception of the fact that projective identification is a phantasy: 'I don't mean to suggest that *we* were responsible for courage or anything in others'. I would dare to hypothesize that this kind of natural pre-disposition that shows itself at an early age, coupled with a capacity to learn from painful experiences, may have made a more mature Dr Bion also a more permeable patient, enabling him to grasp in a smooth, natural way the many truths that Mrs Klein tried to show to the psychoanalytic movement – thirty years later – and perhaps to himself, in analysis.

How can one deal with other people's limitations without attacking them? I think that one way is to realize the phantastic nature of projective identification, which is the same as saying, to understand and be responsible for one's own states of mind. In a later account, sub-titled 'Amiens' (1958), the same Major de Freine is seen as trying to retain a minimum of comfort amidst the horror of the slaughter. In 1919 he was seen merely as a corrupted official. How can arrogance be transformed into self-respect?

I believe that some considerations on the realization of the hallucinatory nature of transference phenomena and of projective identification, explicitly stated by Freud in 1912 and by Klein in 1946, as well as by Bion many times (as for example, Bion 1965, p.132) but often lost sight of, are fundamental to the analytical formation. Also, the psychoanaytical movement is prone to the acritical idolization of many of its personalities, either in universal terms (as with Freud) or in more parochial terms. Idolization and idealization are fairly well understood in terms of transference phenomena under the aegis of narcissistic projection and projective identification, but perhaps its use in group terms leaves much to be desired, if one observes the splitting wars among psycho-analysts that still prevail in the psychoanalytic movement (as opposed to psychoanalysis proper). A fresh look at these problems may consider that through their attitude, training analysts set an example for candidates. In terms of transference, this is what parents offer their children. Children usually imitate their parents (which is called identification) and gradually can leave this primeval model to set up in motion their own unique traits, becoming who they are in reality; adolescence is a contradictory, turbulent, painful interregnum, not always successful, of transgression or from those imitated patterns towards the true self (in Winnicott's terms and also described by Bion in 'Emotional Turbulence' (1977b). As he became older, Bion perceived that he was making projective identifications of his own feelings (even if they were unaccompanied by actions) of cowardice and fear into these people. Bion is seen to try to forgive himself and, consequently, Major de Freine and his previously despised colleagues, the 'bad guys', who functioned as containers to his projective identifications in the Commentary of 1972 (see *War Memoirs* 1997a). Is it a manifestation of gratitude and concern for life, in the sense of Klein's depressive position? He also seems to test his writing method which we might call 'an inner dialogue', later used in the *A Memoir of the Future* trilogy (1975a and 1977a). Let us recall that in the whole autobiographical or quasi-autobiographical cycle (composed of the trilogy, the *Long Week-End* and this volume, *War Memoirs*) he ascribes his most immature aspects to the 'Bion' character.

> *Myself:* I thought your comment that they had gone into Tanks to avoid fighting [p.8] was quite breath-taking in its disparaging insolence. Do you still mean it?[10]

> *Bion:* Let it stand, like my lack of culture, [reference to his lack of knowledge when young] as a monument to my effrontery. I am ashamed and would like to cross it out.

Myself: As long as it serves as a reminder of what we are really like, and not as a slur on 'them'.

Bion: I feel that much of the diary will appear, on this reading, to be an exercise in sheltering my complacency from the chilling blast of truth' (F. Bion 1997 p.201)

Myself: Your description of Méaulte, which was admittedly a horrible camp, a horrible Christmas, and a period of low morale in the troops, is certainly evocative, but I am disagreeably impressed by your sanctimonious priggish-ness – not only in the Army, but at Oxford where you wrote your account. I cannot believe that your army were as bad. If so, it was not surprising that Cook, Homfray and Clifford disliked you as much as you did them.

Bion: I think the 'diary' is a fair enough reflection of me (F. Bion 1997, p.208; author's bold)

Do these comments on companions-in-arms differ from the not-so subdued, behind-the-scenes, 'corridor talks' during coffee-breaks in meetings at psy-choanalytical societies or conferences? Is this disdainful mode any different from the references many a psychoanalyst makes about his or her colleagues? I can observe the existence of a 'critical sense', a product of intelligence and scientific unrest. I regard it as a manifestation of the epistemophilic instinct (Freud 1909, p.245; Klein 1932, pp.115, 153, 247). Under the aegis of the death instinct and immobilized in the paranoid–schizoid position, it expresses itself as hetero-criticism and violence. It transforms itself into morality. Under the aegis of the life instinct it moves freely from the paranoid–schizoid to the depressive position and vice-versa, and it is expressed as self-criticism, love of truth and compassion. It is transformed into ethics and discipline. The pattern is not an outside being, entity or code; it is the person vis-à-vis him/herself.

As he grew more mature, Bion used characters named after friends to express parts of himself. 'Hauser's' conversation with the professional soldier 'Carter' indicates an appreciation of what occurs when love is split off from hate. It also displays with fine detail what happens when a given social reality has a 'stimulating' function or whatever it be. For 'social reality' I understand the encircling context, either macro or micro social environment. For example, this social reality may be a sick organization; too often, social envi-ronments are overcast with projective identifications. In this case, 'stimulating' should be seen in the sense of providing a perversely 'good container' for projective identifications, which follow unobserved, in an authentic 'cross-fire'. Hate follows undisturbed, in the form of contempt of life, lack of scruples and a cunning use of projective identification. Politicians and all sorts of group leaders use it, either conscious or unconsciously. In many focal geographical areas (in Africa, Far East, Middle East, some parts of Central and South America and now in the Balkans again) it lingers in the explicit, more easily apprehended form of the sensuous–concrete counterpart in reality that the word 'war' conjures. But in some periods of history, such as our epoch, the post-World War II age, the formidable caesura of explicit, generalised concrete war does not exist. If it existed, it could more readily display to us the impressive, albeit unobserved, continuity of the death instinct in seemingly more peaceful times. Bion himself talks about 'war among psycho-analysts' in *Memoir of the Future*, Vol. II (1977a); careful publications such as *The Freud–Klein Controversies* (King and Steiner 1991) display the state of mind underlying the burning of books and, therefore, ideas as a timeless posture, which does not dispense with menaces of survival to those who are considered wrong, for they can be deprived of their means to earn a living, even if they are not physically eliminated on the spot. Even within the psychoanalytical movement, a cunning ability to get rid of personal responsibility and ethics, and an abuse of projective identification are too often regarded as 'political ability':

> 'Ah, yes,' said Hauser bitterly, 'this war, like the last war, is to be the war to end war; and the next war, like this war, will be a war to end war, and so on ad infinitum. And all the breakthroughs are the last possible breakthroughs which will break through everything of course, naturally.'
>
> 'I see you are in very good form too – sarcastic as usual. Still, I sympathize with you. I can't honestly say that I believe that this is going to be the last war, and in fact I think it would be a damned bad thing if it was.'
>
> Hauser snorted. 'You had better be careful how you say that kind of think to the Christian contingent. I don't think I should be inclined to air your views too much to Bion and his pals if I were you.'
>
> 'No', said Carter, 'I don't think I would. Still, they're not a bad lot in their way. The trouble about these damned Christians is, of course, that although they're so full of high ideals, and so packed with enthusiasm, and so determined that right will triumph, they fail to appreciate some of the more seamy sides of this business. Then when at last it does get through them, they have a nasty way of cracking up – in my opinion. I remember one poor devil. We used to think the world of him, but he just went west when he discovered his colonel was trying to do a bit of graft on him and had thwarted his possibilities of promotion simply because the colonel himself

was afraid that if he promoted such a promising officer, his own job would be jeopardized. He became unstuck, and the next thing he did was to have a kind of breakdown. This had the effect of proving that the Colonel was quite right, when in fact he was quite wrong.' (Bion 1997a, p.232)

Does the psychoanalytic movement offer a brighter perspective on the relationships between its members? Are they amenable to be managed with well-intentioned laws and bylaws intended to regulate the relationships between human beings whose internal, intrapsychic relationships still follow on under the aegis of the death instincts split off from the life instincts? After World War II, Bion would return to this point:

> To me it seems that in so far as man has set about the regulation of external relationships by law, he has been tolerably successful; the failure arises when it comes to producing any method for dealing with the underlying tensions in human relationships. And yet it is precisely these primitive unconscious tensions that present the fundamental problem in all human relationships. Whenever they obtrude themselves as an intrinsic element in the problem that is being studied, men retreat into further exploration of the possibilities of external regulation. This repeated preoccupation with machinery, being themselves nothing more than a by-product of the failure to grapple with the main problem, never achieves any higher level than the technicalities of police operations, no matter how magnificent the language they are clothed in. (Bion 1947, p.341)

The depressive position

With the aid of his self-criticism Bion maintained a sour, paradoxical relation to his war decorations, some of them ranking among the highest to be awarded for gallantry and skill. There are written indications that he valued them, alongside his university degrees. But *how* did he value them? In *Bion in New York and São Paulo* he stated his strong opinion that the gas chambers in Auschwitz should be preserved in order to prevent forgetting. He always declared that his Distinguished Service Order medal (DSO, one of the highest decorations for non-commissioned officers, second only to the VR) was his 'mark of shame'. All these self-critical 'second thoughts' were included with typically British humour in the *A Memoir of the Future* trilogy (1975a, 1977a), and they turn bitter in its complement, *The Long Week-End* (Bion 1975, 1977, 1979, 1982, 1985). The crystal-clear statements of the Diary, linked with Amiens (1958) and the Commentary (1972) (see F. Bion, 1997), might decisively contribute to prevent self-appointed followers and disciples creating a 'cult of heroes'. This term was used by Freud in a talk with a friend, the gifted writer Arnold Zweig, when trying to dissuade him from writing Freud's biography and 'idolization', as Hans Thorner observed. The Commentary seems to be almost violent in its self-criticism towards a young Bion perhaps recovering from a psychotic bout, but still intoxicated, occupying the paranoid–schizoid position, with fantasies of superiority and leaning towards hiding the truth through splitting and denial. In the Commentary Bion tries to restore what which had once been his own earlier perceptions of 'O' truth. Those perceptions, which were painful and were denied by the young officer, have been transformed up to the point of distortion. In fact, the 'O' truth is ultimately unknowable, but the perception, intuition or using of it are ever at our disposal. We can obtain the truth about Bion's unfavourable opinion of himself when he was 20 years old. It was repressed and denied, transformed to the point of distortion into its contrary, appearing as self-praise, propaganda. Thirty-eight years later, Bion agrees with himself: his opinion is expressed to himself. This leads to the *sense of truth*. To be faithful to himself: a product of analysis ('we hope to introduce the person to his 'real' self'; Bion 1977a, p.44). To be nourished by Truth, the food of the mind – as he puts it in the studies published in *Cogitations* (1960), *Learning from Experience* (1962b), *Transformations* (1965) – and till the end of this life.

In some circles of people who knew Bion personally, there is often a question which I believe false, in so far as it tries to reach absolute truth: was Bion a good soldier? According to himself, he was not. According to some superiors and friends, he was. Such a contradiction, unlike a paradox,[11] obstructs the sense of truth and common sense. What was he? We – those who are alive now and were not witness of facts – shall never know. Enjoying his hard-won maturity, he was nearer his own common sense. Then he admitted that he had been – in his own view, and this does not depend on other people's views – a bad soldier even though he wished to be a good one.[12] And he said it 'loud and clear' to himself without depression or guilt, without evasion or subterfuge, which appears to me to constitute a sense of truth; he shelters now the good and bad object, that in the end are himself, or his true self. This process is often complicated because in some cases one may overtly downsize oneself through verbal self-recriminations with a view to obtaining external consolation; the denial does not subside. In those cases there is a mimicry of the depressive position, which turns out to be untrue. The 'false depressive position' is usually full of verbal acknowledgements of guilt devoid of the living experience of insight into it; a kind of propaganda that often successfully advertises something that person is in reality avoiding experiencing. I think that those living examples, written in a literary form, can really contribute to the more precise observation of the obtrusion of that which Bion himself puts into more theoretical terms, such as 'hyperbole' and 'violence of emotions', in his earlier published work, for example, in the last three chapters of *Transformations*. There he dwells on Klein's observation that it is not only the hate that endangers the object, but also violent love (Klein 1934, p.286). Bion many times said that the wish to be a good analyst (to act out memory and desire) precludes being an analyst. To wish to be a good parent, child, soldier, whatever it be, precludes being a real parent, child, soldier, analyst.

Splitting, denial and absolute truth

There are states of *mindlessness* linked to *splitting* (in the sense given by Melanie Klein) which result in destructive value judgements:

> The rest of the day passed more or less uneventfully except for the fact that the Boche smelt a rat and started to shell our little area. We took cover and lost neither men nor tanks. We simply had the misery of enduring an hour and a half's desultory strafe from 5.9's.[13] In the evening we were cheered by the arrival of three artillery officers who were going up to observation posts to reconnoitre. They stopped to talk, and we had the usual flow of 'news'. The artillery are notorious liars and always cheerful liars. They assured us the enemy would attack the next morning and that they would suffer hopeless defeat; King George had been assassinated and Horatio Bottomley[14] had seized the throne; the Germans had sued for peace, which would probably be signed within three days. With this and earnest protestations of truthfulness they departed! *It's a funny thing, but cheeriness was every bit as infectious as gloom*, and those yarns, with the method of telling, quite set us up for the night. But we were to have a rude shock. Clifford[15] had not been near us since he had departed to Brigade HQ in a state of panic. We had been left entirely to our own devices. (F. Bion 1997, pp.60–61; my italics)

Just before action, the company had found a false refuge in a convent near Meteren:

> At this date things were very bad. It is very difficult to stop in a line for days and expect an enemy attack at any moment. The strain on the nerves is very great, especially when you know there is nothing between the enemy and the sea but your line of troops. Idiot jokes in mess and open talk of fear all

contributed to lower one's spirits, and, as you will hear, I was already in a very low state.

The night's rest and the good food made us feel very much better. We were hardly disturbed by the enemy's shelling of the convent as his fire was erratic; and although there were casualties, they occurred in a different part of the building. (*ibid* p.89)

A kind of progressive self-attack on his own perception, turning him, albeit in a hallucinated way, into an insensitive person, oblivious to the danger and far from self-preservation (depleted of the life instincts) took the young official over as the war went on. To the practising analyst, this entails the impossibility of 'smelling' the 'O' truth.[16] There is an exacerbation of the destructive mental situation of *splitting*. From page 93 onwards the account shows how Bion's survival depended increasingly on chance, as well as on his precocious capacity of discernment. The latter naturally proved to be useful in his later psychoanalytical practice.

It was a weird business – the heat, and the nightmares out of which one started up suddenly in a kind of horror to find the sweat pouring down one's face. *It was almost impossible to distinguish dream from reality.* The tat-tat-tat of the German machine-guns would chime in with your dream with uncanny effect, so that when you awoke you wondered whether you were dreaming. The machine-gun made you think everything was genuine, and only by degrees you recovered yourself to fall into uneasy sleep again. (*ibid.* p.94; my italics)

The situation was extremely serious and it seems that Bion was finally able to get his sense back. The dangerous, life-threatening state would be further elaborated in studies in Second Thoughts (1967): the person is neither dreaming nor awake, there is no discrimination between dead and alive, the psychotic personality does not distinguish animate from inanimate. A forced *splitting* occurs (*Cogitations,* p.133; *Learning from Experience,* p.9 and also Chapter V) or 'anti-alpha-function', as I have proposed to name it (Sandler 1990, 1997a). See also in many parts of *A Memoir of the Future:*

The dreamless sleep ended. The day was as empty of events – facts proper to daytime – as the night had been empty of dreams. Meals were served to both girls. It occurred to them that they had no memory of the food; the 'Facts' of daytime and night were defective, mutilated. They were having dreams – mutilated dreams – lacking a dimension like a solid body that cast no shadow in light. The world of reality, facts, was no longer distinguishable from dreams, unconsciousness, night. Thoughts with and thoughts without a thinker replaced universe where discrimination ruled. Dreams had none of the distinguishing characteristics of mind, feelings, mental representations, formulations. The thinker had no thoughts, the thoughts were without thinkers. Freudian dreams had no Freudian free associations; Freudian free associations had no dreams. Without intuition they were empty, without concept they were blind. (Bion 1975a, p.41)

Having thus rid himself of the apparatus of conscious awareness of internal and external reality, the patient achieves a state which is felt to be neither alive nor dead (Bion 1956, p.38; see also 1957, p.46)

I would begin to be a bit suspicious about that patient: I would wonder whether she really knows the difference between a dream and waking life, or whether she knows the difference between courtship – a love affair – and a psychoanalysis (Bion 1975b, p.5)

It did not take long for interest in life to die out. Soon I found *myself* almost hopeless. I used to lie on my back and stare at the low roof. Sometimes I stared for hours at a small piece of mud that hung from the roof by a grass and quivered to the explosion of the shells. Then suddenly one day I heard that the South Africans on our left were playing the fool. They used to crawl out onto the road on their left at night and try to get hit by the German machine-gun that fired down the road. The news had a curiously bracing effect. I don't know now whether the tale was true – certainly it had been common enough in the earlier part of the war – but I felt things now could be no worse and that actually a gleam of hope had appeared – it was always possible to get badly wounded or perhaps even killed... life had now reached such a pitch that horrible mutilations or death could not conceivably be worse...After all, if you get a man and hunt him like an animal, in time he will become one. I am at a loss now to tell you of our life. Such worlds separate the ordinary human's point of view from mine at that time, that anything I can write will either be incomprehensible or will give a quite wrong impression ('Amiens' in F. Bion 1997, p.94)

The state of mind that phantazises possession of absolute truth was gradually seen as dangerous to life itself. In later years, Bion would profit from this experience when he brought into the psychoanalytical realm the actuality of the fantasies of possessing absolute truth, ideas of full contact with beta-elements, Kant's '*Ding-an-sich*' (thing-in-itself). As the war continued, this dangerous state of mind became more frequent:

> ...a curious kind of excitement that used to come over us in action... I told Hauser that I thought the only thing we could do if we were to be any use at

all was to get out of our place and get with our men. He agreed. I may as well say now that from that point of view of sheer unadulterated lunacy what followed was the maddest and most dangerous thing I ever did. I must have been very nearly mad to do it. But I never *thought* more clearly in my life ('Amiens' in F. Bion, 1997, p.106; Bion's italics)

Femininity

Slowly, the multitude of judgements start to disappear – perhaps in the way that good mothers do not judge their children. After several months of cruel battles Bion begins to use the high temperature of the exhaust pipes of the tanks to boil water in containers improvised from gasoline cans, thus conjuring up a serious manifestation of 'Britishness' otherwise unthinkable: hot tea. Later on, Bion would ingeniously and maternally find a way of getting round still another strenuous job which his men had to face for more than ten uninterrupted hours before battle. They had to sweep mile after mile of ground behind the tanks, to erase the trail left by the tank tracks, which could be spotted by aircraft or reconnaissance balloons. Bion attached a kind of giant sweeper to the back of the bestial weapon, which could thus automatically sweep behind itself.

Can human beings attain happiness? This provides us with a link between motherhood and a baby's expectations. Is happiness a word that has any counterpart in reality? Or can we human beings only experience 'unreal felicity'? Whatever it may be, there is a transience in this event. If the individual is under the aegis of the pleasure/unpleasure principle, he/she abhors the transient nature of life. Those doubts coincide with feminine expressions of care and life among the soldiers: the beer in the canteen, hot meals, good cigars and an officer playing '*Träumerei*' on the violin. Unpleasant surprises put an end to the gaiety: Mount Kemmel, which had been considered a firm conquest, was lost again. 'We got up and looked at the pleasant room and the cheery fire and wondered why we had ever been such fools as to believe they were real' ('Diary' in War Memoirs, p.99). The same situation repeats itself with the episode of the drowning of the noise of the Handley Page bombers protecting the infantry men (*ibid.*, p.103). Is there a moment in life after the stage of the mother–baby pair, when projective identification is not just a phantasy?

The unknown

Apparently Bion faced rather early the need for a kind of discipline and care which he would later call *Attention and Interpretation*. Perhaps this kind of discipline allows for a real analysis, a real life which deserves this name, a life which is not locked in unconsciousness, unconcern, the commonplace, little learning, contempt toward the animated world, superficiality, arrogance, illusion. The micrometric following, by the analyst, in an observant and lively manner, of 'each', as it were, psychic movement in the session seems to me another of Bion's contributions to analytical practice and to psychoanalysis. Foreshadowing this is the need to live through five hours to advance just one mile inside a steel cage filled with carbon monoxide, continuously risking a direct hit which would blow it up instantaneously. This was the tank (Bion 1977, pp.44–45). Is there any practising analyst who endures session after session in order to reach what is often much less than a 'psychic mile' – which in real terms should be called a 'micro-mile' – and is entitled to be exempted from such an effort? What is waiting for us after an insight? Usually, it is a resistance. What is waiting for our perception after the real experiencing of the depressive position? A renewed experiencing of the paranoid–schizoid position, *if* the analysis proceeds. Bion formulated this often denied aspect of Melanie Klein's work, the living tandem movement that dynamically depicts the interplay of the paranoid–schizoid position with the depressive position through a quasi-mathematical symbol: PS–D.[17] The unknown – Freud unearthed the forgotten insights of the German Idealism and called it the unconscious,[18] and later, the id – is the life of an analyst. At least, to those who do suspect that, during a session, the whole of the psychoanalytic theory can constitute a vast paramnesia to fill the void of our ignorance (Bion 1976, 1977b). To try to use the already available body of knowledge as a shield to 'becoming' and to 'being' what one really is, equals scientific push into the unknown. It means that one avoids using theories either as *a priori* pre-patterned moulds repeatedly used to fit clinical data into *a priori* theories or *ad hoc* theories that fit the clinical data. Bion, because of his war experience, the analyst in real analysis, the patient undergoing a real analysis,[19] can probably report their experience in the same way: 'You felt you were being pushed into the unknown' (Bion 1997, p.79).

This seems to be a counterpoint of the bard's insight: 'It's like a barber's chair, that fits all buttocks' (Shakespeare, *All's Well that Ends Well* II, ii, 18). Bion's philosophical background had firm bearings in his life experience. Let us continue with the tank experience: the engine simply did not work for a whole day, but he did not give up: 'The infantry were warned that my tank wouldn't be able to go in after all. We started up again, however, and to our surprise it went like a bird that time to the end!' (F. Bion 1997, p.47). To someone who had this experience and managed to learn from it, David Hume's observation on the pitfalls involved in inductive reasoning becomes crystal clear, rather than a subject of sterile, brainy, philosophical dispute. This is a delicate, and in my opinion still little understood, point in Bion's work – what he said about *reality and truth*, about common sense. I propose the following steps: first, to put up with the multi-dimensional nature of three views, i.e. *A Memoir of the Future*, *The Long Week-End*, *War Memoirs*. Second, to couple this with a paradoxical fact without any attempt to resolve it: the views were written by, and correspond to, four 'different' people: the youngster, the experienced analyst and the older man that are simultaneously the fourth, i.e. one person called Bion. If what I propose proves to be acceptable, we have a situation – the whole of Bion's autobiographical cycle – analogous to the five human senses (or six as Freud suggested, when he regarded consciousness as the sense organ for the perception of psychic reality). Hence we become capable of achieving common sense – each view being analogous to each human sense. Bion, after Locke and Hume, brought into light the common-sense nature of psychoanalysis, already existing in the work of Freud and Klein. It must be neither confused with 'commonplace' nor with 'good sense', a concept used by Descartes and by religion. It concerns the fact that all the 'senses' can apprehend the same reality, even if we do not know exactly what this reality is. It must not be confused with Bachelard's use of the term in French (Bachelard 1938). The common sense is either individual or collective: having at least two senses in common, or, even better, more than two. It allows getting closer to 'O', even if this closeness is transient and fleeting as the Demiurge and the forms, demanding constant adjustment.[20] This concept of common sense in Bion's work is identical to that originally created by Locke, a fact which has generally been overlooked. Given the solid scientific grounding that Bion had in Oxford, it is not surprising to find it in his work. Like Freud, he continuously made use of Bacon, Locke, and Hume, and he allied them with Kant. We cannot know what really happened in the muddy fields of Flanders – 'O'. A verbal transformation can take the form of 'incarnate horror'. The lack of life goes on there. Today most of those who witnessed that life are dead and we do not know what it was. But we know *that* it was and we may intuit its nature.

Doubts regarding the human possibilities of love and concern for truth seem to me this book's leitmotiv. What is the reality of love? What is its possibility in social terms, 'passionate love', according to Bion the highest expression of 'O' itself, or its complementary, matching antithesis in the antithetical pair, 'beastly hatred'? Passionate love is also made apparent in some passages in *War Memoirs* (e.g. p.215) as well as in the very existence of the whole autobiographical cycle in its published form. After all, it is the work of a creative couple, Wilfred Bion and his dedicated wife Francesca. Perhaps love is a permanent state of doubt, of rejecting policies of 'property', or 'thus far and no further', as he writes in the trilogy, on the subject of life and love. Life and love is a flame that is eternal as long as it lasts:

Myself: What upsets you most?

Bion: Your success, I think. I hesitate to say it, because it sounds ungrateful. I cannot imagine what was wrong, but I never recovered from the survival of the Battle of Amiens. Most of what I do not like about you seemed to start then.

Myself: As you had not realized it then, I am surprised that you say so little about events that in retrospect seem utterly horrible.

Bion: I should have thought that there was nothing material excluded .

Myself: Possibly. It may not have struck you as dramatic enough to mention the time, long before Ypres, when you were asleep on the stone floor of a farmhouse that had been levelled in previous fighting. That sickly, sweet stench of corpses which...

Bion: ...we couldn't locate. I remember perfectly. What about it?

Myself: Nothing: that was what was so awful. You were not even frightened. By the time you got to Oxford, you had 'forgotten' it. I don't remember it, but my gut does. I was and am still scared. What about? I don't know – just scared. No, not even 'just' scared. Scared.

Bion: That 'sweet smell of the dead' I remember. It was pervasive. Where was that? I know it was before we had tanks.

Myself: And how could you have been such a damned fool as to let that Boche drag you to the dug-out where his dead pal was? On August 8th it was.

Bion: I remember. Asser was about to die – refusing to surrender. He could have been fighting for something of which I could not be aware. But his death killed me. At least, it made me feel I could never be a man of such intensity that I would knowingly embrace certain death.

Myself: Years after, many years after, I learned that I could hardly claim to love a woman because the woman's love included her love of the father of her children. I do not know. I can only aspire to such love and suffer the uncertainty that it is only an aspiration of which I fall short.

Bion: I had no doubt – do not ask me why, but I repeat *no* doubt – that Asser, nearly a year younger than me, was such a man. I do not feel that about you, who I have survived to become.

Myself: I certainly do not claim it. I am still 'becoming', though. It depends if death forestalls my growth. I can hardly claim more time as of a right. (Bion 1977, pp.209–210)

Acknowledgements

to Mrs. Francesca Bion and Dr Robert Lipgar, who kindly reviewed the original text with painstaking care, granting me the privilege of their many corrections as well as suggestions; to Drssa Parthenope Bion Talamo, for her reading and suggestions; to Prof. Marc de La Ruelle, for his correction of the English language.

References

Bachelard, G. (1938) *A Formação do Espírito Científico (contribuição para uma psicanálise do conhecimento). Brazilian version, por E. S. Abreu. São Paulo: Contraponto, 1996.*

Bion, F. (1997) 'Introductory notes.' In *War Memoirs.* London: Karnac Books.

Bion, W. R. (1917–1919) 'Diary.' In F. Bion (ed) *War Memoirs* (1997) London: Karnac Books.

Bion, W. R. (1947) 'Psychiatry at a time of crisis.' In Francesca Bion (ed) *Cogitations.* London: Karnac Books 1992.

Bion, W. R. (1956) 'Development of Schizophrenic Thought.' In W.R. Bion *Second Thoughts.* London: Heinemann Medical Books, 1967.

Bion, W. R. (1957) 'Differentiation of the Psychotic from the Non-psychotic Personalities.' In W. R. Bion *Second Thoughts.* London: Heinemann Medical Books, 1967.

Bion, W. R. (c. 1960) '*The Tower of Babel – possibility of using a racial myth.*' In F. Bion (ed) *Cogitations.* London: Karnac Books, 1992.

Bion, W. R. (c. 1960) 'Concern for Truth and Life.' In F. Bion (ed) *Cogitations.* London: Karnac Books, 1992.

Bion, W. R. (1962a) 'A Theory of Thinking.' In *Second Thoughts.* London: Heinemann Medical Books, 1967.

Bion, W. R. (1962b) *Learning from Experience.* London: Heinemann Medical Books.

Bion, W. R. (1963) *Elements of Psychoanalysis.* London: Heinemann

Bion, W. R. (1965) *Transformations.* London: Heinemann.

Bion, W. R. (1967) *Second Thoughts.* London: Heinemann Medical Books.

Bion, W. R. (1970) *Attention and Interpretation.* London: Tavistock Publications.

Bion, W. R. (1972) 'Commentary.' In F. Bion (ed) *War Memoirs* (1997). London: Karnac Books

Bion, W. R. (1975a) *A Memoir of the Future. Vol. I: The Dream.* Rio de Janeiro: Imago.

Bion, W. R. (1975b) Clinical Seminars. In F. Bion (ed) *Clinical Seminars and Four Papers.* Abingdon: Fleetwood Press, 1987.

Bion, W. R. (1976) Evidence. In F. Bion (ed) *Clinical Seminars and Four Papers.* Abingdon: Fleetwood Press, 1987.

Bion, W. R. (1977a) *A Memoir of the Future. Vol. II: The Past Presented.* Rio de Janeiro: Imago.

Bion, W. R. (1977b) 'Emotional Turbulence.' In Francesca Bion (ed) *Clinical Seminars and Four Papers.* Abingdon: Fleetwood Press, 1987.

Bion, W. R. (1977c) *The Grid and Caesura.* Rio de Janeiro: Imago.

Bion, W. R. (1979a) *A Memoir of the Future. Vol. III: The Dawn of Oblivion.* Strathclyde: Clunie Press.

Bion, W. R. (1979b) *Bion in New York and São Paulo.* Perthshire: Clunie Press.

Bion, W. R. (1982) *The Long Week-End.* Abingdon: Fleetwood Press.

Bion, W.R. (1985) *All My Sins Remembered.* Abingdon: Fleetwood Press.

Bion, W. R. (1992) In F. Bion (ed) *Cogitations.* London: Karnac Books.

Bond, B. (1968) 'Passchendaele.' In *Historia do Século XX, Vol II.* Edited by J. M. Roberts. Brazilian version, São Paulo, Abril Cultural, 1974.

Bracher, K. (1968) *The German Dictatorship.* New York: Penguin Books, 1991.

Bullock, A. (1997) *Hitler and Stalin: Parallel Lives.* (revised edition, 1998) London: Fontana.

Dirac, P. (1930) *The Principles of Quantum Mechanics.* Fourth edition. Oxford: Clarendon Press, 2001.

Eksteins, M. (1989). *A Sagração da Primavera.* Brazilian version, by R. Eichenberg. Rio de Janeiro: Rocco, 1991.

Fest, J. (1963) *The Face of the Third Reich.* English version, by M. Bullock. London: Pelican Books, 1979.

Freud, S. (1909) 'A Case of Obsessional Neurosis.' *Standard Edition X.*

Freud, S. (1911) 'Psycho-Analytic Notes on an Autobiographical Account of a Case of Paranoia.' *Standard Edition XII.*

Freud, S. (1912) 'The Dynamics of Transference.' *Standard Edition XII.*

Freud, S. (1914) 'On Narcissism.' *Standard Edition XIV.*

Freud, S. (1930) 'The Goethe Prize' Address delivered in the Goethe House at Frankfurt *Standard Edition XXI.*

Freud, S. (1938) 'Constructions in Analysis' *Standard Edition XXIII.*

King, P. and Steiner, J. (1991) *The Freud–Klein Controversies.* London: Routledge.

Klein, M. (1932) *The Psycho-Analysis of Children.* London: The Hogarth Press and the Institute of Psycho-Analysis, 1959.

Klein M. (1934) 'A Contribution to the psycho-genesis of the manic-depressive states.' In *Contributions to Psycho-Analysis*. London: The Hogarth Press and the Institute of Psycho-Analysis, 1950.

Klein M. (1946) 'Notes on some schizoid mechanisms.' In *Developments in Psycho-Analysis*. M. Klein, P. Heimann, S. Isaacs, J. Riviere, (eds) *Developments in Psycho-Analysis* London; The Hogarth Press and the Institute of Psycho-Analysis, 1952.

Law, B. [Viscount Montgomery of Alamein] (1958) *The Memoirs of Field Marshal the Viscount Montgomery of Alamein, K.G.* New York: Signet Books.

Lyth, O. (1980) 'Obituary: Wilfred Ruprecht Bion.' *International Journal of Psycho-Analysis* 61, 269.

Sandler, P. C. (1987) 'The Long Week-End.' *International Journal of Psycho-Analysis 14*, 273.

Sandler, P. C. (1988) *Introdução a 'Uma Memória do Futuro', de W. R. Bion.* Rio de Janeiro: Imago Editora Ltada.

Sandler, P. C. (1990) *Fatos: A tragédia do conhecimento em psicanálise.* Rio de Janeiro: Imago Editora Ltada.

Sandler, P. C. (1997a) 'The apprehension of psychic reality: Extensions of Bion's theory of alpha-function.' *International Journal of Psycho-Analysis 78*, 43.

Sandler, P. C. (1997b). *A Apreensão da Realidade Psíquica. Vol. I.* Rio de Janeiro: Imago Editora Ltada.

Sandler, P. C. (1999) 'Um desenvolvimento e aplicação clínica do instrumento de Bion, o Grid.' *Rev. Bras. Psicanál 33*, 13, 38.

Sandler, P. C. (2000) *A Apreensão da Realidade Psíquica. Vol. III: As Origens da Psicanálise na Obra de Kant.* Rio de Janeiro: Imago Editora Ltada.

Sandler, P. C. (2002) 'O Desassossego de Russell, as Irrelevâncias de Dirac' (Origens inéditas du obra de Bion) *IDE 35*, 69–84.

Tálamo, P. B. (1997) 'Aftermath.' In W. R. Bion *War Memoirs*. London: Karnac Books.

Taylor, A. J. P. (1950–1967) *Europe: Grandeur and Decline.* New York: Penguin Books, 1991.

Thorner, H. A. (1981) 'Notes on the desire of knowledge.' *International Journal of Psycho-Analysis 62*, 73.

Endnotes

1.   As soon as this paper was completed, the psychoanalytic movement was struck by an unpleasantly sad surprise: the untimely disappearance of Drssa. Parthenope Bion Talamo. As was the custom in a four-year history of mutual collaboration, Drssa. Parthenope Bion Talamo was reviewing this manuscript; she already had kindly given some ideas on it. I dedicate the present text to her memory.

2.   Unless otherwise indicated, all quotations refer to *War Memoirs* (Bion, 1997). The reader must bear in mind that all the names Bion use in his books are fictional, out of his natural courtesy and deep respect to his fellow men.

3.   At second ' Bion's Writings Around the World', extra-official meeting at IPAC, San Francisco, 1995.

4.   I proposed elsewhere an aid to grasp its meaning and usage though a tri-dimensional version of the Grid; it was awarded the 'Durval Marcondes Prize', given by the Associação Brasileira de Psicanálise to papers written by training analysts, 1999 (Sandler, 1999).

5.   The choosing of a literary presentation sometimes fuels hostile questioning about the psychoanalytical status of some works. One may be reminded that Freud won a Literature Prize (the Goethe Prize, 1930). Bion's autobiographical cycle is useful to the practising psychoanalyst. It resembles Freud's and, perhaps surprisingly, Goethe's work. Not only in the formal, dialogic structure but also in the way that Goethe, just like Freud and Bion, was one of those wise men whose broadness of knowledge was so remarkable that it defies any attempt at classification. Goethe was a scientist, a poet, a philosopher. His autobiographical cycle, *Wilhelm Meister*, which I take to include *Dichtung und Wahrheit*, *Werther* and *Faust*, is one of the most effective testimonies of real human nature. Shakespeare inspired Goethe; both inspired Freud and Klein; those four were perhaps Bion's most fundamental intellectual forebears.

6.   During one week in 1914 two million young men from the main European capitals enthusiastically enlisted themselves to fight (Eksteins 1989; Sandler 1987).

7.   Kant's 'criticism' or critique is a method first expounded in his work *Critique of Pure Reason*. He displays the flaws of rational thinking and formal, classical logics when the issue is the apprehension of reality, especially deductive and inductive methods, as well as showing some of the traps of dogmatic metaphysics. Freud based his discovery of psychic reality and the unconscious realm as a form of existence of its own, vis-à-vis material reality, on Kant's differentiation of immanent, sensuously apprehensible phenomena and the transcendent, ultra and infra-sensuous realm of noumena. The investigation of the roots of psychoanalysis in the work of Kant is published elsewhere (Sandler 1997b, 2000).

8.   I am using a concept that tries to make a constant conjunction of two observations: Bion's linkage between arrogance and self-respect (*On Arrogance*, 1957) and T. S. Eliot's observation that self-criticism produces poetry and hetero-criticism (criticism directed at persons other than oneself) produces poetry.

9.   In a seemingly psychotic adolescent foolhardiness, young Bion moved heaven and earth to enlist at 17, after being rejected on the grounds of age and perhaps augmenting it artificially, using his father's prerogatives as a colonial engineer serving in India. See *The Long Week-End* (Bion, 1982, pp.98–118).

10. In the beginning of the Diary (F. Bion 1997), Bion boasts that the tank soldiers are superior people; and he also records his opinion that more seasoned infantry soldiers joined the Tank Corps in order to evade direct combat.

11. For the differentiation between contradictions and paradoxes, see Sandler 1997b.

12. I had the opportunity to confirm this interpretation of mine with Mrs Bion's ideas and experience with her husband. She, kind as ever, was gracious enough to confirm to me that Dr Bion maintained deep respect towards those who he saw as 'real soldiers', even though he would not include himself among them. Hence the paradoxical situation, that one can observe under the paradox of the sense of the truth, without trying to resolve it, regarding his war decorations as 'marks of shame', as he depicts them in *A Memoir of the Future* and *The Long Week-End*, while at the same time he used these decorations of war on important occasions in his whole life, including them with his titles, following his name as the author of many of his books.

13. This refers to the diameter, in inches, of fragmentation howitzers with very precise aiming which were utterly destructive and hazardous projectiles, much feared by soldiers because they cruelly injured people in an almost indescribable, appalling way. They were a typically German military speciality: maximum destructive power with maximum mechanical precision and speed.

14.   King George was a known alcoholic who lacked competence to be a real king. As a result some demagogues and professional speakers, seasoned in the skills of rhetoric, perceived a void in which to act – and to make money. Among these Horatio Bottomley was perhaps the most successful. He showed a striking similarity to John Bull, which gave him mythical clout. He made a remarkable fortune with his 'patriotic' speeches.

15.   The battalion commander at that moment.

16.   Or 'pursuing truth O' ('Reality: psychic and sensuous', in *Attention and Interpretation*).

17.   The more popular interpretation of Klein's original interplay between the positions debased it into a static concept pervaded with idealized ideas of cure. The so-called 'neo-Kleinians' understand that PS should be regarded as madness, a pathological state. Conversely, they regard D as the goal of that which they see as a successful analysis, as if mind could be a paralysed entity allowing its 'beholder' to live in a paradise-like 'cured' or 'analysed' state.

18.   '*The unconscious is the true psychical reality; in its innermost nature it is as much unknown to us as the reality of the external world, and it is as incompletely presented by the data of consciousness as is the external world by the communications of our sense organs.*' (Freud 1900, *The Interpretation of Dreams*, p.613; Freud's italics).

19.   '*P.A.*: Mystery is real life; real life is the concern of real analysis, Jargon passes for psycho-analysis, as sound is substituted for music, verbal facility for literature and poetry, trompe l'oeil representations for painting.' (Bion 1977, p.80)

20.   Bion was explicit in many of his works, as for example, *Transformations* (for example, pp.136, 136, 147) and *A Memoir of the Future* (for example, vol. I, p.56) of his respect towards Plato's dialogues especially *The Republic*, whose metaphor of the cave and shadows he quoted often. One of the most used photos of him displays his own copy of Plato's works. Bion's emphasis on Plato served as an inspiration to my own research on Freud's origins in Plato's observations. These observations also caused some of Aristotle's attacks on him. Plato posited the existence of ideal forms, or simple forms, that corresponded to the unknowable ultimate reality that were, nevertheless, real and the origin of everything else. Plato also formulated the existence of an untiring and ever-erring demiurge, a mythological entity that tried to copy the forms, being doomed to eternal failure and eternal reformulation. This corresponds, according to my own research, to Freud's concept of unconscious and conscious; and to Kant's noumenic and phaenomenic realms (Sandler 1997b).

3

Gregariousness and the Mind

Wilfred Trotter and Wilfred Bion

Nuno Torres

Devil: …I do not cultivate theories; theories are a symptom of gregarious animals when they function as members of a group. I am special, individual, a victim of disapproval.

Bion, The Dawn of Oblivion (1979)

It is reasonably consensual that Bion's scientific production can be divided roughly at least into two clear stages: the 'group period' and the 'psycho-analytic period'. Both periods are clearly marked by his analysts. The first period is marked by the analysis with John Rickman,[1] and the second one with Melanie Klein. One of John Rickman's ultimate aims was to apply psychoanalytic knowledge to the study of groups (Rickman, 1957) and Bion shared it; they've worked together on groups for many years. In Bion's words: 'There is no corpus of knowledge that does for the study of the group what psychoanalysis does for the study of the individual…a subject which today has begun to assume clearer outlines' (Bion 1948, p.82).

Later, Bion would follow Melanie Klein's advice and abandon the group studies in favour of psychoanalysis of individuals. The separation of these two periods is so sharply linked to Rickman and Klein, that Bion wrote and published 'Group dynamics: a review' (Bion 1952), his last paper on groups, the year after Rickman's death on July 1951. He reformulated his earlier group dynamics theory as manifestations of psychotic mechanisms described by Klein, and would not write again on groups until 1970 (*Attention and Interpretation*),

It is the aim of this paper to show that there is a third major influence on Bion's scientific ideas, although much hidden in the background: Wilfred Trotter. Trotter represents one influence that can be considered no less fundamental than Rickman and Klein, and certainly more inclusive, as it can be seen traversing all of Bion's work, unlike that of Rickman and Klein which are in some ways mutually exclusive.[2] In Wilfred Trotter we can find the conceptual roots for several original propositions and fundamental conceptions concerning group dynamics and the functioning of the mind in general, which were foreign to earlier psychoanalytic propositions:

(a) the study of the factors which lead to group morale (good group spirit)

(b) preference for groups with 'suspended leadership' instead of authority-based ones

(c) man as a gregarious animal

(d) group mentality, and its conflict with individual needs

(e) the triad of group instinctual basic behaviour, plus a social *valency*

(f) the mind's necessity for truth and certainty, and the problem of intolerance to uncertainty

(g) the importance and difficulties of learning by experience

(h) the focus on the 'development of the mind' instead of the alleged 'cure'

(i) the conflicts between the new idea and establishment (status quo)

(j) the importance of accepting mental turbulence instead of adherence to stable-minded states

(k) the crucial need for an adequate system of communicating ideas

(l) the mental 'digestion' of raw sensory material into food for thought

(m) the mind as a muscle

(n) the danger of human extinction.

The analysis of these issues is not merely an exercise in historic archaeology. It can throw some light onto some of Bion's conceptions, frequently taken as 'enigmatic and deliberately half-formulated' (Hinshelwood 1994, p.ix).

Who was Trotter?

Wilfred Batten Lewis Trotter (1872–1939) was, according to Strachey, one 'English man of science and wide education born at the middle of the nineteenth century' (Cheshire and Thoma 1991), a surgeon and sociologist whose writings on the behaviour of man in the mass popularised the phrase 'herd instinct'. He had been a surgeon at the University College Hospital, London, since 1906, a professor of surgery there since 1935, and held the office of honorary surgeon to King George V from 1928 to 1932. In the history of surgery he is especially noted for his work on the regeneration of sensory nerves in the skin.

Furthermore, his role in the history of the British psychoanalytical movement is a pioneering and central one; he had attended the first International Congress of Psychoanalysis in April 1908, and brought its ideas to England. He was the great friend and staunch supporter of Ernest Jones. The latter says that he was, 'apart from Freud, the man who mattered most in my life' (Jones cit. in Gillespie 1979). According to Ernest Jones:

> He was one of the first two or three in England to appreciate the significance of Freud's work, which I came to know through him...he followed the development of Psycho-Analysis to the end of his life (he revised the translation of the Moses book, for instance)... He was a member of the Council of the Royal Society that conferred their Honorary Membership on Professor Freud and he attended him medically after his removal to England. (Jones 1940)

In 1905, Trotter and Jones shared an office in Harley Street, and they shared enthusiastically theoretical interests:

> Together they discussed far-reaching plans for improving the future of civilization based on a full knowledge of the biological, including psychological, motivation of man... Jones and Trotter had begun their study of abnormal psychology by reading William James, Frederic Myers and Milne Bramwell, then the French school, and above all Janet...Then, through Trotter, Jones discovered Freud, first through reading the Dora analysis... Trotter and Jones had already appreciated that the secrets to be discovered were outside of consciousness, but they did not know how to explore unconscious mental processes until Freud showed the way, namely by the technique of 'free association'. (Gillespie 1979, pp.276–277)

With a growing interest in Freud's workings, Trotter and Jones decided to learn German for the purpose of going into the matter further (Jones 1945). For a variety of reasons, their professional ways separated; Jones become a psychoanalyst and Trotter remained a brain surgeon. Nevertheless, they would be linked by family for ever; in 1910 Trotter married Jones' sister.

Trotter was also the role model for the editorial policy decision about the terminology of the existing standard edition of Freud's works (Cheshire and Thoma 1991, p.433). According to MacCurdy, Jones borrowed from Trotter the use of the word 'rationalization', an assertion which is strongly contested by James Glover (Glover 1924.)

In his masterpiece, *Instincts of the Herd in Peace and War* (1916), Trotter's main idea is that there exists one instinct that was as yet incompletely described by psychology, the *herd instinct*. This instinct would represent the natural tendency to association – i.e. gregariousness – of some biological organisms. Charles Darwin had referred to the existence of a social instinct deeply ingrained in all social animals as the origin of moral and consciousness in man (Darwin 1871). Trotter not only retakes Darwin but also the contributions of Karl Pearson and Boris Sidis about the biological and psychical significance of gregariousness. According to Trotter, Pearson called attention to the enlargement of the selective unit effected by the appearance of gregariousness, and to the fact that therefore within the group the action of natural selection becomes modified. (Trotter 1916, p.24). Sidis' concept inspiring Trotter is the idea of *suggestion* as a mechanism to serve gregariousness. In short, the assumptions underlying the concept of herd instinct are: a) gregariousness is a natural vector of living beings, which gives advantage to the species facing the laws of natural selection b) the weaknesses of the rational mind are consequences of suggestibility imposed by herd instinct c) the main problem of the human species is how to reconcile the rational mind and gregariousness, both of which are the foundations of its evolution.

These ideas were received quite enthusiastically at those times. The book was printed six times from 1916 to 1921, but with time it was relegated to a merely historic status and nowadays is only available in second-hand book shops, even though it was re-edited in 1953. In 1917, it was given a long and favourable notice by William A. White in the Psycho-analytic Review. Augusta Bonnard, in her review of the book, wrote:

> What remains is a storehouse of brilliant and stimulating inferences, leading to curiously faulty conclusions. For instance, Trotter's postulation of a 'gregarious instinct' may be quite wrong, but his working through of its modes of operation is descriptive of much that still awaits clarification in our theory in regard to the ego-ideal and the superego. When one combines this subject-matter with his plea that the otherwise much praised new discipline of

psycho-analysis gives too little due to the repressing forces which successfully vanquish unwelcome instincts, he provides a remarkable forecast of the redresses still being made in metapsychology.

That this book on sociology, written by a distinguished surgeon for the lay public, should still call for republication is the most practical proof of its intrinsic value. (Bonnard 1954)

Actually, the criticisms made of Trotter by the Freudians are centred in their refusal of a social/herd instinct *per se* distinct from sexual instinct or libido.[3] Freud himself always refuted the concept of a primary social instinct, and always saw social intercourse and group phenomena as manifestations of a) *libido* 'diverted from its aims', and b) *identification* (Freud 1913, 1921). In the 1980s Friedman proposed that they were both right, and tried to reconcile Trotter's and Freud's ideas grounded on 'what evolutionary biologists are now calling the altruistic line of motivation in human life' (Friedman 1985).

Furthermore, Trotter's ideas were not only crucially important in Bion's concepts along his entire work, as we shall see, but they represented also an important paradigm discussed in Freud's (1913, 1921) incursions into groups, and Hadfield's (1923) conception of instincts.[4] Trotter, among others, 'provided the basic material for most British students of social psychology during the 1930s, including Bion and Rickman' (Harrison 2000, p.27), and Rickman actually noted that he agreed with the 'herd instinct' (Rickman 1950, p.165). Malcolm Pines mentions also that Trotter was one great influence on Norman Glaister, one of the 'forgotten pioneers' of the therapeutic community movement (Pines 1999).

Wilfred Trotter and Wilfred Bion

The role of Wilfred Trotter in Bion's life is a very remarkable one. They met around 1927 when Bion did his medical housemanship at University College Hospital, having won the Gold Medal in Surgery, as Trotter's attendant dresser. Bion greatly admired Trotter (Lyth 1980; Bléandonu 1994; Francesca Bion 1995); Trotter, this mature and honest man, who was also a gifted brain surgeon, left an outstanding impression on Bion's personality:

Towards the end of his life Bion acknowledged that Trotter had remained a role model for him through his professional career…Trotter won the young man's loyalty…identifying with Trotter and his self-confidence helped Bion to modify his severe super-ego. He could tolerate making mistakes, as even a past master like Trotter could sometimes be wrong (Bléandonu 1994 pp.38–39).

In what concerns Trotter's influence in Bion's scientific production, the situation is not so clear: 'In his autobiography Bion does not make mention that Trotter was the first to turn his mind to the problem of the psychology of group behaviour' (Bléandonu 1994, p.39).

Trotter's book *Instincts of the Herd in Peace and War* was to set Bion to thinking (Boris 1986, p.161), and was to prove an important influence on Bion's interest in, and nascent theories about, group behaviour (Francesca Bion 1995). Francesca Bion went a step further when she, by accident, came across that book and read it:

> Trotter makes observations which remind one strongly of Bion's later views. He speaks of man's 'resistiveness to new ideas, his submission to tradition and precedent'; of 'governing power tending to pass into the hands of a class of members insensitive to experience, closed to the entry of new ideas and obsessed with the satisfactoriness of things as they are'; of 'our willingness to take any risk other than endure the horrid pains of thought'. (Francesca Bion 1995)

However, Bion's explicit references to Trotter are actually slender, and even contradictory. Only once did he place Trotter's book *Instincts of the Herd* in his bibliographic references: in 'Group dynamics: a review' (Bion 1952) but only to follow Freud in refuting the idea of the 'herd instinct', while in the previous chapters Bion borrows Trotter's concepts of gregariousness and man as a herd animal (Bion 1961, p.91, 95), as we shall see in detail later. In 1973–74 he refers to Trotter as 'my chief surgeon', curiously as a prelude to talking about common wisdom:

> We like to think that our ideas are our personal property, but unless we can make our contribution available to the rest of the group there is no chance of mobilising the collective wisdom of the group which could lead to further progress and development. (Bion 1978, p.29)

In a *Memoir of the Future* he referred to Trotter twice, presenting him as the author of the idea that the 'group as a whole is greater than the sum of its parts' and also in a personal way (Bion 1991, pp.111 and 223).

The background ideas of Trotter in Bion's work

As we have said, Trotter's ideas can be seen traversing all of Bion's work, however much in the background, and they seem to have worked as seeds in a fertile land.

The focus on the morale of the group

One of the aims of Trotter, initially impelled by First World War issues, was to apply the newborn science of psychology to the study of the functioning of the morale of the social group. In the preface of *Instincts of the Herd in Peace and War* Trotter states:

> If it is war becoming…more and more completely a contest of moral forces, some really deep understanding of the nature and sources of national morale must be at least as important a source of strength as the technical knowledge of the military engineer and the maker of cannons (Trotter 1916, p.6)

and also:

> A satisfactory morale…gives smoothness of working, energy and enterprise…while from the individual it ensures the maximal outflow of effort with a minimal interference from such egoistic passions as anxiety, impatience and discontent. A practical psychology would define these functions and indicate means by which they are to be called into activity (*ibid* p.7)

Precisely the focus on morale was shared and developed by Bion in his first three papers (Bion 1940, 1946; Bion and Rickman 1943). In *"The War of Nerves": Civilian reaction, morale and prophylaxis* (1940), Bion analysed war from the point of view of phantasy and anxiety of the enemies, as a 'war of nerves' – a real 'contest of moral forces' – between the enemies. Some prophylactic measures to prevent the lowering morale of civilian populations submitted to air raids are proposed.

In 'Intra-group tensions in therapy' (1943), written with Rickman, the problem of the morale in a rehabilitation wing is centrally addressed, and devices were ready to transform the Northfield Hospital into a battalion ready to fight against neurosis. Bion's and Rickman's aim was the 'acquisition of knowledge and experience of the factors which make for a good group spirit' (Bion and Rickman 1943), disregarding the traditional mental hospital culture of individual care and sedatives. What they searched for was a totally different approach, the morale of the group-as-a-whole, one which clashed with a culture which gave precedence to the health of the individual (Hinshelwood 1999). This morale-oriented device, although abruptly terminated in six weeks under circumstances analysed elsewhere (Trist 1985; Hinshelwood 1999; Harrison 2000), was to leave a profound influence on the people who worked with Bion and Rickman and was to be integrated in the second Northfield experiment, mainly in the activity-oriented groups. One of the most prominent was Tom Main (later one of the leaders of the so-called 'therapeutic community movement'), who approached the larger system of the whole hospital in the same manner as Bion approached the Rehabilitation Wing (Hinshelwood 1999).

In 'The Leaderless Group Project' (1946), Bion again takes up Northfield and the theme of morale as a therapeutic agent: 'morale had to be raised to the point where the real enemy could be faced. The establishment of morale is of course hardly a pre-requisite of treatment; it is treatment, or a part of it' (Bion 1946, p.79). In this revolutionary idea of transforming the traditional ward into a 'therapeutic community', one can hear the echo of Trotter's proposal that a good morale would 'cure' neurotic symptoms such as anxiety, impatient and discontent, while regretting 'that atmosphere of the consulting room and the mad-house which does so much to detract from its pretensions to be a psychological system of universal validity' (Trotter 1916, p.91).

The 'suspension of leadership' group approach

The 'suspension of leadership' was one of the main characteristics of Bion's group technique. This 'suspension of leadership' must not be understood as 'anarchic' or ultimately leaderless. It is rather a revised notion of traditional leadership, which stressed the 'participatory/democratic set of relations among members in a sophisticated group' (Lipgar 2000, personal communication). As Bion stated: 'The group always make it clear that they expect me to act with authority as the leader of the group, and this responsibility I accept, though not in the way the group expect' (Bion 1961, p.82). Bion's style of leadership tried to resist the emotional pressure the group throws on the leader to support the idea that he can 'magically' solve problems. Its sole activity was instead to make interpretations of the phenomena in the group as these developed. In this way he gave back to group members the responsibility for dealing with the problems of being in a group as grown-up people, which was, according to Bion, precisely the best way for starting *really* to resolve them. This 'suspension of leadership' approach was present in the very beginning of Bion's work with groups in the army: a) the 'leaderless group project', b) the 'regimental nomination experiment' and c) the 'Northfield experiment', and goes on to the Tavistock experiences from 1948 until 1951.

In the 'leaderless group project', established for the War Office Selection Boards (WOSB), the main idea was to observe a group of candidates in a real-life situation in which no lead was given about organisation or leadership: 'these were left to emerge and it was the duty of the observing officers to watch how any given man was reconciling his personal ambitions, hopes and fears with the requirements exacted by the group for its success' (Bion 1946, p.78).

In Northfield groups and seminars, 'he allowed the group to evolve, and would then comment only when it became clear to him what might be happening. This approach usually left the group feeling perplexed and wondering what the relevance of his contribution was' (Harrison 2000, p.187–8).

This 'suspended leadership' position, which deliberately refused the mythical role of 'the Doctor' contrasted with that of other psychiatrists – for instance, with the Foulkes' more traditional leadership style in Northfield, in which Foulkes 'took the position of an educator and discussion tended to revolve around his comments':

> Foulkes tended to get people thinking about the details of therapeutic practice. He was a healer dedicated to create more healers. Bion, in contrast, had another aim. It was not to heal – not in a direct sense. He wanted the group members to assist in thinking about the group for themselves – it was an ontological research: What is the nature of a group? And what is the place of a human person within a group of other persons? Bion came to see this research, *in itself*, as having curative properties, as it would advance the maturity of the members of the group who undertook the research. (Hinshelwood 1999, p.477)

The 'suspension of leadership' device was maintained and developed in his 'experiences in groups' at Tavistock Clinic. There, the group movements anxiously in search of a leader obtained the first insights.

The advantages of this, as we could call it, subversion of values was addressed by Trotter (1916),[5] in analysing the factors that gave advantage to England in the First World War, and reflecting about leadership: 'Susceptibility to leadership is a characteristic of relatively primitive social types, and tends to diminish with increasing social complexity (Trotter 1916, p.248). This conclusion springs from the division of gregariousness, or herd instinct, into socialised and aggressive types, represented respectively by England as 'bees' and Germany 'wolves'. Trotter's conclusion was that the victory in one of 'nature's august experiments' (First World War) belonged to the socialised type. The altruistic and moral equality of its members won over the aggressive type, with its severe limitations on the participation of the individual in the social unit, rigid segregation of society and social instinct, which express themselves through leadership:

> During the war itself the submission to leadership that England showed was …to a great extent spontaneous, voluntary, and undisciplined, and gave repeated evidence that the passage of inspiration was essentially from the common people to its leaders rather than from the leaders to the common people. When the current of aspiration sets persistently in this direction…it is very plain that the primitive type of leadership that has led so many civilisations to disaster is no longer in unmodified action (Trotter 1916, p.249)

Both quotations found feedback in, and clarify, Bion's 'suspension of leadership' approach. The selection of officers in the WOSB was achieved through a 'spontaneous,[6] voluntary, and undisciplined' experimental situation. In the 'Regimental nomination experiment', the passage of inspiration from the common people to its leaders, addressed and prescribed by Trotter, is even more obvious:

> Bion proposed that, in addition to the usual nominees (to officer posts)…a regiment that had shown itself to be a good unit should be given the privilege of sending to a Board candidates voted on by every soldier in the name of the regiment… Each man entered on a secret ballot the names of those he considered should go forward to a WOSB. (Trist 1985, p.12)

As regards the 'primitive character of the sensibility to the leadership', proposed by Trotter, Bion's words are clearly congruent: 'Either the desire for a leader is some emotional survival operating uselessly in the group as an archaism, or else there is some awareness of a situation, which we have not defined' (Bion, 1961, p.39).

Trotter's and Bion's mistrust of traditional leadership had very similar reasons: both considered that it was a phenomenon ruled by atavistic instincts, eventually detached from contact with reality and thinking processes. According to Trotter, the preconception according to which the leaders are *a fortiori* more competent than the common people to solve the problems of the group is a serious mistake:

> There need [to be a political leader] be no specially arduous training, no great weight of knowledge either of affairs or the human heart, no recep-

tiveness to new ideas, no outlook into reality. Indeed, the mere absence of such seems to be an advantage; the successful shepherd thinks like his sheep, and can lead his flock only if he keeps no more than the shortest distance in advance. He must remain, in fact, recognisable as one of the flock, magnified no doubt, louder, coarser, above all with more urgent wants and ways of expression than the common sheep, but in essence to their feeling of the same flesh with them. (Trotter 1916, p.116)

In addition, traditional leadership had more to do with superficial appearance than with reason or true merit:

This instinctive feeling inclines them to the choice of a man who presents at any rate the appearance and manners of authority and power rather than to one who possesses the substance of capacity but is denied the shadow. (Trotter 1916, p.117)

Bion persisted in his 'suspension of leadership' approach, in spite of all the anxiety and mistrust raised by it. His experiments in the army were systematically terminated as if victims of sabotage by the system, at least in Bion's way of feeling. (Sutherland 1985; Trist 1985). In what concerns the groups in Tavistock:

His [Bion's] role was stressful much of the time, and Rickman and I were not sufficiently on his wavelength to take the pressure off…despite the denial mechanisms in the group the impact was profound; two members developed duodenal ulcer symptoms before the group finished, and three decided to have personal analysis subsequently. (Sutherland 1985, p.52)

One can suspect that this inner strength was in part inspired by Trotter's prophetic words:

If society is to continue to depend for its enterprise and expansion upon leadership, and can find no more satisfactory source of moral power, it is…highly probable that civilizations will continue to rise and fall in a dreadful sameness of alternating aspiration and despair. (Trotter 1916, p.247)

In fact, Bion took to pieces the group's unconscious idealisation of him as an *a priori* God-like type of leader, and valued the conscious *co-operation* of all the members of the group.

Theoretical advances in 'Experiences in Groups'

Trotter's ultimate assumption about 'group psychology' was that it was continuous with individual psychology, an idea that precedes Freud's similar argument (Freud 1921). As Trotter puts it:

> Sociology has, of course, often been described as social psychology and has been regarded as differing from ordinary psychology...the assumption being made that society brings to light a special series of mental aptitudes with which ordinary psychology, dealing as it does essentially with the individual, is not mainly concerned. It may be stated at once that it is a principal thesis of this essay that this attitude is a fallacious one... The two fields – the social and the individual – are regarded here as absolutely continuous; all human psychology...must be the psychology of associated man, since man as solitary animal is unknown to us, and every individual must present the characteristic reactions of the social animal if such exists. (Trotter 1916, p.11–12).

Trotter considered man a social/gregarious animal, and the mental phenomena were directly deductible from that condition: 'The gregarious mental character is evident in man's behaviour, not only in crowds and other circumstances of actual association, but also in his behaviour as an individual, however isolated' (Trotter 1916, p.42). This is also Bion's assumption in his *Experiences in Groups*, and the conceptions presented there can only be clearly understood if we bear that in mind: 'In fact, no individual, however isolated in time and space, should be regarded as outside a group or lacking in active manifestations of group psychology' (Bion 1961, p.169); and also: 'that part of the individual's mental life, which is being incessantly stimulated and activated by his group, is his inalienable inheritance as a group animal' (*ibid.* p.91)

Trotter's main idea was that there exists one instinct – besides sex, self-preservation and nutrition – that was not yet described by psychology, the *herd instinct*. This instinct would represent the natural tendency of biological organisms to associate, first in multiple-cell (metazoa) forms and then in gregarious forms as bee-swarms, herds, hordes and societies. Bion, while assimilating this idea, replaced the term 'herd instinct' by the physical-chemical term *valency*: 'The counterpart of co-operation in the basic assumption group is what I have called valency – a spontaneous, unconscious function of the gregarious quality in the personality of man' (Bion 1961, p.136). Furthermore, Bion's conception of a triad of basic instinctive group dispositions (flight/fight, pairing and dependence basic assumptions) is parallel with Trotter's triad of basic instincts: self-preservation, sex, nutrition.

Trotter (1916–18)	Bion (1948–51)
Basic instincts:	*Basic assumptions:*
Self-preservation	Flight/fight
Sex	Pairing
Nutrition	Dependence[7]
Factor of group cohesion:	*Factor of group cohesion:*
Herd instinct/gregariousness	valency/groupishness

Table 3.1 Some Parallel Concepts in Trotter and Bion

According to Trotter, the interference of the herd instinct in reason would be the cause of man's inability to use his rational potential, in spite of possessing a very potent mind:

> It is of cardinal importance to recognise that belief of affirmations sanctioned by the herd…goes on however much such affirmations may be opposed by evidence, that reason cannot enforce belief against herd suggestion, and finally that totally false opinions may appear to the holder of them to possess all the characters of rationally verifiable truth (Trotter 1916, p.39).

Trotter had stated that this impairment of rational abilities in the group should be one of the main themes of investigation in psychology (*ibid.* p.39). And, in what looks like a true dialogue with his old master who had passed away a decade before, Bion states:

> The group accordingly will often wrestle with intellectual problems that, one believes, the individual could solve without difficulty in another situation… One of the main objects of our study may well turn out to be precisely the phenomena that produce these perturbations of rational thought in the group. (Bion 1961, p.40)

Bion confronted these same rational impairments in his *Experiences in Groups*, and stated very similar ideas that we can identify as an empirical confirmation of Trotter's theoretical formulation. As did Trotter, Bion pointed to the valency/herd instinct as responsible for the mindless states associated with group life:

> I wish also to use it [valency] to indicate a readiness to combine on levels that can hardly be called mental at all but are characterised by behaviour in human beings that is more analogous to tropism in plants than to purposive behaviour. (Bion 1961, pp.116–117)

The 'sense of vitality' that according to Bion was achieved in these instinctual states, the basic assumption groups, is well described by Trotter: 'for re-embodiment in the herd at once fortifies courage and fills the individual with moral power, enthusiasm, and fortitude' (Trotter 1916, p.143).

The concept of *group mentality* has also a parallel in Trotter, at least in its characteristics of a primitive kind of uniformity and unanimity in opinions and conduct among the group, which belongs more to an irrational herd than to a human set. Trotter refers to it as 'sensitiveness to the behaviour of the herd', and 'voice of the herd':

> manifestations of the same tendency to homogeneity are seen in the desire for identification with the herd…each of us in his opinions and his conduct … is compelled to obtain the support of a class, of a herd within the herd… anything which tends to emphasize differences from the herd is unpleasant. In the individual mind, there will be an unpleasant dislike of the novel in action or thought. It will be 'wrong', 'wicked', 'foolish', 'undesirable', or as we say 'bad form'… It is sensitiveness to the behaviour of the herd which has the most important effects upon the structure of the mind of the gregarious animal, and therefore of that of man. The effect of it will clearly be to make acceptable those suggestions which come from the herd, and those only… Of two suggestions, that which the more perfectly embodies the voice of the herd is the more acceptable. The chances an affirmation has of being accepted could therefore be most satisfactorily expressed in terms of the bulk of the herd by which it is backed…anything which dissociates a suggestion from the herd will tend to ensure such a suggestion being rejected. (Trotter 1916, pp.32–33)

Bion's definition of group mentality stresses also the pleasant uniformity, but he went much further and pointed out the anonymous and unconscious nature of it:

> Any contributions to this group mentality must enlist the support of, or be in conformity with, the other anonymous contributions of the group. I should expect the group mentality to be distinguished by a uniformity that contrasted with the diversity of thought in the mentality of the individuals who have contributed to its formation. (Bion 1961, p.50)

> This term [group mentality] I use it to describe…the unanimous expression of the will of the group, an expression of will to which individuals contribute anonymously. (*ibid.* p.59)

> Group mentality is the unanimous expression of the will of the group, contributed to by the individual in ways of which he is unaware, influencing him disagreeably whenever he thinks or behaves in a manner at variance with the basic assumptions. (*ibid.* p.65)

These two parallel concepts have the advantage of overcoming the vague and imprecise concept of 'suggestion', hitherto used in group psychology. The *voice of the herd* and *group mentality* are expressions of a tacit, unspoken agreement between the elements of a group as to what issues are acceptable to the well-being of the whole, and no more a mysterious kind of passive credulity, as implied in the concept of *suggestion*.

The conflict between group mentality and individual needs was another idea developed from a sketchy thought by Trotter:

> The appearance of the fourth instinct [herd instinct] introduces a profound change, for this instinct has the characteristic that it exercises a controlling power upon the individual from without…with the social animal controlled by herd instinct it is not the actual deed which is instinctively done, but the order to do it which is instinctively obeyed. The deed, being ordained from without, may actually be unpleasant, and so be resisted from the individual side and yet be forced instinctively into execution. (Trotter 1916, p.48)

Bion coined the term *group culture* to denote the product of this conflict between group mentality/voice of the herd and the individual:

> …it is the nature of the group to deny some desires in satisfying others, but I suspect that most resentment is caused through the expression in a group of impulses which individuals wish to satisfy anonymously, and the frustration produced in the individual by the consequences to himself that follow from this satisfaction…the group meets this challenge by the elaboration of a characteristic culture of the group (Bion 1961, p.54–55)

The theoretical advances in understanding experiences in groups allowed a new vision of group phenomena; the human association could now be seen as a whole entity (and not as a sum of individuals), in which several powerful, unconscious/instinctual forces bind the individual elements even when these are physically isolated. These forces are seen as the legacy of the gregarious condition of the human animal, or at least a product of the earlier emotional experiences in the basic social/gregarious unit – the family – and are independent of the development of the intellectual machinery of rational thinking.

Epistemology and the growth of the mind

After leaving his work on groups, Bion centred his attention in the psychoses. This transition is less abrupt than it appears at first glance, since the last conclusions in his last paper on groups are as follows:

> The understanding of the emotional life of the group...is only comprehensible in terms of psychotic mechanisms. For this reason advances in the study of the group are dependent upon the development and implications of Melanie Klein's theories of internal objects, projective identification, and failure in symbol formation and their application in the group phenomena... (Bion, 1952 p.247)

In the following stage of his work, he applied and developed Klein's theories in a very creative and productive manner, but it is not the aim of this paper to analyse this so vast domain. His thinking becomes gradually more and more independent of strictly Kleinian theories (and eventually critical of them and of his own use of them). He developed his own theories, and the problem of scientific status of psychoanalysis and other epistemological matters become his prime concern. It is in the 'epistemological period', from 1962 onwards (Bléandonu 1994), that Trotter's background influence can be seen regaining importance. Simultaneously, the continuity of individual and group psychology become once more the focus, and in 1970 Bion retakes group psychology (see *Attention and Interpretation*). Trotter seems to be one of the links between epistemology and group psychology in Bion's thinking.

Bion introduced the epistemological debate into psychoanalysis as no one had done before. It was a matter of growing importance to search for truth instead of the apparent cure or improvement of the patient, alongside his work on individual psychoanalysis. He ended up addressing the ultimate truth, 'O', a mystical approach (Amaral Dias 1991, 1992; Grotstein 1993), and the result of love of truth and aesthetic sensibility (Grinberg *et al.* 1975).

If epistemology is the inquiry into the human conditions for knowledge, it can also be seen as an inquiry into the natural tendency of the human mind for accepting lies, which prevents the cognition of truth. This 'lie question' was a high priority agenda to Bion. However, Lie and Truth are in themselves ideal concepts devoid of practical significance if we don't attach to them some sensory-based models – as Bion did: truth is the nourishment of the mind, while lies are its poison. As the human intellect does not have the abilities to embrace truth most of the time, the simple answer to a question is a poison for its developing, since it is doomed to become a lie because of the inadequacy of the intellect to grasp its new meaning. As the empiricist trend, well represented by Hume, proposes, followed by both Trotter and Bion, 'suspension of judgement'[8], is required to prevent the lie:

> the judgements of conscience vary in different circles and are dependent on local environments…they are not advantageous to the species to the slightest degree beyond the dicta of the morals current in the circle in which they originate. (Trotter 1916, p.41)

> Almost any answer appears to make truth contingent on some circumstance or idea that is itself contingent. (Bion 1965, p.38)

Heisenberg and his *principle of uncertainty* become one of Bion's references. However, there is another problem: the human mind needs *certainty*, the *sense* of truth; as Trotter stated, 'the desire for certitude is one of profound depth in the human mind, and possibly a necessary property of any mind' (Trotter 1916, p.34), and Bion completed: 'the failure to bring about…a common sense view induces a state of debility…as if starvation of truth was somehow analogous to alimentary starvation' (Bion 1962a, p.119). Owing to this need, humans are likely to easily give up the mental pain of uncertainty, and exchange it for the common-sense view, a sense of correlation (Bion 1962a) between the members of the group. From that can spring the paradox that one isolated man's belief can easily be a delusion, while one delusion shared by the group can easily be a belief. Very frequently the latter happens in the group, as in Bion's -*K* link ('the protective coat of lies') and ψ ('theory used as a barrier against the unknown' – Bion 1963, p.18). Once more Trotter, 'amused by the mysterious viability of the false' (Kothari and Mehta 1998) had pointed it out earlier:

> …it is of cardinal importance to recognise that belief of affirmation sanctioned by the herd…goes on however much such affirmations may be opposed by evidence, that reason cannot enforce belief against herd suggestion and finally that totally false opinions may appear to the older of them to possess all the character of rationally verifiable truth, and may be justified by secondary processes of rationalization which it may be impossible directly to combat by argument. (Trotter 1916 p.39)

The idea of intellectual impairment inherent to the functioning of the group was not new in Bion's and even Trotter's days. It springs from Le Bon, was referred to by McDougal, Freud, amongst others and can even be traced back earlier, to Kierkegaard, in his famous assertion 'wherever there is a crowd there is an untruth.' (Clark 1999). What is new in Trotter, again developed from Hume's conceptions (the fallacious nature of the human mind), is the idea that intellectual impairment is not limited to the physical mob. Rather it is present in the mentality of the individual, because he is under the influence of the group even when he is alone:

> Man is not, therefore, suggestible by fits and starts, not merely in panics and in mobs…but always, everywhere, and under any circumstances. The capricious way in which man reacts to different suggestions has been attributed to variations in his suggestibility. This…is an incorrect interpretation of the facts which are more satisfactorily explained by regarding the variations as due to the differing extent to which suggestions are identified with the voice of the herd. (Trotter 1916, p.33).

This is also Bion's innovation: the *moral* outlook that suffocates both intellectual development and learning from experience is not only a result of group collusion but is ultimately characteristic of a preponderance of the super-ego over the functions of the ego (Bion 1965, p.38). Meanwhile, Freud in *Civilisation and its Discontents* (1908) had defined the super-ego as a coercive entity simultaneously inner and external; the guardian of consensus and correlation of conduct, as we might say, controlling objective behaviour as well as repressing and moulding subjective desires and thoughts.

The empiricist, the one who searches for truth from empirical data instead of from the judgements of the mind (ideas), proposes that experience, combined with suspended judgement, is the only learning method to trust.[9] When empirical data, evidence, doesn't fit the dictates of morality – the shared assumptions of the herd – humans must evade evidence and experience:

> Man's resistiveness to certain suggestions, and especially to experience, as is seen so well in his attitude to the new…the new has always to encounter the opposition of herd tradition… Experience, as is shown by the whole history of man, is met by resistance because it invariably encounters decisions based upon instinctive belief. (Trotter 1916, pp.34–35)

> …The acceptance of any proposition is invariably the resultant of suggestive influences, whether the proposition be true or false, and…the balance of suggestion is usually on the side of the false, because education being what it is, the scientific method – the method, that is to say, of

experience – has so little chance of acquiring suggestionizing force. (*ibid.* p.40)

These ideas are very close to Bion's formulation of the hatred of learning by experience:

> They [patients in the group] also show, as in psychoanalysis, that they do not have much belief in their capacity for learning by experience... Now all this, and more like it, really boils down to the hatred of the process of development ... there is a hatred of having to learn by experience at all, and lack of faith in the worth of such a kind of learning. A little experience of groups soon shows that that this is not simply a negative attitude; the process of development is really being compared with some other state...something like arriving fully equipped as an adult fitted by instinct to know without training or development exactly how to live and move and have his being in a group. There is only one kind of man that approximates to this dream...the man who is able to sink his identity in the herd. (Bion 1961, p.89)

This hatred is ultimately a characteristic of the basic assumption group and of the psychotic part of the personality, both of which are grasped as two sides of the same coin by binocular vision.

Trotter had stated that anxiety, i.e. mental pain, is the price to pay for the process of learning – mental growth: 'In matters that really interest him, man cannot support the suspension of judgement which science so often has to enjoin. He is too anxious to feel certain to have time to know (Trotter 1916, p.35). According to Freud, anxiety is the result of the danger of destruction of libidinal cathexis of the ego, or loss of personal meaningfulness (Grotstein 1991), and it can be so intense that the individual would discard his own apparatus for empirical reception – consciousness – and so become psychotic (Bion 1962a, 1962b). Bion's idea of psychosis as an attack to the thinking apparatus is partially linked with the failure of maternal love (reverie), i.e. primary libidinal cathexis, in Freudian language. The circle closes at the point when the group implies psychotic-like operations of preventing learning by experience. At this conceptual crossroads, we find the basis for the idea that social systems are associated with primitive defences against psychotic anxiety (Elliot Jacques (1955), Isabel Menzies-Lyth (1959), an issue also elaborated by Bion:

> the assumption underlying loyalty to the K link is that the personality...can survive the loss of its protective coat of lies, subterfuge, evasion and hallucination and may even be fortified and enriched by the loss. It is an

assumption strongly disputed by the psychotic and *a fortiori* by the group, which relies on psychotic mechanisms for its coherence and sense of well-being. (Bion 1965, p.129)

– and also addressed by Trotter: 'reason intrudes as an alien and hostile power, disturbing the perfection of life and causing an unending series of conflicts (Trotter 1916, p.35).

Bion was very sensitive to the epistemological criticisms of psychoanalysis as a science, and worked hard to deal with them. Trotter, the 'biological father' of British psychoanalysis, pointed out a question that would cross Bion's work at least from 1962 onwards: is psychoanalysis promoting mental growth or only adaptation to the conformed, stable-minded norm, despising the search for truth?[10] In the words of Trotter:

> However precious such a cure [psychoanalytic] may be to the patient, and however interesting to the physician, its value to the species has to be judged in relation to the 'normal' to which the patient has been restored – that is, in relation to the question as to whether any move, however small, into the direction of an enlargement of the human mind has been made. (Trotter 1916, p.90)

Almost in direct response to that, Bion stated: 'In psychoanalytic methodology the criterion cannot be whether a particular usage is right or wrong, meaningful or verifiable, but whether it does, or does not, promote development' (Bion 1962b).

Trotter's remark was an extension of his concepts of normality and mental instability, and the social pressure to neutralise disturbing new ideas:

> The mental stability, then, is to be regarded as, in certain important directions, a loss; and the nature of the loss resides in a limitation of outlook, a relative intolerance of the new in thought, and a consequent narrowing of the range of facts over which satisfactory intellectual activity is possible. (Trotter 1916, p.55)

Trotter believed that the mental instability was the result of a conflict between rational independence and pressure of the norm by herd instinct, and an inner, unresolved conflict between lies and search for truth. The subjugation of the type of people who were mentally unstable and termed degenerates, and incarcerated in mental hospitals, and the dominance of stable-minded types of people in society forced the narrowing of mankind's intellectual development. This was responsible for many cyclic social disruptions. The consensus of the stable-minded group was achieved through discarding possibilities of intellectual progress and evolution. Bion transported this question straight into the psychoanalytic institutional group:

> ...[I] repeat reasons for mistrusting 'cure' or 'improvement'...because the tendency to equate psycho-analysis with 'treatment' and 'cure' with improvement is a warning that the psychoanalysis is becoming restricted; limitation is being placed on the analysand's growth in the interest of keeping the group undisturbed. (Bion 1967, p.157)

He also said:

> ...even psycho-analysts seem to be unaware of the expanding nature of their universe... If my suspicion that this is so is found by experience to be correct, the difficulties of the patient...are significant for both the analysand and analyst when growth is taking place. (*ibid.* p.137)

From this problem spring many original and disturbing contributions by Bion. The desire for 'cure' starts to be seen by him with suspicion, and it was quickly extended to *desire* in general, as well as *memory* and even understanding (Bion 1970) as far as they block out new meanings by total saturation of the preconception. The importance in Bion's work of accepting mental turbulence and preventing the 'poisonous' nature of stable-minded saturation of preconception is addressed in Chapter 7 of this book by Robert Hinshelwood.

However, the set of epistemological problems doesn't end in the eventual production of truthful enunciates – mental growth – through learning by experience. Once some degree of mental sophistication is achieved by an individual, how does he *communicate* it to his fellow men? Trotter stressed that the capacity for adequate and precise intercommunication between human minds would make the difference in the possibility of human evolution. Exactly like communication between cells and organs is the essential form of co-ordination of complex organisms.

> The enormous power of varied reactions possessed by man must render necessary for his attainment of the full advantages of the gregarious habit a power of intercommunication of absolute unprecedented fineness...how momentous is the question as to what society does with the raw material of its minds to encourage in them the potential capacity for intercommunication. (Trotter 1916, p.62)

From the date on which Bion started to work in psychoanalytic training, the 'accuracy of communication' issue emerged: 'I have experience to record, but how to communicate this experience to others I am in doubt. This book

[*Learning from Experience*] explains why' (Bion 1962b). The self-revision of his earlier papers presented in *Second Thoughts* (Bion 1967) is dominated by the same concern; how to communicate accurately (to patients, colleagues, laymen, and even to himself) psychoanalytic experience? This issue became a first order concern: 'If this communication cannot be made, the future development of analysis is imperilled and the successful discoveries made so far could be lost to the world' (Bion 1992, p.173).

Trotter's analogy between human groups and a complex biological organism takes us up to another point of our inquiry.

Psycho-somatic and somato-psychic parallelisms

Maybe one of the most enigmatic concepts proposed by Bion was the *proto-mental system*. Although, as far as we are aware, from 1952 onwards the term 'proto-mental' disappears from his writings, the idea and theoretical elaboration of phenomena in which mental and physical are undifferentiated continues under other terms (e.g. ß elements; soma-psychotic portion of personality; psychosomatic innervations), and in other contexts (Meltzer, 1984). This concept is the extreme corollary of the integrated 'binocular vision' between somatic and psychological which Bion used in his work. It was not totally well received in Klein's vertex, which stressed the purely psychological object relations in contrast with the instinctual/physiological ground of Freud's model of the mind (Gomez 1997; Sutherland 1985). In order to clarify his psycho somatic/soma-psychotic models, Bion justified himself in a very expressive way:

> For myself, I have found it impossible to interpret the material presented to me by these patients as a manifestation of purely psychological development divorced from any concurrent physical development. I have wondered whether the psychological development was bound up with the development of ocular control in the same way that problems of development linked with oral aggression co-exist with the eruption of teeth. (Bion 1950, p.22)

This protomental vertex can be traced back to Trotter's original intuitions. It was Trotter's attempt, apparently in the footsteps of Darwin, to make psychology and sociology a consistent part of evolutionary biology (Miller 1983), and in this he was fertile in finding somatic-based correspondences to psychic phenomena: 'It [gregariousness] was not at all widely looked upon as a definite fact of biology which must have consequences as precise and a significance as ascertainable as the secretion of the gastric juice or the refracting of the eye' (Trotter 1916, p.21).

Furthermore, we can also find in Trotter's somatic analogies the seeds of Bion's contributions in the themes of (a) the conflicts between the new idea and *status quo*, (b) the mind as a muscle, in evacuatory phenomena, and (c) the mental 'digestion' of raw sensory material into food for thought, in psychic integration and growth. According to Trotter:

'The mind likes a strange idea as little as the body likes a strange protein and resists it with similar energy…a new idea is the most quickly acting antigen known to science' (Trotter 1939, p.186). From this visionary assertion, Bion developed a series of reflections concerning the reception of new ideas by the mind and the group, and the possible outcome of this conflict (Bion 1970).

According to Bion's model of the mind, the psychic entities can be ultimately divided into two fundamental categories: unassimilated (ß) and assimilated (α) by the mind. The unassimilated elements are also the ones expelled by 'the ability to believe in the possibility of ridding himself of unwanted emotions' (Bion 1992, p.181), just like foreign bodies which gravitate around the self's perception: 'any unwanted idea is converted in a ß element, ejected from personality, and then becomes a fact of which the individual is unaware, though he may be aware of feelings of persecution stimulated by it' (Bion 1992, p.182). The very act of expelling an idea/thought/emotion is made possible by the inability to distinguish between thoughts and things, an idea suggested by Trotter: 'Feeling has relations to instinct as obvious and fundamental as are the analogies between intellectual processes and reflex action' (Trotter 1916, p.15). Following Trotter, Bion used the attention to muscular reflex actions to understand the schizoid–paranoid mechanism of evacuation of ß elements:

His failure to distinguish thoughts from things contributes to a sense that the actual meaning of the words, as that would be understood in a rigid motion transformation, is expelled as air from his lungs is expelled. Conformably with this the patient seems to feel that his mind is an expelling organ like a lung in the act of expiration…the patient is using his eyes, and the mental counterpart of his capacity for vision, as evacuatory musculature. (Bion 1965, p.131)

The assimilated elements are the metaphorically digested ones, which can be used for non-psychotic mental functioning and mental growth. Trotter also referred to the digestive model of the mind: 'An event experienced is an event perceived, digested, and assimilated into the substance of our being and the ratio between the number of cases seen and the number of cases assimilated is the measure of experience' (Trotter 1932, p.98) – and was closely followed by Bion: 'I am reminded that healthy mental growth seems to depend on truth as the living organism depends on food. If it's lacking or deficient, the personality deteriorates' (Bion 1965, p.38).

The first assimilation of raw sensory data into the mind (Tα), or mental digestion, must be made with the help of maternal reverie. Bion even proposed the idea of a 'psychosomatic alimentary canal' in the baby, which received love (reverie) instead of milk (Bion 1962b, p.34).

All these somatopsychic/psychosomatic models can be framed into a vision of sociology and psychology as a part of evolutionary biology.[11] In Bion's model, the development of the mind follows embryonic-like steps which are grounded in biological process, and that reveal their origins in the primitive (psychosomatic/somatopsychotic) processes presented in psychosis and group dynamics.[12] Just as the biological maturation of the human embryo recapitulates all the evolution of life on earth, the psychic and social characteristics of humans are based on an adaptation and development of primeval characteristics:

> P. A. I have no doubt of the 'fact' of religion as a part, perhaps an unalienable part, of human character. I have even seen a mouse assume what looked like an attitude of religious beseeching when being tortured by a cat that had caught it. Is that a religious impulse? Or is it an attitude we have learned from animals – to take when in a hopeless situation – (Bion 1979, p.87)

In much the same way, the processes of thinking are seen as grounded and intimately linked with somatic (including physiochemical) processes:

> P. A. If it is true that living matter derives from the heat engendered by the reaction of oxygen with protoplasm then I can see that brain substance might derive from the 'decay' of involuntary muscle, and the mind likewise from the energy released by the degeneration of athletic ability (*ibid.* p.39)

This vertex allowed Bion also some curious and amusing games of words. In the next one, intestinal problems and a social institution are equated:

> P. A. It had never occurred to me that the costum[e]s authorities were sociological haemorrhoids, but I see what you mean. (*ibid.* p.73)

In the following example, the parallels of biological and psychic conception, and somatic and mental pain, are emphasised:

Somite Twenty-four: I've got a stomach-ache.

Alice: At last – something I do understand; I have the advantage of knowing pregnancy.

Fourteen years: Neither of you knows how painful it is to have an idea.

Twenty-two years: You? I didn't know you ever had an idea.

Fourteen years: I and my friend Thirteen have had ideas – even religious ones. (*ibid.* p.29)

Some subsequent contributions concerning the beginning of mental life in the foetus use Bion's concept of *protomental* (Bianchedi, E.T. *et al.*, 1997; Mancia, 1981; Proner 2000), a concept where not only biological and psychic but also social phenomena are taken as undifferentiated. The apparently odd conception of man as a developing global organism in which biology, psyche, and society (cells, individuals, groups, etc.) are completely continuous and interdependent as a vital flux, is getting more and more evidence in this globalisation era. However, these ideas were far from straightforwardly optimistic to both Trotter and Bion.

The concept of 'group diseases' (Bion 1961, pp.102, 108) springs from this vertex. J. A. Halliday[13] addressed the primary function of emotional conflict in psychosomatic affection stressing the environmental settings, including cultural demands, over the needs of emotional expression of individuals. He proposes the concept of the 'sick society', linking social group dynamics, individual psychology and somatic diseases:

> The prevalence [of psychosomatic diseases] is related to changes in the communal environment considered psychologically and socially. The incidence of a psychosomatic affection in a community rises and falls in response to the changes of social environment, that is, to changes of environment regarded in its psychological aspects rather than its physical aspects. (Halliday 1948, p.48)

Eric Wittkower[14] found, in an immense study of hundreds of tuberculosis patients, that 'situations which rouse aggressiveness or endanger the delicately poisoned security system of the patients often precede the onset of symptoms of tuberculosis' (Wittkower 1949, p.137). Bion tried to articulate both these contributions in his concept of the protomental system and 'group diseases'. A 'group disease' would be the manifestation of an impairment of the transformation of bodily and emotional raw experiences into meaning and thinking, impairment which was forced by the sophisticated group culture (Bion 1961, p.102). The conceptual seeds of these scientific hypotheses can also be traced back to Trotter, who had pointed out the theme of psychosomatic/somatopsychic group diseases:

> Certain mental and physical manifestations, which have usually been regarded as disease in the ordinary sense, are due to the effects upon the mind of the failure to assimilate the experience presented to it into a harmonious unitary personality. We have seen that the stable-minded deal with an unsatisfactory piece of experience by rejecting its significance. In certain minds such a successful exclusion does not occur, and the unwelcome experience persists as an irritant, so to say, capable neither of assimilation nor rejection... Now, we have already seen that a gregarious animal, unless his society is perfectly organised, must be subject to lasting and fierce conflict between experience and herd suggestion. It is natural, therefore, to assume that the manifestations of mental instability are not diseases of the individual in the ordinary sense at all, but inevitable consequences of man's biological history and exact measures of the stage now reached of his assimilation into gregarious life. The manifestations of mental instability and disintegration were at first supposed to be of comparatively rare occurrence and limited to certain well known 'diseases', but they are coming to be recognised over a larger and larger field, and in great variety of phenomena. (Trotter 1916, p.56–57)

The rationale of 'group diseases' was also addressed by Freud (1908) in his paper 'Civilised sexual morality and modern nervous illness'. There, Freud establishes a causal connection between the morality of the civilisation (repression of sexuality and aggressiveness) and the growing rate of psychoneuroses in the population. The direct link between social rules and disease has a radical expression in the case of the taboo (one of the first society rules) in primitive societies. The violation of the taboo often leads to a sudden mysterious illness and death of the violator, correlated with its own anguish and dread (Freud 1913).

The dread of human extinction

As a scientist of the 19th century, Trotter was strongly impressed by the 'Copernican revolution' made by Darwin and other pioneer scientists, which took mankind away from the centre of the putative preference of deity, and of Nature's favour. As any other species, man evolved from primitive beings, and was equally subject to a possible extinction:

> Without some totally revolutionary change in man's attitude towards the mind, even his very tenure of the earth may come to be threatened...after all man will prove but one more of nature's failures, ignominiously to be swept from her work-table to make way for another venture of her tireless curiosity and patience. (Trotter 1916, p.65)

One of Trotter's influences was surely Sir Charles Lyell, the great pioneer of geology, whose conclusions suggested that all species, including man, were ephemeral (Wilson 1999). Painful as it is, this idea was quickly out of fashion in the post-war *zeitgeist* until thermonuclear threats and, above all, ecological impairments, started to become evident in the late 20th century. Bion, however, insisted on it throughout his entire work, from *Group Dynamics:*

> History of life on this planet shows that decay of a species is often associated with over-development of some portion of its organism ... is there a possibility of similar over-development of mental functioning? (Bion 1952, p.247)

– to *The Dawn of Oblivion:*

> P. A. ...I do not see why he [the man] should not be another of Nature's discarded experiments. (Bion 1979, p.91)

This emphasis evokes an aura of oracular dread and gravity, that brings to the foreground the fragility of our existence and the responsibility for our destiny, for we are the only animal able to think about how our mind directs our thoughts and actions.

Trotter and Bion, the missing link

One of the questions that certainly arise is 'Why didn't Bion quote Trotter more often?' The answer could be the simplest one: he forgot him. Francesca Bion tells us that Trotter's book *Instincts of the Herd* (1916) was not in Bion's personal library and 'It may have been among those he lost during air raids over London in the early thirties and by the fifties it was out of print' (Francesca Bion, 1995). When Bion wrote *Second Thoughts* (and in commenting on the 'Imaginary twin' paper) he observed that 'he [the patient] must have been the first patient to make me wonder whether the idea of cure was not introducing an irrelevant criterion in psychoanalysis (Bion 1967 p.135). This statement attests to the fact that by that time Bion had totally forgotten the link between this idea and its author, Wilfred Trotter.

Interestingly, later in the same book Bion made some curious comments about forgetting important papers:

> Only in this way [forgetting] is it possible to produce the conditions in which, when it is next read, it can stimulate the evolution of further development. There is time to do this only with the best papers; but only the best papers have the power to stimulate a *defensive* reading (of what the paper is about) as a substitute for experiencing the paper itself – what I have elsewhere called transformation under K as contrasted with transformations under O. (Bion 1967, p.156)

Malcolm Pines has observed that we must look also for other reasons, like identification and rivalry (Pines 2000, personal communication). In what concerns identification, the process of forgetting would be a part of the transformation under O. Trotter seems to be an intimate part of Bion's personality, one of its functions or factors. It would also be worthwhile to inquire if Wilfred Trotter would not be in some way an 'imaginary twin' of Wilfred Bion.

Acknowledgements

I am indebted to Professor Robert Hinshelwood for his encouragement in the elaboration and publication of this paper and to Malcolm Pines and Robert Lipgar for their thoughtful and helpful suggestions on earlier versions. I also thank Zé Gabriel for his revision, Luis Sousa Ribeiro for his teachings and inspiration, and my wife Filipa for her support. This research was conducted with funding from the Foundation for Science and Technology (Fundção para a Ciência e a Tecnologia) of Portugal.

References

Amaral Diàs, C. (1991) *Ali Babá – Droga: Uma Neurose Diabólica do Século Vinte.* Lisbon: Escher.

Amaral Diàs, C. (1992) *Aventuras de Ali Babá nos Túmulos de Ur: Ensaio Psicanalítico Sobre a Somatopsicose.* Lisbon: Fenda.

Bianchedi, E.T. *et al.* (1997) 'Pre-natals/Post-natals: The Total Personality.' Available in www.sicap.it/~merciai/papers/bianc2.htm

Bion, F. (1995) 'The days of our years.' *The Journal of Melanie Klein and Object Relations 13*, 1.

Bion, W. R. (1940) '"The War of Nerves": Civilian reaction, morale and prophylaxis.' In E. Miller and H. Crichton-Miller (eds) *The Neuroses in War.* London: MacMillan.

Bion, W. R. (1946) 'The Leaderless Group Project.' *Bulletin of the Menninger Clinic 10*, 77–81.

Bion, W. R. (1948) 'Psychiatry in a time of crisis.' *British Journal of Medical Psychology 21*, 2, 81–89.

Bion W. R. (1950) 'The imaginary twin' in W. R. Bion, *Second Thoughts* (1967) London: Karnac Books.

Bion, W. R. (1952) 'Group dynamics: A review.' *International Journal of Psychoanalysis 32*, 2.

Bion, W. R. (1961) *Experiences in Groups and Other Papers*. London: Routledge.

Bion, W. R. (1962a) 'A Theory of thinking.' In *Second Thoughts* (1967) London: Karnac Books.

Bion, W. R. (1962b) *Learning From Experience*. London: Heinemann.

Bion, W. R. (1963) *The Elements of Psychoanalysis*. London: Karnac Books.

Bion, W. R. (1965) *Transformations*. London: Heinemann.

Bion, W. R. (1967) *Second Thoughts*. London: Karnac Books.

Bion, W. R. (1970) *Attention and Interpretation*. London: Tavistock (Reprinted Karnac, 1984; also in *Seven Servants* (1977).)

Bion, W. R. (1978) *Bion in New York and Sao Paulo*. Perthshire: Clunie Press.

Bion, W. R. (1979) *The Dawn of Oblivion*. Perthshire: Clunie Press.

Bion, W. R. (1990) *A Memoir of the Future*. London: Karnac Books.

Bion, W. R. (1992) *Cogitations*. London: Karnac Books.

Bion, W. R. and Rickman, J. (1943) 'Intra-group tensions in therapy.' *Lancet 2*, 678–681.

Bléandonu, G. (1994) *Wilfred Bion: His Life and Works 1897–1979*. London: Free Association Books and New York: Guilford Press.

Bonnard, A. (1954) 'Review of "Instincts of the Herd in Peace and War".' *International Journal of Psycho-Analysis 35*, 78.

Boris, H. N. (1986) 'Bion re-visited'. *Contemporary Psychoanalysis 22*, 159–184.

Cheshire, N. and Thoma, H. (1991) 'Metaphor, neologism and "open texture": Implications for translating Freud's scientific thought.' *International Review of Psycho-Analysis 18*, 429–455.

Clark, A. (1999) 'A study in character: Luke Spencer, Existentialist.' *General Hospital Review, 4.*

Darwin, C. (1871) *The Descent of Man*. Available at www.yorku.ca/dept/psych/classics/Darwin/Descent/descent4.htm.

Flügel, J. C. (1927) 'Sexual and social sentiments'. *British Journal of Medical Psychology 7*.

Freud, S. (1908) 'Civilised sexual morality and modern nervous illness.' In A. Dickson (ed) *Group Psychology, Civilisation and its Discontents and other Works*. Harmondsworth: Penguin.

Freud, S. (1913) *Totem and Taboo*. New York and London: Norton.

Freud, S. (1921) *Group Psychology and the Analysis of the Ego*. New York and London: Norton.

French, J. R. P. (1941) ' The disruption and cohesion of groups.' *Journal of Abnormal Psychology 36*, 362–377.

Friedman, M. (1985) 'Toward a reconceptualization of guilt.' *Contemporary Psychoanalysis 21*, 501–547.

Gillespie, W. (1979) 'Ernest Jones: The bonny fighter.' *International Journal of Psycho-Analysis 60*, 273–279.

Glover, J. (1924) 'Problems in dynamic psychology: Review of John T. MacCurdy's "A Critique of Psycho-Analysis and Suggested Formulations".' *International Journal of Psycho-Analysis 5*, 379–385.

Gomez, L. (1997) *An Introduction to Object Relations*. London: Free Association Press.

Grinberg, L. *et al.* (1975) New *Introduction to the Work of Bion*. New Jersey: Aronson.

Grotstein, J. (1991) 'Nothingness, meaninglessness, chaos, and the black hole III: Self- and interactional regulation and the background presence of primary identification.' *Contemporary Psychoanalysis 27, 3*, 1–33.

Grotstein, J. (1993) 'Towards the concept of the transcendent position: Reflections on some of "the unborns" in Bion's *Cogitations.*' A contribution in the *Special Issue:* 'Understanding the Work of Wilfred Bion' for *The Journal of Melanie Klein and Object Relations, 11*, 2, 55–73.

Hadfield, J. A. (1923) *Psychology and Morals.* London: Methuen & Co.

Hadfield, J. A. (1950) *Psychology and Mental Health: A Contribution to Developmental Psychology.* London: George Allan and Unwin.

Hadfield, J. A. (1954) *Dreams and Nightmares.* Harmondsworth: Penguin.

Halliday, J. L. (1948) *Psychosocial Medicine.* London: Heinemann.

Harrison, T. (2000) *Bion, Rickman, Foulkes and the Northfield Experiment.* London: Jessica Kingsley Publishers.

Hinshelwood, R. D. (1994) Foreword, in G. Bléandonu (1999) *Wilfred Bion; His Life and Works 1897–1979.* London: Free Association Books and New York: Guilford Press.

Hinshelwood, R. D. (1997) *Therapy or Coercion: Does Psycho-Analysis Differ from Brain-Washing?* London: Karnac Books.

Hinshelwood, R. D. (1999) 'How Foulkesian was Bion?' *Group Analysis 32*, 469–488

Jaques, E. (1955) 'Social systems as a defence against persecutory and depressive anxiety.' In P. Heimann, M. Klein and R. Money-Kyrle (eds) *New Directions in Psychoanalysis.* London: Tavistock Publications.

Jones, E. (1940) 'Wilfred Trotter.' *International Journal of Psycho-Analysis 21*, 114.

Jones, E. (1942) 'The concept of a normal mind.' *International Journal of Psycho-Analysis 23*, 1–8.

Jones, E. (1945) 'Reminiscent notes on the early history of psychoanalysis in English-speaking countries.' *International Journal of Psycho-Analysis 26*, 8–10.

Kothari, M. and Mehta, L. (1998) 'The cloning bandwagon.' *Issues in Medical Ethics 6*, 1, 17–19.

Lewin, K. and Lippitt, R. (1938) 'An experimental approach to the study of autocracy and democracy.' *Sociometry 1*, 292–300.

Lyth, O. (1980) 'Wilfred Ruprecht Bion (1897–1979).' *International Journal of Psycho-Analysis 61*, 269–273.

Mancia, M. (1981) 'On the beginning of mental life in the foetus.' *International Journal of Psycho-Analysis 62*, 351–357.

Meltzer, D. (1984) 'A Klein–Bion model for evaluating psychosomatic states.' In *Studies in Extended Metapsychology.* Perthshire: Clunie Press.

Menzies Lyth, I. (1959) 'The functioning of social systems as a defence against anxiety,' reprinted in *Containing Anxiety in Institutions: Selected Essays, Vol. I.* Free Associations Books, 1988.

Miller, J. (1983) 'Crowds and power – some English ideas on the status of primitive personality.' *International Review of Psycho-Analysis 10*, 253–264.

Payne, S. (1957) Foreword in J. Rickman (1957) *Selected Contributions to Psychoanalysis.* London: Hogarth Press and Institute of Psychoanalysis.

Pearson, K. (1897) *The Chances of Death.* London: Edward Arnold.

Pines, M. (1999) 'Forgotten pioneers: The unwritten history of the therapeutic community movement.' *Journal of the Association of Therapeutic Communities 20*, 1.

Proner, K., (2000) 'Protomental synchrony: Some thoughts on the earliest identification processes in a neonate.' *The International Journal of Infant Observation 3*, 2, 55–63.

Rickman, J. (1938) 'Need for belief in God.' In J. Rickman (1957) *Selected Contributions to Psychoanalysis*. London: Hogarth Press and Institute of Psychoanalysis.

Rickman, J. (1950) 'The factor of number in individual and group dynamics.' In J. Rickman (1957) *Selected Contributions to Psychoanalysis* (1957). London: Hogarth Press and Institute of Psychoanalysis.

Rickman, J. (1957) *Selected Contributions to Psychoanalysis*. London: Hogarth Press and Institute of Psychoanalysis.

Saravay, S. M. (1975) 'Group Psychology and the Structural Theory: A Revised Psychoanalytic Model of Group Psychology.' *Journal of American Psychoanalytical Association 23*, 69–89.

Sidis, B. (1898) *The Psychology of suggestion: A Research into the Subconscious Nature of Man and Society*. New York: D. Appleton company

Strachay, J. (1966) 'General introduction' and 'some technical terms.' In *Standard Edition of the Work of Sigmund Freud 1*, xiii–xxvi.

Sutherland, J.D. (1985) 'Bion revisited: Group dynamics and group psychotherapy.' In M. Pines (ed) *Bion and Group Psychotherapy*. London: Routledge and Kegan Paul.

Trist, E. (1985) 'Working with Bion in the 1940s: The group decade.' In M. Pines (ed) *Bion and Group Psychotherapy*. London: Routledge and Kegan Paul.

Trotter, W. (1916) *Instincts of the Herd in Peace and War*. London: Unwin.

Trotter, W. (1932) 'Art and science in medicine.' In W. R. Trotter (ed) *The Collected Papers of Wilfred Trotter* (1941). London: Geoffrey Cumberlege, Oxford University Press.

Trotter, W. (1939) 'Has the intellect a function?' In W. R. Trotter (ed) *The Collected Papers of Wilfred Trotter* (1941). London: Geoffrey Cumberlege, Oxford University Press.

Wallerstein, R. S. (1963) 'The problem of the assessment of change in psychotherapy.' *International Journal of Psycho-Analysis 44*, 31–41.

Wilson, A. N. (1999) *God's Funeral*. London: John Murray Publishers.

Wittkower, E. (1949) *A Psychiatrist Looks at Tuberculosis*. London: The National Association for the Prevention of Tuberculosis.

Endnotes

1.   Rickman was in his turn analysed by Freud, Ferenczy and Melanie Klein. In Bion's words (about the Wharncliffe Memorandum): 'It was a fascinating account... punctuated with generous tributes to the merits of what were assumed to be my ideas, but never once betraying the least awareness of how much the scheme he was describing was the child of his own [Rickman's] creative imagination (Payne 1957, p.12). A discussion concerning Rickman's decisive influence on Bion's earlier work in groups can be found in Tom Harrison's book *Bion, Rickman, Foulkes and the Northfield Experiments* (see References).

2.   Although Rickman considered himself for many years a Kleinian, Mrs Klein and Rickman never seemed to get along, mainly because of theoretical disagreements (Bléandonu 1994, p.47). Mrs Klein seemed to be 'out of sympathy, if not actively hostile', to Bion's work with groups (Sutherland 1985).

3.   A contemporary (1927) discussion of this theme can be found in the paper 'Sexual and
          social sentiments' by J. C. Flügel (see References).

4.   J. A. Hadfield was the 'only person with a psychodynamic orientation working in a
          British University…at University College, where Bion studied medicine'. Later, Bion
          was analytically trained by Hadfield in the Tavistock. The 'Hadfieldeans' were a pow-
          erful group in the Clinic in the 1930s (Bléandonu 1994, pp.42–43). Hadfield dis-
          agreed with Freud about the aetiology of psychoneuroses. According to him neuroses
          were due to a feeling of deprivation of protective love in childhood, and not to the re-
          pression of sexual love (Hadfield 1950, p.121). Bion would somehow reconcile their
          discordance in his study of groups: 'Since the pair relationship of psychoanalysis can
          be regarded as a part of the larger group situation, the transference relationship could
          be expected…to be coloured by the characteristics associated with the pairing group.
          If analysis is regarded as part of the total group situation, we could expect to find sex-
          ual elements prominent in the material there presented' (Bion, 1961, p.166).

5.   Trotter's work addressed this much earlier than papers by Lewin and Lippitt (1938)
          and French (1941) on democratic and leaderless groups, which are considered by Har-
          rison (2000) as the influences in Bion's 'Leaderless group project'.

6.   In fact, one of the procedures in the leaderless group situations in the Edinburgh's
          WOSB was called 'spontaneous situations' (Trist 1985, p.7).

7.   The connection between the *nutrition instinct* and *dependence basic assumption* is aug-
          mented by a spiritual factor: 'the first assumption is that the group exists in order to be
          sustained by a leader on whom it depends for nourishment, material and spiritual'
          (Bion 1952, p.235) The placement of spirituality in Bion's 'dependence' basic as-
          sumption can be seen as partly inspired by Rickman's ideas of (a) 'a need to believe in
          God' (Rickman 1938), and (b) the correlation between dependency on the group and
          endowment to it of phantasised characteristics of the idealised parents (Harrison
          2000, p.51). Hadfield also puts emphasis on the dependence of the child upon its par-
          ents for comfort, happiness and life itself (Hadfield 1954, p.20), as do J. L. Halliday
          (1948) and E. Wittkower (1949), both of whom are central references in the elabora-
          tion of Bion's *protomental system* (Bion 1961).

8.   'A total suspension of judgement is here our only reasonable resource' (David Hume,
          Dialogues Concerning Natural Religion (1777)).

9.   Parenthetically it must be said that Bion expanded empiricism to the idealist domains
          when he, following Freud, considered that the 'psychical qualities' received by con-
          sciousness are also to be considered empirical data as much as sensory data received by
          the senses. This epistemological position allowed him some rest in what concerns the
          scientific status of psychoanalysis. A discussion of this theme can be found in *Cogita-
          tions* in the chapter 'Need for study of scientific method'.

10.   A problem that is in other terms also addressed by R. D. Hinshelwood's recent ethi-
          cally-based question *Psychoanalysis: Therapy or Coercion?*. However, the importance of
          this question to both Trotter and Bion was more than an ethical issue, it corresponded
          to worries about the survival of man on the face of the earth. In those days Ernst Jones
          wrote his paper 'The concept of a normal mind' (1942) in an attempt to solve Trotter's
          challenge. Later, in 1963, Robert S. Wallerstein takes up this theme in his paper 'The
          problem of the assessment of change in psychotherapy' (1963).

11.   It is beyond the remit of this paper to discuss the importance of the 'quantum revolu-
          tion' in the process of abandoning mechanistic/inanimate models in contemporary
          science, which so deeply affected Bion. We will only stress that this subject was impor-
          tant enough to him:

'I hope that in time the base will be laid for a mathematical approach to biology, founded on the biological origins of mathematics, and not on an attempt to foist on biology a mathematical structure which owes its existence to the mathematician's ability to find realisations that approximate to his constructs, amongst the characteristics of the inanimate.' (Bion, 1965, p.105)

12. It is interesting enough that even the development of a 'group-mind' can be seen as analogue to the development of the infant's mind, starting in a baby-like phase with a 'circumscribed regression of the psychic systems to oral stage derivatives', and subsequent maturation of the social intercourse of the group into more sophisticated, Oedipal and post-Oedipal stages (Saravay, 1975).

13. Halliday was also supported by John Rickman.

14. Who also worked with Bion in the 'Leaderless Group Project'.

4

'Group Dynamics: A Re-view'

Matias Sanfuentes

Introduction

In reviewing the first edition of Bion's paper 'Group Dynamics: A Re-view' (1952), published in the *International Journal of Psychoanalysis*, it dawned on me that this version of the article was different from the one published by him three years later. It was apparent that important aspects of the second variant of the paper did not appear in the first edition. This motivated me to review both versions and attempt to analyse the principal changes that Bion made to his first paper. This paper tries to describe the principal differences that exist between them, and to clarify what may have influenced him to make these modifications. I will briefly describe the main characteristics and conceptual developments of the first edition. Then I will analyse the principal changes that Bion would make. To this end I will organise the discussion into five sections that represent, for me, the most substantial theoretical advances in his ideas about groups. These sections examine the following topics: 1. Bion's relation to Freud's group concepts; 2. regression; 3. thought; 4. countertransference; 5. psychotic mechanisms and early stages of the Oedipus complex.

Wilfred Bion has been one of the major figures in the history of psychoanalysis. He generated important ideas both in the field of individual psychoanalysis and group processes. These ideas have had great sway in the development of both fields. As Malcolm Pines stresses with regard to the group sphere, *Experiences in Groups* is probably the shortest and most influential text in group psychotherapy' (Pines 1985, p. xiii). Bion started his work with groups in the 1940s. He developed creative and productive experiences during the Second World War, working as a military psychiatrist in the selection and rehabilitation of soldiers. From 1946 onwards, he directed the Tavistock Clinic's multiple group projects, which included group activities with students, industrial managers and patients. He was trying to find a conceptual frame of reference for the group situation, homologous with the psychoanalytic method, that would enable him to deal with the clinical material that emerged in it (Trist 1985). The result of these experiences was published in *Human Relations* (1948–51). He left his work with groups towards the end of the forties, instead dedicating himself exclusively to individual psychoanalysis. As he said in 1977, 'I have not abandoned groups but the urgency of work to be done with individual analyses leaves me no time for anything else' (Bléandonu, 1990 p.88).

In 1952 Bion published his paper 'Group Dynamics: A Re-view'. This paper was published three times from 1952 to 1961. The first version appeared in a special issue of the *International Journal of Psychoanalysis* dedicated to M. Klein on the occasion of her seventieth birthday. The second one was part of the book that reproduced the papers published in the special issue of the *International Journal of Psychoanalysis*, and other additional ones. This book was edited by M. Klein *et al.* under the title *New Directions in Psycho-analysis*, and was published in 1955. The paper's third appearance was in 1961 as part of the book *Experiences in Groups* that compiled some of the papers written by Bion concerning group dynamics.

It is interesting to highlight that Bion modified some sections of the first version of the article, when it was published for the second time in 1955. Although most of the original text kept its former organisation, he changed some parts of the previous edition. He utilised new psychoanalytic concepts for the comprehension of group processes, such as the early stages of Oedipus complex and regression. Moreover, he included some clinical material, drawn from group sessions, in order to support his ideas. He incorporated headings into the text to organise the development of his principal concepts, and two summaries about the principal ideas discussed: one in the middle of the text and the other at the end. He also increased the length of the paper by several pages. This second version was re-published again in the compilation of 1961 without new modifications.

I have found in the secondary literature few references concerning these changes. Most of the literature fails to highlight the differences between these two. They seem to presuppose that the paper was published three times without modification. However, Bléandonu (1990 p.84) mentions the importance that the Kleinian theory acquired in Bion's group concepts, when

'Group Dynamics: a Re-View' was republished in 1961. Sutherland (1985 p.66) for his part, in allusion to the first version of the paper, maintains that 'the culmination of his works on group dynamics did not become widely manifest until ten years later'. However, the paper's theoretic transformations had occurred several years before, and not in 1961, as these authors suggest.

By contrast, Scheidlinger clearly distinguishes between the two variants of the article. In a painstaking study, he analyses Bion's work with groups and he clearly specifies that they are quite different papers. 'In his later contribution in 1955 Bion went even further, claiming that "basic assumption" phenomena could be understood only in terms of "psychotic" mechanisms' (Scheidlinger 1960, p.36). Yet, he neither analyses the differences between the articles, nor gives any clues on to what might have encouraged Bion to develop his paper a bit further. Rather, he sharply criticizes Bion's group ideas by detailing what are, according to him, his main theoretical weaknesses.

Consequently, the causes of the paper's modifications have to be searched in the period from 1952 to 1955. Bion himself left the main clues in the first version of the paper, in which he stresses the necessity to continue the investigation of the topic in the light of the Kleinian ideas. 'Advances in the study of the group are dependent upon the development and implications of Melanie Klein's theories of internal objects, projective identification, and the failure in symbol formation and their application in the group situation' (Bion 1952, p.247). For this reason we need more evidence for what Bion was doing during these years.

He was fully dedicated to individual psychoanalysis and to the study of the relationship between thought and language in psychosis. He, along with Hanna Segal and Herbert Rosenfeld, was analysing psychotic patients, almost without any modification of the classical technique, inspired by Klein's work. Bion presented a paper in 1953 to the '18th International Psycho-analytical Congress' called 'Notes on the theory of schizophrenia', which was published in 1954 in the *International Journal of Psychoanalysis*. Later he modified this paper and published it in 1955 under the title 'Language and the schizophrenic' in the book *New Directions of Psycho-Analysis*. Both papers represented his evolution in the study of schizophrenic thought, which he would continue developing during the following years. The series of articles that he published in the *International Journal of Psychoanalysis* during the 1950s were the result of this productive research.

Bion had been in analysis with Melanie Klein since 1945, and her ideas had permeated his own views with great intensity. His analysis finished in

1953, and important changes had taken place in his life during the course of it. He had been accepted as a member of the British Psycho-analytical Society in 1950 after reading his membership paper 'The imaginary twin'. He had become one of the most distinguished of Klein's students. He had got married for the second time in 1951, and his wife had given birth to a boy in 1952. In 1955 he was father again for a third time. As Bléandonu (1990, p.93) points out, during these years, 'he found a new psychic equilibrium'. Both his marriage and work became the support and focus of his life. He was able to build a family and to father two more children. His intellectual activity was at its height as he published a new paper almost every year. Psychoanalysis awoke his powerful creativity and sharp wit, enabling him to expand the scope of his observations and ideas.

Within this context Bion published 'Group dynamics: A re-view' for the first time. In this paper he reviewed his previous ideas that were related to his work with groups during the last decade, and which he had published in *Human Relations* some years before. The author picked up the distinction that he had formerly established between two different states of mind that individuals in a group can develop: the 'work group' and the 'group basic assumptions'. He also resumed discussion of the phenomena of the proto-mental system and specialised work groups. He re-examined these ideas from the Kleinian perspective that, at this period, represented for him the most important theoretical reference point.

Therefore, what made this paper distinct and different from his previous works about group dynamics was the incorporation of Kleinian ideas. It gave him the possibility to think afresh his previous work, in the light of the Kleinian theory of the early phases of mental development, and the pathological forms of such development. The consequences of this productive review appear clearly illustrated in Eric Trist's (1985) account of his experiences working with Bion as an observer in the therapeutic groups that the latter ran at the Tavistock Clinic. According to Trist, something that really bothered Bion was the difficulty in grasping what caused the alternation of the basic assumptions during group processes. He was only able to solve this problem when 'he sought an explanation in Melanie Klein's theory of the early psychotic phases of personality development' (Trist 1985, p.34).

Consequently, Bion found in the psychotic mechanisms described by Klein, a new framework for the comprehension of emotional life in groups. In the paper's first version he considered that her theories of internal objects, and the mechanisms of projective identification, helped him to understand the operation of the basic assumptions. He also related these latter phenomena to Klein's ideas of failure in the capacity of symbol formation. According to him, in the work group, individuals employ the symbol formation in the process of verbal communication. On the other hand, in the basic assumptions they are not in a condition to use these verbal abilities with the precision conferred by the capacity to form and use symbols. In the latter, words are not interpreted as symbols 'but as sounds having pre-verbal significance' (Bion 1952, p.246). Therefore, in the basic assumption the individuals lose the capacity of symbolisation and they remain unaffected by the stimuli that would prompt the development of such a capacity. 'In the basic assumption group the individual *is* the totem animal. He is not identified with it, or equated with it, he is it' (*ibid.* p.245).

At the end of this edition, Bion affirmed that progress in the study of the group would be dependent on the developments of Kleinian theory. He left a gate open for further elaborations, and he clearly stated in the article's conclusions three possible groups of phenomena that may direct following investigations on the subject. They were the process of depersonalisation, the failure in symbol formation, and the comprehension of the basic assumptions in terms of psychotic mechanisms. Bion actually continued the work that he had previously left unfinished. In spite of the fact that he did not carry on new clinical activities with groups, he applied the concepts he built up in the field of the individual psychoanalysis to the understanding of group phenomena. These developments were part of the second version of his article that was published in 1955.

In order to analyse the main differences between both articles, I will try to establish the principal modifications that he made to the first edition, and what might have influenced him to do so. I shall organise the discussion into five sections, in which I will pick up what I consider to be the most important conceptual variations.

1. Bion's relation with Freud's group concepts

Between both versions, Bion's attitude towards Freud's group work changed considerably. Scheidlinger (1960) states that in the paper's second version, Bion appeared less critical with Freudian group theories than in the previous one. In the first article, he thought that his own group ideas were divergent from Freud's ones. 'We have reached a point at which my description of the group is sufficiently far removed from that which Freud proposed' (Bion 1952, p.237). He attributed these differences with Freud to the fact that the latter derived his group ideas from a bi-personal psychoanalytic setting. By contrast, in his last work, Bion saw his own perspective as a complement of the Freudian group outlook. 'Freud's view of the dynamics of the group seem to me to require supplementation rather than correction' (Bion 1955a, p.475; 1961, p.187).

In the last work, Bion specified his own ideas more accurately with regard to Freud. He felt himself more confident to demarcate his conceptual differences with Freud. 'Groups would, in Freud's view, approximate to neurotic patterns of behaviour, whereas in my view they would approximate to the patterns of psychotic behaviour' (Bion 1955a, p.470; 1961, p.181). This sense of confidence and certainty concerning his theories is also depicted through the discussion that Bion developed about the mental process that governs the relationship between group members and the leader. In 1952 he discussed the relationship between the group and the leader using the mechanisms of splitting and projective identification to conceptualise it, without relating his perspective to Freud's. 'The individual splits off his aggressiveness and projects it into the leader' (Bion 1952, p.245). In his second version, Bion contrasted directly his own vision with Freud's. For the latter, the identification of the individuals with the leader depends on the process of introjection. For Bion, this identification depends 'not on introjection alone but on a simultaneous process of projective identification' (Bion 1955a, p.467; 1961, p.177).

Thus in his new paper, Bion dared, with more clarity and precision, to set out and specify different solutions to what Freud had stated before. It reveals Bion's independence of mind, allowing him to search for new answers when the previous ones did not satisfy him, and to envisage the phenomena studied by him, even though it meant moving away from the paths of his predecessors.

2. Regression

In the first paper Bion maintained that one of the phenomena that may lead to further investigations in the group field was the process of depersonalisation. There, he stated that individuals in the group lose their 'individual distinctiveness' in a process 'indistinguishable from depersonalisation' (Bion 1952, p.246). Three years later he conceptualised this depersonalisation as a phenomenon of regression that individuals suffer as being part of a group.[1] I think we need to emphasise the point that this was the first time that Bion used and applied the concept of regression in the course of his work. The author affirms that the individual, who is in contact with the emotional life of the group, resorts, as a massive regression, to primitive mental mechanisms typical of the earliest phases of mental life. He stresses that this contact 'would appear to be as formidable to the adult as the relationship with the breast appears to be to the infant' (Bion 1955a, p.441–442; 1961, p.141–142). Thus, according to Bion, the group has a mobilising quality for the individual, who experiences an intense process of regression in his/her mode of mental functioning. The individual in the group has the task 'to meet the demands' that the group life involves. Failure to satisfy such demands discloses a regressive phenomenon, which entails the individual losing his/her 'individual distinctiveness' indistinguishable from depersonalisation.

What may explain the change and evolution that Bion suffered in relation to this topic? Perhaps his greater comprehension of the primitive layers of mental functioning, and of the deep levels of regression that individuals experience in psychoanalytic treatments, especially psychotic patients? Maybe he could have been influenced by Heimann and Isaacs' paper on regression, published in 1952 in Klein and her collaborators' anthology, *Developments of Psycho-analysis*? Although this paper was originally presented in 1943 as part of the 'controversial discussions' that took place within the British Psychoanalytical Society, the publication of the book in 1952 may have swayed Bion. When it was published it had important repercussions, becoming 'the clearest, most systematic and comprehensive account of her [Klein's] theory of the developmental positions' (Bléandonu 1990, p.96). Far from establishing a final answer, these explanations offer some useful traces for possible causes of his theoretic development.

It is important to highlight that Bion has a particular viewpoint concerning the eliciting regressive pull that group life exerts. Many other group theorists do not share this perspective. In fact they strongly criticise this viewpoint. As Schermer points out, Bion is more inclined to consider that the bringing into play of the group's regressive influence through the primitive basic assumptions states is 'omnipresent' (Schermer 1985, p.143). Thus something inherent in the group would provoke retrogressive movements in group dynamics, which would not be attributed to conditions of group malfunction. According to Bion, such inherent characteristics of groups would be constituted by psychotic patterns of functioning, which are the ultimate wellspring of group life.

With regard to these issues, Miller (1998), through what he calls the 'biogenetic perspective', offers a different outlook to the 'psychoanalytic' one that predominated in the papers written by Bion about groups during the

1950s. The author describes, as part of the infant's instinctual primate inheritance, the existence of an instinct of 'groupishness'. He depicts this as 'a propensity to combine with others in collective, simultaneous, and instantaneous mobilisation of survival drives directed to survival of the group' (Miller 1998, p.47). He also considers as part of this instinctual inheritance, the existence of 'instinctive survival drives towards dependency and fight–flight and the (latent) drive to reproduction'. He sets out that the combination of both groups of drives entails an instinctive tendency towards the emergence of the group's three basic assumption states. The author concludes that these forms of group functioning always exist, and they are never completely supplanted by the work group. They are the result of the regressive 'instinctiveness' that is elicited from the group phenomenon. This instinctiveness, according to Bion, would arise in the individual's mental life not as a consequence of new instincts that are brought into play. These instincts are always in play, and moreover they form part of the individual's 'equipment as a herd animal' (Bion 1952, p.239). Accordingly, for the author, the physical congregation of a group only allows for the demonstration of group characteristics, 'but it has no significance for the production of group phenomena' (*ibid.* p.238–9; 1955, p.461; 1961, p.168).

3. Thought

In the second edition Bion resumed the discussion developed in his previous work about the role of symbol formation in the group member's mental life. In his first work he stressed that 'the "language" of the basic assumption group is therefore a method of communication devoid of the precision conferred by a capacity for the formation and use of symbols' (Bion 1952, p.245). In the second publication he added more by stating that the 'language' of this group mentality, rather than primitive, is 'debased'. 'Instead of developing language as a mode of thought, the group uses an existing language as a mode of action' (Bion 1955a, p.474; 1961, p.186). This important statement would come from the study of the language and thought of psychotic patients, which he dealt with during these years. As he stated in his paper 'Language and the schizophrenic' (1955b, p.226), the schizophrenic employs language 'as a mode of action in the service either of projective identification or of splitting the object'. He 'uses words as things, or as split-off parts of himself, which he pushes forcibly into the analyst'.

Therefore he might have applied these ideas, drawn in the field of individual psychoanalysis, to the comprehension of group phenomena, especially of thought perturbations observed by him in the groups that he had run. Moreover, through the idea of 'the language as a mode of action' he was adumbrating what some years later he was going to conceptualise as the mental apparatus's manipulation of 'beta elements'. In accordance with the author's later developments, 'beta elements are not amenable to use in dream thoughts but are suited for use in projective identification...they are objects that can be evacuated or used for a kind of thinking that depends on manipulation of what are felt to be things in themselves as if to substitute such manipulation for words and ideas' (Bion 1962, p.6).

4. Countertransference

Bion formed part of the group of psychoanalysts that during the fifties stimulated the utilisation of the mechanism of countertransference as a tool to facilitate access to the patient's inner world. In the second version of the paper, he illustrated through some clinical material the operation of the mechanism of projective identification in group phenomena and the countertransference responses that the analyst experiences as a result. 'In group treatment many interpretations, and amongst them the most important, have to be made on the strength of the analyst's own emotional reactions... The experience of countertransference appears to me to have quite a distinct quality that should enable the analyst to differentiate the occasion when he is object of projective identification and when he is not' (Bion 1955a, p.446; 1961, p.149). Three years before, Bion only described the role of projective identification in the group, and he did not make reference to the analyst's employment of the countertransference mechanism as a clinical tool. 'The individual splits off his aggressiveness and projects it into the leader. His wish to fight, to nourish, to choose a partner or his parents, all are in turn deposited in some external figure' (Bion 1952, p.245).

Hinshelwood (1999) states that Bion, along with Segal and Rosenfeld, had an important role in the post-Kleinian developments of a new conception of countertransference. This new conceptualisation stressed the 'relational aspects of the transference–countertransference' by linking them with the use of the mechanism of projective identification. The author also affirms that Bion (1959, 1962) initiated a different form to describe and envisage the relationship between analyst and patient. By utilising the model of the mother and the infant, he describes it as the 'container and contained'. The function of 'containing' the distress of the infant (patient) on the side of the mother (analyst) arises as a central feature. This implies the latter's capacity of transforming distress into a metabolised experience more able to be tolerated by the former. 'The knack is to feel the dread and still retain a balance of mind' (Hinshelwood 1999, p.802).

Perhaps Bion's advances in the study of the analyst's management, in the psychoanalytic setting, of the primitive object relations and defensive mechanisms that the psychotic patient employs, gave him the clarity and conviction to describe the utilisation of this mechanism in the context of the group. He was using countertransference responses in his work with schizo-phrenic patients as a powerful guide. 'My interpretation depends on the use of Melanie Klein's theory of projective identification, first to illuminate my countertransference, and then to frame the interpretation which I give the patient' (Bion 1955b, p.224). Yet, as Bléandonu (1990, p.108) states, 'when the concept of countertransference began to appear in the psychoanalytic literature of the 1950s, Bion had encountered the phenomenon a good ten years earlier'. Therefore, Bion's experiences with groups gave him an intuitive knowledge that some years later he was able to conceptualise and then apply to group processes. This happened when the evolution and maturity of his ideas allowed him to do so.

5. Psychotic mechanisms and early stages of the Oedipus complex

When Bion finished his article in 1952, he knew that a better comprehension of the functioning of the basic assumptions could be achieved through his advances in the study of the psychotic mechanisms. 'The understanding of the emotional life of the group, which is a function of the basic assumptions, is only comprehensible in terms of psychotic mechanisms' (Bion 1952, p.247). After three years, his conceptions on the subject had progressed enough. In this context, he picked up the figure of the Sphinx in the Oedipus myth. He identified the leader of the work group with the 'enigmatic, brooding, and questioning sphinx from whom disaster emanates' (Bion 1955a, p.456; 1961, p.162). He maintained that the analyst's interventions provoke intense levels of anxiety and extremely primitive fears. According to him, when the group is an object of inquiry, it establishes contact with 'primitive phantasies about the contents of the mother's body', which are characteristic of the para-noid–schizoid position. Thus, psychotic anxieties connected with primitive Oedipal conflicts are brought about when investigation is carried out on the level of the basic assumptions. Bion envisaged that the basic assumptions arise as reactions against fundamental phenomena that he links with an 'early primal scene worked out on a level of part objects, and associated with psychotic anxiety and mechanisms of splitting and projective identification' (Bion 1955a, p.457; Bion 1961, p.163).

Thus, what Bion had enunciated before, as a possibility for the development of his research about groups, was some years later conceptualised in a more definitive form. He employed Klein's concepts of the primitive stages of the Oedipus complex, and the connection of epistemophilia with the early sadism of the first phases of language development, in order to understand the group's primitive forms of mental functioning. According to him 'the central position in group dynamics is occupied by the more primitive mechanisms that Melanie Klein has described as peculiar to the paranoid-schizoid and depressive positions' (Bion 1955a, p.475; Bion 1961, p.188). These psychotic patterns entail for him 'the ultimate sources of all group behaviour' (Bion 1955, p.476; Bion 1961, p.189). He states that these patterns need to be unfolded within the group in order to achieve any therapeutic progress. Accordingly, he is very sceptical that any successful therapy might be developed before the working through of these primitive aspects.

Therefore, what Bion was using for the comprehension of the schizophrenic thought he was utilising to apprehend group dynamics as well. Perhaps his work with schizophrenic patients and the ideas that he drew from this task exerted such a strong power on his thought, that he felt the necessity to re-examine his conceptions about group life? His last paper depicts how these ideas intensively pervaded his group outlook. With this paper he concluded a deep reinterpretation of the ideas that he had formulated by working with groups during the 1940s. In this reinterpretation, the power of the destructive psychotic aspects that are characteristic of the early phases of personality development created a strong explicative force for the understanding of the deepest features of group life. They allowed him to re-conceptualise the fragile and unstable nature of group dynamics. From this new framework, the group arises as the ideal arena for the unfolding of the dismembering action of the group members' psychotic aspects on their thought and their connection with reality.

Conclusion

From the analysis of both papers it is possible to conclude that Bion made important changes to the second version. He included some Kleinian concepts as well as his own ideas drawn as the result of studying psychotic thought. This was in fact his last attempt to comprehend group dynamics in an integrative form. He returned to the analysis of groups in his book *Attention and Interpretation* that was published in 1970. However, this later conceptual foray was not the result of being re-engaged in the world of group projects, but rather, a revision from a 'different vertex'.

What stands out for me, from the differences found between both versions, was Bion's wish to give the article a more definite form. It implied variations either in his conceptual developments or in the presentation of his ideas. The later edition appears more formal and better organised. It includes clinical examples to illustrate his concepts, and it does not leave open questions undeveloped, as he had done in his previous work. From this perspective, his former article could be seen as a first effort to re-examine group dynamics in the light of Kleinian ideas, but ultimately, as an unfinished theoretic attempt. Therefore, it is possible to say that his new endeavour was the result of the evolution that Bion's thought had taken during these years.

In the course of these years Bion was achieving a new stability. As Bléandonu (1990, p.103) stresses, 'after his second marriage, the story of his life began, slowly, to be eclipsed by his work'. And this work was closely linked with the evolution not only of his life and personal ideas, but also of the British psychoanalytical context in which he was inserted[2]. Kleinian theory had acquired a more definite status, and its followers began to apply it to cultural and social phenomena as well as the clinical field. In the latter is highlighted the application of Klein's ideas to the study of psychosis, which represented in these years one of the most attractive fields of research.

It is difficult to answer with precision how this context could have influenced Bion in his task of reviewing his previous work about groups. However, the context would, no doubt, have been important in a period in which he 'considered himself first and foremost a Kleinian' (Bléandonu 1990, p.91). Perhaps as Miller affirms, it was the second instance of 'Bion's deference to her [Klein's] theories' (Miller 1998, p.43). Anyway, what arises with more clarity is that Bion perhaps felt something to be unfinished in his first text; three years later he returned and completed it.

Acknowledgements

I am greatly indebted to Bob Hinshelwood and Robert Lipgar for their helpful comments and valuable encouragement on the development of this paper.

References

Bion, W. R. (1948–51) Experiences in Groups.' *Human Relations* vols. I-VII.

Bion, W. R. (1952) 'Group dynamics: A re-view.' *International Journal of Psycho-Analysis 33*, 235–247.

Bion, W. R. (1954) 'Notes on the theory of schizophrenia.' *International Journal of Psychoanalysis 35*, 113–118.

Bion, W. R. (1955a) 'Group dynamics: A re-view.' M. Klein *et al.* (eds) *New Directions in Psycho-Analysis.* London: Maresfield Library, 1985.

Bion, W. R. (1955b) 'Language and the schizophrenic.' M. Klein *et al.* (eds) *New Directions in Psycho-Analysis.* London: Maresfield Library, 1985.

Bion, W. R. (1959) 'Attacks on linking.' *International Journal of Psychoanalysis 40*, 308–315.

Bion, W. R. (1961) *Experiences in Groups.* London: Tavistock Publications.

Bion, W. R. (1962) *Learning from Experience.* London: Maresfield, 1984.

Bion, W. R. (1970) *Attention and Interpretation.* London: Tavistock Publications.

Bléandonu, G. (1990) *Wilfred Bion: His Life and Works 1897–1979.* London: Free Association Books, 1996.

Heimann, P. and Isaacs, S. (1952) 'Regression.' In M. Klein *et al. Developments in Psychoanalysis* (1989). London: Karnac Books.

Hinshelwood, R. D. (1999) 'Countertransference.' *International Journal of Psychoanalysis 80*, 797–818.

Miller, E. (1998) '*Are basic assumptions instinctive?*' In Talamo P. Bion, F. Borgogno and S. A. Merciai, *Bion's Legacy to Groups.* London: Karnac Books.

Pines, M. (1985) Introduction to *Bion and Group Psychotherapy.* London: Routledge, 1992.

Scheidlinger, S. (1960) 'Group processes in group psychotherapy: Trends in the integration of individual and group psychology.' *American Journal of Psychotherapy 14*, 104–120, 346–363. Republished in S. Scheidlinger (1982) *Focus on Group Psychotherapy.* New York: International Universities Press.

Schermer, V. L. (1985) 'Beyond Bion: the basic assumption states revisited.' M. Pines (ed) *Bion and Group Psychotherapy.* London: Routledge, 1992.

Sutherland, J. D. (1985) 'Bion revisited: Group dynamics and group psychotherapy.' In M. Pines (ed) *Bion and Group Psychotherapy.* London: Routledge, 1992.

Trist, E. (1985) 'Working with Bion in the 1940s: The group decade.' In M. Pines (ed) *Bion and Group Psychotherapy.* London: Routledge, 1992.

Endnotes

1.   He states this even though, for Bion, the gathering of a group in a particular place and time has no significance for the development of group phenomena. The individual, though isolated, 'should [not] be considered as outside a group or lacking in active manifestations of group psychology' (Bion 1952, p.239; 1955a, p.461; 1961, p.169).

2.   Herbert Rosenfeld and Hanna Segal were working with psychotic patients and publishing papers on the subject. The former published five papers about the treatment of schizophrenics from 1947 to 1954. The latter published a paper on the same topic in 1950, an article on aesthetics in 1952, and two more in 1953 and 1954. The last of them was related to schizoid mechanisms. Paula Heimann for her part published a couple of papers in 1952, one about the early stages of the Oedipus complex and the other

on defence mechanisms in paranoid states. Donald Winnicott published his fundamental paper 'Transitional objects and transitional phenomena – a study of the first not-me possession' in 1953, and in 1955 an article about regression in psychoanalytic treatments. In July of 1951, Bion's influential and close colleague, John Rickman, died. In 1953 Elliot Jaques published *On the Dynamics of Social Structure.* In 1952 S. H. Foulkes created the Institute of Group Analysis. He also published two papers in 1954 and 1955 related to group psychotherapy.

5

Anthropological Psychoanalysis

Bion's Journeying in Italy[1]

Claudio Neri

Bion held his last seminar in Rome on 17 July 1977. Francesco Corrao, on behalf of all the participants, expressed his gratitude for the lessons which had been given.

Bion thanked the participants for their gratitude and added that he hoped he would not seem rude if he compared Corrao's description of his contribution to something of which he was aware but did not much like – the nearest image he could give was of a leaf falling from a tree without our being able to tell on which side it would land.

At first I didn't perceive the fact that he was expressing perplexity about how his contribution would be received and worked through. I was more struck by the image he was using than by the content. In 1977, Bion was getting on in years and although in good health, he did not know what the future held for him. The image of the falling leaf remained in my mind as a farewell: his goodbye to the people with whom he had spent a week of fervent work.

Continuing with his speech, Bion quoted a few lines from Yeats' 'Solomon and the Witch' and a short passage from Shakespeare: 'Journeys end in lovers meeting, / Every wise man's son doth know.'

At the very moment in which we were to part, Bion was pointing out the need to look ahead, thinking about the possible outcomes of the meeting which had taken place.

In fact, he ended his speech by saying that he did not think that journeys ended in lovers meeting, but that they began at that point, asking further on what the group might give birth to, what thought or action.

2003

To my mind, three of Bion's theories have been developed in an original way in my country; they are:

1. the 'container↔contained relationship' model

2. the notion of 'PS↔D oscillation'

3. the intuition of the existence of 'thoughts without a thinker'.

Furthermore in Italy, Bion's particular view of psychoanalysis has been understood and his model for promoting the thinking activity has been assimilated.

I will deal with this theme straight away, because of its more general aspects. I will then develop his treatment of 'container↔contained,' 'PS↔D' and 'thoughts without thinker.'

A way of conducting a discourse

The particular model of thinking and talking which Bion called 'speculative imagination' was introduced into Italy, enhanced by the brilliant light of Sicily and the Mediterranean, by Francesco Corrao. I am referring to the colors and intensity of the light in Sicily, but above all to the intensity and depth of Sicilian culture, a culture that is directly descendant from Greek, Arab and Norman traditions. Francesco Corrao identified deeply with Bion through a connection of a common object of love: psychoanalysis. If the statement 'one can love the mind of a man' is true, it is true that Corrao loved the thought and way of Bion's thinking. Corrao (1998a, 1998b) placed Bion's thoughts into his mind and when he brought them to the Italian psychoanalysts' attention, they were transformed for having lived in his mind.

The primary function of speculative imagination is to give the germ of thought an opportunity to come to life. The second function is to allow it to be communicated, to pass through the barriers of conformity, hypocrisy, cynicism and apathy.

Speculative imagination – as far as I have understood – is made up of a third of courage, a third of dramatization and the remaining part of observation and scientific method. Courage lies in saying exactly what one thinks and feels at the moment of the session, making only slight adjustments which may help the patient (or the members of a group) to a better use of communication. An illustration of courage is Bion's saying to the participants at the Rome seminars that he didn't know how they would work through his contribution.

Dramatization consists in privileging the use of images and in suggesting that an intervention be a cue for a dialogue (of two or more voices), which is open to unpredictable developments. The reference at the beginning of this paper where Bion quotes from Yeats and Shakespeare is a fine example of dramatization. The scientific component is offered by the relationship the analyst forms with the facts of the session and by the genuineness with which he accepts that his hypothesis be open to discussion.

Speculative imagination can be used not only in meetings of analyst and analysand (and between the analyst and members of a group with analytic aims), but every time there is a meeting among psychoanalysts, too. Several examples of this are shown in the interventions in which Bion tells his colleagues of the discoveries which are progressively giving weight to his 'psychoanalytic anthropology,' and represent as many different expressions of it.

First, I want to give a brief definition of 'psychoanalytic anthropology.' Anthropology is a compound term which is derived from two Greek words, 'anthropos' which means man and 'logos' which means reasoning, discourse and word. Anthropology therefore, is a reasoning upon human nature, or more precisely, a reasoning on man. The specific task of psychoanalysis, according to Bion, is to develop a discourse on the most primitive and archaic aspects of man, which goes together with the more evolved ones (language and thought). These aspects of the nature of man persist in civilization as living animal and ancestral remains: remains that may manifest themselves in various ways and reawaken suddenly, without warning.

I would now like to present the illustrations taken from Bion's seminars.

In *Italian Seminars* (1985), he says that the suffering and limitations of capabilities that the patient suffers can actually be sited in aspects of his personality that are not removed or denied, but are living archaic residuals that have never emerged. He also says that there is evidence of survival, 'gill slits,' and that if these residuals (remaining from when man was an aquatic animal) exist as far as the body is concerned, why should there not be, somewhere, something that concerns what we define as our mind. Still with the course of *Italian Seminars*, Bion sketches a portrait of man, using a science-fiction form:

war between 'man who is dominated by the basic assumption of fight/flight' which is dramatized in the figures of 'adrenal gland' ('adrenalists,' 'adrenalin producers'), and 'man dominated by the basic assumption of coupling.' This is shown in 'gonadic' figures. This war may lead to complete destruction, so it is necessary for Homo Sapiens ('Man who is able to think') to intervene. As Bion (1985) wrote:

> ...Adrenal glands...might emerge inside the human mind...and so...find expression, aided by the film business, by film projectors and by mass advertising, [in] a modern presentation of fleeing and fighting... Perhaps someone would like to write the scene of a war film between the Adrenalists and the Gonads. Maybe we would all end up by being impotent and sterile or maybe we could make the world impossible to live in as we become overpopulated... Perhaps it will not be just a film, perhaps in this very same moment we will have to prepare ourselves mentally and mobilize our capacity to face up to future dangers. These future dangers will seem to be so enormous, as compared both to our current and past dangers that our present dangers will appear to be just a trailer. One must feed the capacity to think in a way which becomes more able and more robust than it currently is.

Courage

Freud (1920) knew about this type of problem, as we can see from his note on the prehistory of analytical technique where, regarding free association, he spoke about creative writing, making reference to Ludwig Borne, 'The art of becoming an original writer in three days.' Borne spoke about the necessity of jotting down notes on 'everything that came into one's head' for three days in a row, as the method for becoming a writer. He then said that in reality it was moral courage that an individual lacked, not ideas.

The feeling of risk is an unavoidable experience for anyone using speculative imagination. The analyst can perceive either a personal risk or a risk concerning his patient, the risk that he may waken a sleeping tiger, triggering forces beyond his control. Therefore, one must be rather courageous to face up to such an unpredictable event.

In the adrenal glands example that I have shown above, courage (the primary component of speculative imagination) lies in Bion's way of expressing his thoughts openly to colleagues who might misunderstand or mock him.

Dramatization

Dramatization is evident in the use of the 'remains of the fish' image on which the sufferings and limitations of the patient might depend.

According to Bion, dramatizing doesn't mean just describing but giving a shape to that which is in dynamic evolution. Dramatizing doesn't mean recalling something that had already been lived, but letting that part of the past which was made up of trauma and not recallable, live (Cavalletti 2000, p.xxi).

I will relate a short account. Sometimes, when there is a new member in a small therapeutic group, it may happen that the old members speak about an episode which is unknown to the newcomer. He may ask: 'What are you speaking about?' Very often the others answer: 'Everything that happened a long time before your arrival.' We may interpret the refusal of giving explanations as rivalry of the siblings toward the newborn baby. We may also follow a different line of interpretation, which focuses on a real difficulty. Such a difficulty can be better explained if the answer of the old members were formulated in the following terms: 'We could tell you about the facts, but that would not give you very much idea as to what was happening in the group. To do that we would have to let it happen again.'

Dramatization is a way of reenacting something that happened at a different moment or in a different place, something that can be recalled, but recalling is not sufficient to convey all the emotions, feelings and turmoil. To do so, one would have to recreate the same situation and atmosphere. Bion was conveying emotions, feelings and turmoil to the participants at the Rome seminars, through his use of poems and images.

The scientific aspect of speculative imagination

In the example I have given, the scientific aspect lies in the suggestion of a hypothesis, which differs substantially from Freud's hypothesis of the unconscious. This hypothesis takes on part of Ferenczi's theory (1924) in a new form. The form in which the hypothesis is given, however, is closer to Galileo's and Einstein's method than to Ferenczi's.

I'm referring to 'mental experiments,' which are crucial to some moments of the history of science. An example of preliminary 'mental experiment' is the question that the adolescent Einstein asked himself. He was rowing a small boat on a lake surrounded by high hills. The sun rose over the edge of the hills and Einstein asked himself how fast he should row in order to prevent the sunlight from touching him. The most famous mental experiment was the 'platform experiment.' One can see how this mental experiment is closely linked to the theory of relativity and to the idea that privileged observers do not exist. Einstein imagined a railroad station with a very long platform. Two people were positioned on the platform, observers A and B. A train passes through the station at a certain speed. In the train there is another observer, C. At a certain moment, Tx, a gun is fired on the train. The observers hear the shot at different times: T1, T2, T3, because of the speeds of the train and of the sound. Einstein assumed that there is not only one privileged referral time, but all were at the same level. Now passing to the solar system, in accordance with the theory of relativity, it is not correct to assume that the earth only goes around the sun. It is not correct to assume the sun as the only one privileged point of reference; we can also consider the Earth, or even Mars, as a point of reference.

Getting back to Bion, it is important to underline that in his use of the image of 'something in the mind, which is the correspondent to the archaic residuals of the gills,' the metaphoric thickness is very thin. Bion's aim is not to evoke a scenario, but to conduct an 'analytical mental experiment.'

> The peculiarity of mental experimentation (or thought experimentation – Gedankenexperiment) is such that while 'freedom' of imagination has to lean towards the extreme (indeed, to see links which were not previously seen, as in Poincaré's descriptions), at the same time, thought must be 'self-disciplining,' limiting the spectrum of the imaginable to the planning of future experiments...and/or to the compatibility with the 'corpus' of theoretical hypotheses which are deemed to be relevant. [... It is this type] of 'mental experiment' that Bion tries to set in motion through the use of faculty or 'non-logical' acts even though they are self-regulated by thought (as 'imaginative conjecture,' 'rational conjecture,' and speculative imagination...or even 'idea generators,' or as Joyce called them, 'mother ideas.' (Di Paola 1995, p.104)

Speculative imagination in Italy

Speculative imagination, in its Italian form, has become richer in images whilst the scientific part is of lesser degree. Furthermore, it has improved by taking the needs and vulnerability of the patient into consideration. Great store is held in these in the formulation and choice of moment of intervention, which the analyst makes. The necessity of being authentic and courageous, for the analyst, remains unchanged.

Beyond the close circle of those who have been into Bion's work in great depth, there are many psychoanalysts in Italy today who lean towards the interpretation as invention or trace of an image or hypothesis which is able to activate both a response of the analysand's and a transformation of that which is taking place in the session. I believe that this way of viewing interpretation, at least in part, is an effect of the impact of the idea of Bion's 'speculative imagination.'

A particular view of psychoanalysis

The theory of speculative imagination acquires even more sense if seen from Bion's point of view of psychoanalysis.

I spoke previously of Bion's 'psychoanalytic anthropology'. I shall now better explain what I meant by that with the aid of an analogy. Along with many psychoanalysts, two artists continue to come to mind both when studying Bion's view of psychoanalysis and recalling his ties with Italy. Alberto Burri and Pino Pascali were rather anomalous compared to other postwar Italian artists as they were not 'intellectuals' or 'left-wing,' and while being on friendly terms with other artists, they did not belong to any particular artistic movement. Burri – who is also regarded as the major Italian painter of the period – was a doctor and had started painting during the last years of World War II while he was a prisoner of war in Texas. Some paintings, such as the famous 'Sacks,' show cuts and stitches in the cloth – stitches put in by an expert surgeon's hand, but which leave the wound visible. Of his other works, 'The Clays' create cracked earth on the surface of the painting – earth or clay that has cracked when dried in the sun because of the drought. Other works by Burri were created by ripping a part of the smooth layer of a sheet of plywood to show two adjacent surfaces – one smooth and the other rough. Looking at them, one gets the same effect as when contemplating the countryside where a large field is composed of brown ploughed clods on one side and green, newly sprung, waving wheat on the other.

Pascali loved motorcycles and speed. He produced several works entitled 'Anthropology.' They are more like do-it-yourself, (DIY) than proper sculptures – 'nests' made of straw, 'tree-houses' made of nets, wood and ropes. These are nests, houses and passages in which a primitive man might have moved about. Another piece of work, '32 sq. m. of Sea' was made by colouring a large quantity of water with blue aniline. In a short film, 'Measures of the Earth,' shot on the beach at Fregene, one can see Pascali measuring sandy areas with a tape and other tools (cf. Christov Bagargiev 1997).

Like Burri and Pascali, Bion uses the simplest and most precise tools. Like them, he searches for a measure for man, man who is not alone or isolated, but part of a flock; that means, man who is subjected to the forces which are active in the flock. Moreover, Bion is interested in measuring man under extreme conditions, when the flock is subjected to very strong pressure and in turn exerts powerful constraints on man – man subject to the drive to be part of the flock, to attack or to run with the crowd, man faced with terror and stupidity, a thinking man.

Work-group mentality and primitive mentality[2]

What I just said may remind us of Bion's hypothesis of rational or work-group mentality as opposed to primitive mentality.

The terms 'rational group' and 'work-group' correspond to two chronological moments and two stages of Bion's development. To begin with he speaks (1943) of a 'group with a rational structure,' referring to those aspects of collective mental life which maintain a level of behaviour linked to reality such as the awareness of the passing of time and the ability to follow methods which may be roughly called scientific. Such methods may still be rudimentary (like that of the monkey using a stick to reach a banana) but they are different from simple motor activity (like that of a monkey flinging itself against the bars) and from the automation of actions promoted by primitive mentality.

Later Bion (1961) replaced the name 'rational group' with 'work-group.' As he himself says: 'In some groups with which I was concerned, what I had called 'rational group' was spontaneously called 'work-group.' The name is concise, and since it expresses well an aspect of the phenomenon which I wish to describe, from now on I shall use this term.' The term 'work-group' used by Bion makes it clear that a learning activity is necessary if a participant is to be able to make a contribution to the achievement of the group's aims. This term also shows that participation in the work-group implies having developed some skills which Freud had indicated as characteristic of the individual's Ego, i.e. attention, verbal representation and symbolic thought.

The second group mentality described by Bion is primitive mentality. Primitive mentality corresponds to the tendency to give automatic replies. It is a dimension in which it is hard not to become completely involved. To illustrate this characteristic I shall tell the tale of a friend with a sense of humour: 'My first contact with politics was one day many years ago. Nationalism and Fascism were just beginning. I was at Middle School and I was very proud to have had this first contact with politics, and anxious to tell my family all about it. When I went home to lunch, I met my brothers and my father, an old gentleman with a liberal education. Full of enthusiasm, I began to tell them that the High School boys had arrived, and that we had gone to the other schools in a procession to get the boys to come out. We had gone all round the town. My father asked me: "What were the reasons for the demonstration? What did you want?" I replied: "I don't know, but we were all shouting 'Fast-belt, Fast-belt.'

My brothers burst out laughing. It took me some time to understand that I had joined the procession out of step. In fact they were shouting: "Bel-fast, Bel-fast."

The more the group functions according to primitive mentality, the more limited the space for the individual. It is important for the therapist to be aware of this, and in particular of the fact that the group can limit people's liberty by requiring them to adjust to a certain collective functioning. This adjustment is demanded both regarding thought (through the elimination of dissonant thoughts) and emotion. For instance, the group may exert coercion in the sense that everyone must be happy and show themselves to be so. If those forces which tend to limit freedom to express oneself and to think prevail, then individuals lose their uniqueness and become interchangeable. Therefore, the group therapist's task is not to force individuals to form a group (as in the case of a mass group) but to slow down processes that are too swift and disruptive, and to underline the peculiarities, differences and rights of the individuals.

According to Bion, primitive mentality is supported and pervaded by three phantasies which alternate in the group. Bion defines them as 'basic assumptions' to indicate how fundamental and indisputable they are. In a recent paper (1991), his daughter Parthenope Bion Talamo speaks about them as follows:

> In a broad outline of Bion's theory...he declares that the attempts made by human beings united in a group to develop creative conduct (in whatever field) may be disturbed and even completely broken off by the emergence of thoughts and emotions as rooted in unconscious phantasies concerning the 'true' motives for the foundation of the group.

There are three main classes into which these phantasies fall: 1. 'religious,' the phantasy of depending totally on an absolute and dominant figure; 2. that of 'coupling' according to which the group is said to be formed with the sole aim of reproduction, a class which merges into the religious one when the product of mating, whether it be a person or an idea, is seen as a messiah who is still to come; 3) fight/flight, a basic phantasy according to which the group gets together in order to deal exclusively with its own preservation, and this depends exclusively on attacking the enemy in mass or in fleeing from it.

In *Experiences in Groups*, Bion describes the two mentalities (work-group mentality and primitive mentality) as co-present and opposing. In other words, primitive mentality and work-group mentality do not constitute a sequence. This is a very precise point in Bion's work. It is necessary to clarify three points. First, in Bion's thinking, both primitive mentality and work group mentality are a genetic endowment of human beings and thus cannot be annulled. Second, there is real growth only through conflict of that which is primitive and that which is mature. Only growth occurring on the developed side is apparent and is built upon a sandy foundation. Third, development of technology doesn't coincide with growth of man. Quite often, it is just the opposite. Technological development may conceal the fact that man (as someone who is responsible for his primitive drives) has not developed. Evolved man (expression of the work-group) and regressed man (expression of primitive mentality) are present in both the caveman and his modern descendent, technological man. Actually, in technological man, the primitive mentality – if it does not meet adequate opposition in the work-group – is all the more dangerous in so far as it is masked by a sophisticated logic and endowed with immeasurable power. Adequate opposition to the primitive mentality could be the expansion of a worldwide movement which, for example, opposes a nuclear war or destruction of the ecological environment.

The active presence of the work-group mentality and primitive mentality, both in the group and in each of the participants, puts the individual in a situation of conflict, which cannot be resolved. If he participates in the work-group, he feels deprived of warmth and strength, if he adheres to the group as a basic assumption, he knows he may find it impossible to pursue his own ends as a thinking and reflecting individual. Participating in a group dominated by primitive mentality is revitalising, even when it leads to catastrophe, while when we detach ourselves from our herding nature, we suffer a sense of limitation and realise how deeply dependent on others we are and we feel alone.

On the other hand, this conflict between work-group and primitive mentality is also essential, and it is the origin of transformations. In Bion's opinion there is no true growth where the evolutionary aspect is detached from the primitive aspect. It is only when what is evolved comes into resonance with what is primitive and drags it out of its isolation, that there is real development of the group and of the personality of the individual.

More about Bion's particular view of psychoanalysis

Returning to Bion's particular view of 'psychoanalysis as anthropology,' and completing this quick sketch, I should like to mention two more characteristics.

The first lies in the belief that the analyst's (and the analysand's) acceptance of responsibility implies overstepping the boundary of the horizon of knowledge that had previously been laid down. In other words, the ethical duty of a psychoanalyst is not to adjust to certain norms of behaviour, but to expand the fields of knowledge and accept responsibility for the new point of view which has been reached. According to Bion, psychoanalysis is a tool for research, a probe exploring the unknown, not a container for what is already known.

Another important part of Bion's view of psychoanalysis is in considering it a 'truth-verifying process,' a process, through which a person becomes him/herself, whoever that may be. Bion believes truth is 'reality,' 'food for the mind.' For him, truth is also 'what evolves,' 'the non-finished.' Truth has a general, or rather, a universal character there is one truth, which evolves in multiple forms.

In the truth-verifying process, different forms of truth, even though contradictory, do not exclude one another, but on the contrary, are linked to each other. We might say, for example, that without the conception of truth A (Freud's theory of the unconscious), the expression of truth B (the theory of living archaic residuals) would be insufficient or might even never have been able to emerge. The relationship between two truths can perhaps best be compared to the love of Tristan and Iseult: in the sense that they are the protagonists of a 'truth-verifying novel or process' in which they are linked to one another in life and death in an indissoluble way (cf. Reale 1997).

Entering psychoanalysis is like entering a truth-verifying process which does not only concern what becomes known, but also concerns the people (the analyst and the analysand) engaged in the research. We become truth, we do not possess it.

It follows that Bion's 'truth-verifying process' hypothesis, spotlights the transforming effect, the active character of truth (cf. Gargani 1996).

I would now like to examine the impact of these two characteristics of Bion's view on Italian psychoanalysts. The assumption that psychoanalysis is a probe exploring the unknown promoted an original temporal conception. One may say that a patient is anxious because he underwent a trauma when he was an infant. Taking advantage of the image of the probe, one may also say that he is anxious because of something that still hasn't happened. That is, the votes are in the ballot-box which is waiting to be opened.

A second consequence is the accent on a particular aspect of the interpretation of dreams and other clinical material during the sessions. That is: interpretation is seen not so much as clarifying underlying unconscious or pre-conscious meaning, but as a contribution to a very special dialogue, a dialogue in which the two parties become more and more involved, in the sense that it becomes ever more important for each person and increasingly related to what is essential.

Container   contained relationship

I will now move from a general to a more detailed view and briefly consider some of Bion's other ideas which have been developed in Italy in an original way. The first one is the 'container↔contained relationship' model.

Pierandrea Lussana (1998 and 1999) pointed out the difference between the notion of Melanie Klein's 'projective identification' and Bion's 'container–contained relationship' model. The Kleinian theory assumes that the position of the two parties who are engaged in the analytical relationship is a fixed one. The patient 'launches' the 'projective identification content' and the analyst receives it. The analyst takes it on board, works through its implications and responds through verbal interpretations. In the Kleinian view, the analyst is the only agent who is capable of transforming the content of projective identification. On the contrary, when considering the analytic relationship from the point of view of Bion's 'container–contained relationship' model, the stress is on reciprocity and the mutual undertaking in which analyst and analysand, from time to time, take the role of container or contained. In Bion's model, the mind of the analyst is not the sole performer of the transformation. The transformation is carried out mainly through the interchange of the analysand and analyst, both as container and contained.

Luciana Nissim Momigliano (1984) goes even further, developing an original idea of psychoanalysis as 'two people talking in the consulting room.' The analysand is considered as having a completely active role in the course of the analysis.

'PS   D' oscillation

The major contributions to the development of the 'PS–D oscillation' theory in Italy have been provided by Giovanni Hautmann (1981 and 1999) and by Bion's daughter, Parthenope Bion Talamo (1981).

Before entering into this matter, I would like to give a short definition of Bion's 'PS↔D oscillation' theory. PS is the initial for the paranoid–schizoid position. D stands for the depressive position. Bion takes the two terms from Kleinian theory, but he puts new wine into an old barrel.

Melanie Klein worked through the notions of both paranoid–schizoid and depressive positions in quite considerable depth, in connection to the evolving process that a child must pass through in order to reach a more stable relationship with an object. That is, for Melanie Klein the only worthy movement is from paranoid–schizoid towards the depressive position. Any movement in the other direction is considered as being regressive and in fact, pathological. In numerous sections of his work, Bion declared complete acceptance of Melanie Klein's formulations and further, considered them as a milestone within the psychoanalytical world. However, to one side of Klein's theory, Bion developed his own model.

For Bion, that is: oscillation is not between paranoid–schizoid and depression, but between dispersion and integration. For Melanie Klein, as I said before, there is evolution from the paranoid–schizoid position to the depressive position, whilst for Bion there is oscillation between PS and D. For Bion, remaining only or too long in 'D' leads one to a stereotyped form of mind and at the end, to stagnation of thought. To continue functioning, it is necessary to oscillate once more from D to PS.

Of course, dispersion is accompanied by some feelings which are usual in a fragmented state of mind, and integration is accompanied by a slight depressive mood. 'Bion…said that following an effective interpretation, both patient and analyst felt sad… Feelings of sadness associated with separation and loss were the inevitable consequence of an effective interpretation and would always be mutual, however gratifying the analytic process may be' (Mason 2000).

Bion's theory also considers the existence of a principle, which is able to bring order and shape: a 'chosen fact,' a 'significant configuration.' This principle, when one is able to grasp it, activates the oscillation from dispersion to integration.

Giovanni Hautmann and Parthenope Bion Talamo agree on the fact that the PS↔D oscillation should be considered a fundamental mechanism of thought, just as the systolic and diastolic mechanisms are of the heart. They also agree on the need for the analyst to 'contemplate' void and chaotic confusion, which are typical of the paranoid–schizoid position – while maintaining his ability to think and dream. Their opinions differ with regard to the analyst's bringing about a crisis of crystallized beliefs, and therefore triggering D↔PS oscillation. Bion Talamo takes a more 'wait and see' stance, with Hautmann a more active one.

As for myself, I believe that – in certain circumstances – these interventions are useful and desirable. Even in these cases, the analyst, however, must limit himself to using the tools offered by the setting.

I find Giovanni Hautmann's precise descriptions of how Bion was able to activate 'thinking,' thus causing D↔PS oscillation, particularly fascinating. Hautmann also demonstrates how Bion repeatedly and actively questioned all the situations in which he himself, the analysand or the group had reached a finished formulation and a point of emotive equilibrium. The 'thinking' process is presented as a series of moments, where every safe moment is followed by a fracture and a consequent need to face painful instability in a 'to and fro' game which lends importance to the becoming rather than the being, to thinking rather than to thought (understood as what has already been thought).

An illustration of PS   D oscillation[3]

I would like to present an illustration using the notes taken by one of the participants in Bion's seminars in Rome.

Bion sometimes began his seminars by making general considerations, and more rarely, he just waited without saying anything. Then after a little while, someone from the audience would ask a question.

On asking the question, the interlocutor put himself in front of a thought which organized itself and, in turn, became the 'question.' A field of interest was set up. Emotions and thoughts which were up to that point rather vague would begin to take shape within a cognitive and affective condition that was characterized both by the intense expectation of verifying one's own convictions and by the desire to receive confirmation and support from Bion (oscillation from PS to D).

The characteristic trait was that, apparently, there wasn't any reply given. Bion developed his discussion, which seemed not to have anything to do with the question that had been asked. In this way he shifted the emotional and theme context, which had been set up in such a way that the participants were taken by surprise. The designated interlocutor and the group of participants underwent the effects of the destruction of the emotional and theme field into which they had set themselves (oscillation from D to PS).

Nevertheless, at the same time Bion's discussions produced new seeds of thought which brimmed with core significance that he had been able to seize upon from the question that the interlocutor had asked, but was not aware of. This core had been enriched by Bion's thoughts and expressed through a verbal form which was poetic and enriched with images.

Further, using a silence of either longer or shorter duration, the group assimilated the deception. The participants managed to master the confusion and the corresponding tormenting surprise blows. Once more, 'seeds of thought' gathered in another 'question' (oscillation from PS to D.) Once again, the audience were exposed to the frustration and emotional swirling of contact with Bion's spirit (oscillation from D to PS.)

An uneasiness spread through the participants, there was almost a cocktail of both negative and positive elements. The dominating reaction was to grab desperately onto the need to understand. 'To understand' meant struggling to pick up on the way in which Bion, in his answer, had elaborated upon the 'manifest contents' of the question.

This was the exact opposite of what Bion was aiming at. In his Rome seminars he wanted to show that one had to free oneself from codified language and thought forms in order to be able to pick up on something that, although inseparable from those forms, went beyond them. Thought then, freed from 'institutional language,' would have looked for, and found, other efficient forms of expression and communication.

Thoughts without thinker

Bion upheld that thoughts exist both prior to and independently of the subject who thinks them; the thought function, then, comes only after the thoughts. If one wanted to propose the first reference from a purely philosophical point of view, it would be Plato, or whilst regarding contemporary philosophy, 'World 3' which Popper (1963) spoke about, 'a world of thoughts without a subject who does the thinking.' The difference between Popper's World 3 and Bion's thoughts without thinker is that the latter are active and evolve (cf. Dazzi 1987).

Once again, I think it opportune to make reference to Bion's seminars. Bion started the seminar, which was held in Rome on 15 July 1977, by saying that he was thinking that when there are many individuals present, there are also many thoughts without thinkers and that these thoughts without thinkers were, therefore, in the air somewhere.

This proposed consideration, which was sparked off by the idea that in the room, 'in the air,' there could be a lot of 'thoughts without thinkers,' led to the formulation of an original model of 'Field,' which has been developed mainly by Antonello Correale (1991), Eugenio Gaburri (1997) and the members of the Group Research Centre 'Il Pollaiolo,' in Rome and Palermo.

According to this model, the 'field' is the place (both mental and theoretical) where emotions and sensations are accumulated and shared by the members of the group.

The people forming a group are immersed in the field, which is limited by links (L, H, K). The field is the third element, which exists between the 'thoughts without thinker' and 'the thinker.'

Another starting point of the Italian psychoanalyst is Kurt Lewin's (1935) fundamental work. However, it is important to point out that only the more general methodological ideas of Lewin were incorporated by the Italians, not his specific model. More precisely, I am referring to Lewin's approach for observation of psychological phenomena. Lewin doesn't search for regularities, but for interaction of a set of elements within a field. Whether an event 'occurs often or seldom has nothing to do with the [sought after] law' (Desilet 1999). In following Lewin's approach, the Italians are searching for the interaction within the 'field' which is represented by the group and the group session. However, differently from Lewin, they have not tried to state these interactions in terms of forces or dynamics.

Another important researcher who made an important contribution to the 'field theory' from a very original point of view, was Foulkes with his idea of 'matrix.' Foulkes' ideas have been assimilated by Italian psychoanalysts, not directly, but through inter-subjective psychoanalysis.[4] Mitchell (1988) 'considers relationships with others, not drives, as the basic stuff of mental life.' He goes on to say that from his perspective, people are portrayed as being shaped by and are inevitably embedded within a matrix of relationships with other people, struggling both to maintain their ties to others and to differentiate themselves from them. In his vision, the basic unit of study is not the individual as a separate entity whose desires clash with an external reality, but an interactive field within which the individual arises and struggles to make contact and articulate himself. Analytic enquiry entails participation in, and observation of, and uncovering and transformation of these relationships and their internal representations (Wright 2000).

Although these two streams of ideas made important contributions to the construction of the Italian model of 'field,' the latter has kept its originality: the fact that field is seen as something between the members of a group or the analytical couple (the thinker) and emotions, feelings and non-thought thoughts (the thoughts without thinker). A second original point is, that working through implies the fact that thoughts stay for a long period in an undefined reservoir (the field) before they can really be worked through. We believe that good wine is not just pure fermented grape juice but one that has to rest for a period in wooden barrels in well-controlled temperature and humidity conditions in a cellar.

Bion between past and future

In conclusion, I will say a few words about the topicality of Bion's teaching. Bion is not a pre-modern but a post-modern thinker, 'postmodern,' not in the chronological sense, nor in the sense of a removal and relocation of modernity. That is, not in the sense of an impossible return from the modern point of view, but inasmuch as it implies that many routes that had previously been followed by modernity seemed to be blind alleys. At the same time however, through modernity, possibilities of comprehension which are radically new have appeared (Bauman 1993).

Bion is not a psychoanalyst belonging to the period of crisis in psychoanalysis, he is a psychoanalyst of the new beginning of psychoanalysis. Bion sees the limits of psychoanalytical practice and technique, but he also announces its fundamental value: the things that make it unique.

He writes that an activity like psychoanalysis can in certain periods be fashionable, and that fashion changes. He adds that he has lived long enough to have had the experience of recognizing a situation in which psychoanalysis was very fashionable among the intelligentsia – as he was sure that many of us could recall moments in which particular points of view and beliefs were fashionable. He remembers when it was very fashionable to read *The Forsyte Saga*, then the book was forgotten until later on, when there was a revival, thanks to the dominance of television and of seeing with our own eyes. Thus history is renewed, or so it seems. However, Bion continues, admitting that this was a difficult point to write, what was really important was the true saga of the Forsytes, the fundamental history, the facts and the reality. The only name he could give to these was 'truth,' which is not influenced by a fashion or by anything at all we might happen to think about it.

Bion invites psychoanalysts to widen the cracks in the surfaces of customs and beliefs, and starting from the concrete experience, to take care to leave more room for the fundamental history, for the truth that exists in a particular psychoanalytic setting or in a group analysis.

An analytical approach – such as Bion's – sustains the analyst and gives him the security he needs when required to stand his ground, which I believe often occurs.

Moreover, an approach to analytical work such as Bion's guarantees a stimulus. It makes both the analyst and the patient aware of the fact that despite endless doubts, even if sometimes everything may appear worthless, and we may feel worthless ourselves, there is an answer. The answer is 'that you are here – that life exists and identity, that the powerful play goes on, and you may contribute a verse' (Whitman 1855).

References

Baumann Z. (1993) *Postmodern Ethics.* Oxford UK and Cambridge USA: Blackwell Publishers.

Bion, W. R. (1943) 'Intra-group tensions in therapy:' *Lancet 2:* 678–781 (27 Nov. 1943). Also in *Experiences in Groups* (1961).

Bion W. R. (1961) *Experiences in Groups.* London: Tavistock Publications.

Bion W. R. (1985) *Seminari Italiani.* Roma: Borla.

Bion W. R. (1997) *Taming Wild Thoughts.* London: Karnac Books.

Bion Talamo P. (1981) 'PS↔D.' *Rivista di Psicoanalisi, XXVII,* 3–4, 626–628.

Bion Talamo P. (1991) *Aggressività, bellicosità, belligeranza.* Unpublished.

Cavalletti, A. (2000) 'Leggere "Spartakus", prefazione.' In Jesi, F. (2000) *Spartakus – simbologia della rivolta.* Torino: Bollati Boringhieri.

Christov Bagargiev, C. (1997) 'Città natura.' In *Catalogo delta mostra internazionale di arte Contemporanea 'Città natura'.* Roma: Fratelli Palombi Editori.

Corrao F. (1998a) *Orme I.* Milano: Cortina Editore.

Corrao F. (1998b) *Orme II.* Milano: Cortina Editore.

Correale A. (1991) *Il campo istituzionale.* Roma: Borla.

Dazzi N. (1987) 'Note sulla lettura dell'opera di W. R. Bion.' In C. Neri *et al.* (a cura di), *Letture Bioniane,* Roma: Borla.

Desilet, G. (1999) 'Physics and language-science and rhetoric: Reviewing the parallel evolution of theory on motion and meaning in the aftermath of the Sokal hoax.' *The Quarterly Journal of Speech LXXXV,* 4, 339–354.

Di Paola, F. (1995) *Il tempo della mente. Saggio sul pensiero di Wilfred Bion.* Ripatransone (AP) Edizione Sestante.

Ferenczi S. (1924) *Thalass Versuch einer Genitaltheorie,* Wien: International Psychoanalytischer Verlag.

Freud, S. (1920) Quoted in Bion Talamo, P. (1981) 'An "ethical code" for authors?' In Piccioli, E. *et al.* (1996) *Writing in Psychoanalysis.* London: Karnac Books.

Gaburri E. (ed.) (1997) *Emozione e interpretazione, Psicoanalisi del campo emotivo.* Torino: Bollati-Boringhieri.

Gargani A. (1996) Presentazione di Gruppo di Claudio Neri. *Gruppo e Funzione Analitica XVII*, 1, 16–25.

Hautmann G. (1981) 'My debt toward Bion: From psycho-analysis as a theory to psycho-analysis as a mental function.' *Rivista di Psicoanalisi XXVII*, 3–4, 573–586.

Hautmann G. (1999) *Il mio debito con Bion.* Roma: Borla.

Lewin, K. (1935) *A Dynamic Theory of Personality. Selected Papers.* New York: McGraw-Hill Book Company Inc.

Lussana, P. (1998) *Gli elementi della psicoanalisi (Bion) come teoria delle emozioni o delle esperienze emozionali.* In Bion Talamo, P. *et al.* (eds) *Lavorare con Bion.* Roma: Borla.

Lussana, P. (1999) 'Introduzione alla teoria ed alla tecnica della supervisione.' *Rivista di Psicoanalisi. XLV*, 3, 465–473.

Mason, A. (2000) 'Bion and Binocular Vision.' *International Journal of Psycho-Analysis 81*, 983–989.

Mitchell, S. (1988) *Relational Concepts in Psychoanalysis.* Cambridge, MA: Harvard University Press.

Neri C. (1995) *Group.* London and Philadelphia: Jessica Kingsley Publishers, 1998.

Neri C. (1998) *Bion in Italia.* In C. Bion Talamo, F. Borgogno, S. A. Merciai (eds) *Lavorare con Bion.* Roma: Borla.

Neri C. (1999) 'Une pièce, où des gens parlent et discutent. Le modèle implicite de groupe chez W. R. Bion.' *Revue Française de Psychanalyse. Vol. LXIII* 3, 859–865.

Nissim Momigliano, L. (1984) '"... Due persone che parlano in una stanza..." (Una ricerca sul dialogo analitico).' *Rivista di Psicoanalisi XXX*, 1.

Popper, K. (1963) *Conjectures and Refutation: The Growth of Scientific Knowledge.* London: Routledge.

Reale G. (1997) 'Storia di una vita retta.' *Il Sole 24 Ore*, 108, 21.

Shakespeare W. (1969) *Twelfth Night or What You Will*, in *Complete Works of W. Shakespeare, Vol. III.* Philadelphia: Handy Stratford Edition.

Whitman W. (1855) *Leaves of Grass.* New York: Penguin Books 1944.

Wright F. (2000) 'The use of the self in group leadership: A relational perspective.' *International Journal of Group Psychotherapy L*, 2, 181–199.

Yeats W. B. (1984), *The Poems* edited by Richard J. Finneran. New edition. London: Macmillan.

Endnotes

1.   This paper is an expansion upon a previous publication: Neri, 1998.

2.   Those readers who are familiar with this concept or who have read my book *Group* (Neri 1995) can go directly to the next section.

3.   This illustration has already been published in Neri, 1999.

4.   The idea of 'matrix' was regarded both as too vague and too ontological in Italy. Foulkes' ideas were assumed to be opposed to Bion's, the reference for the Italians was to Bion. Nowadays, however, these preconceptions don't exist any more.

Part II

Bion's Context

Contemporaries and Refinements

6

Pairing Bion and Foulkes

Towards a Metapsychosociology?

Dennis Brown

Half-jokingly I once suggested (Brown 1985, p.216) that rather than hope Bion and Foulkes would pair posthumously, we should work to integrate their contributions. I had argued that Bion's idea about Basic Assumption states reflects the negative processes in groups, the dark side of a group's capacity to work together creatively, and that they are more likely to predominate in certain conditions. These include the way they are conducted and the organisational culture. Examples of the former include a remote and mystifying style and talking only to the group-as-a-whole; of the latter, settings which discourage free communication and shared responsibility, which Foulkes believed were essential for healthy growth and development. Bion emphasised the difficulties in the relationship between individual and group, Foulkes the inextricability and creativity of the relationship. Thus Foulkes talked to the group and to individuals, holding that group interpretations inevitably address most members, and that individual interpretations are saying something to all.

Bion described the problem of psychoanalysis as, 'Growth and its harmonious resolution in the relationship between the container and the contained, repeated in individual, pair and finally group (intra- and extra-psychically)' (Bion 1970,15–16). Now, more than ever, I am convinced that the work of Foulkes and his followers helps us to illuminate and resolve that problem. If we work towards integrating the ideas of Bion and Foulkes, we could arrive at a metapsychosociology. A lot of the spadework has already been done. I wish to use some of it.

Freud developed his *metapsychology* to conceptualise the vicissitudes of instinctual drives within the individual, culminating in the so-called structural theory of a personality structured into ego, superego and id (Freud 1923); each part a sub-system of the whole. Similarly, a metapsychosociology would need to visualise a series of systems and subsystems. These could embrace several elements (De Mare 1972): (a) *structure*, incorporating the group beyond the individual isolate; (b) *processes* such as a development of a sense of belonging, identification, and differentiation from others. These would have to include both positive and negative processes, in the sense that they are or are not compatible with both self-respect and respect for others; and (c) *contents* such as values, good/bad, simplicity/complexity, uniformity/diversity. These would include the value accorded to 'individualism' and to group-belonging and participation. Bion summed this up in his idea of humans being group animals at war with their groupishness (Bion 1961); Foulkes's contrasting idea is that groups provide the matrix out of which individuality emerges (Foulkes 1973). In Freud's metapsychology the superego is, as it were, the Trojan horse in which the social breaches the individual. A Foulkesian metapsychology will allow for the influence of the social at all levels of individual and group interaction.

Beyond the vicissitudes of individual development, the stuff of our everyday clinical work, such a theory, could help us to account for the impact on groups of individuals of social trauma, conflict and oppression, as well as the subtler blockages to co-operative work epitomised by the basic assumptions. To do this we need to be aware of the operation of the social unconscious as well as the individual unconscious and the way the context influences what goes on within it.

I have begun to think again about Bion and his unworked out non-relationship with Foulkes, helped by the thinking of a new generation of group analysts, notably Morris Nitsun (1996) and Farhad Dalal (1998), both of whom are to a degree critical of Foulkes. In addition I want to bring in the systemic approach of Agazarian, and group relations thinkers influenced by Bion (Lawrence 2000, Turquet 1974). These have been further illuminated by Earl Hopper's attempts to link psychoanalysis, group analysis and sociology (Hopper 1997), and by the work of others who have applied group analytic ideas to organisational consultancy. They have helped me to integrate both my experience of working as a clinician, and participation in the work of the European Association for Transcultural Group Analysis. This has inevitably involved thinking about transcultural and intercultural phenomena; respectively focusing on similarities and communication across cultures, and differences and failures of communication. The crucial significance of boundaries is illustrated by work on the body image, briefly reported here as a metaphor for group identification, holding and containing. It is explored using the concepts of bi-logic (Matte-Blanco 1975, 1988) and the vicissitudes of intersubjectivity (Brown 1994).

1. Morris Nitsun

Morris Nitsun (1996) challenges Foulkes's excessive optimism about therapeutic groups, and recognises that groups as well as individuals can be the source of aggression and destructiveness. In developing his concept of the Anti-Group, the ever-present potential for destructiveness shadowing creative group processes ('the Pro-Group'), he suggests that basic assumption groups are manifestations of Anti-Group processes (page 66). '[The] basic assumptions undermine the capacity of the group to achieve its purpose. The group is preserved – or there is an attempt to do so – but at the expense of personal and group development.'

Nitsun cautiously but powerfully extends the concept of the anti-group to 'natural groups' – to families and to organisations, and to social cultures. What he calls 'the indivisible link between individual and group, person and culture' involves different levels of the organisational whole in a complex way. He uses a mirroring analogy in which the anti-group is a prism in which the psyche and the social world 'act as containers for each other, mutually reflecting each other in an ongoing cycle' (Nitsun 1996, p.268). Unlike Dalal (v.i.) he starts with an intra-psychic phenomenon – failure of the environmental mother to provide a context in which to acquire a creative relationship to self and other – to group relationships in family and social groups. He does however go on to consider social failures to care for people suffering scarcity and basic requirements for life and dignity.

In his conclusions (Nitsun 1996, p.286), Nitsun proposes three integrated perspectives: the dialectics, ecology, and aesthetics of groups.

(a) Dialectics refers to a continuous cycle of mutual creation and negation, in a sense of Foulkes *and* Bion, construction *and* destruction. The group is never one thing, defined and static, 'it becomes what it is in the interplay of different modes of experience'. Nitsun is wrong though, I think, to counterpoint anti-group basic assumption states with being stuck in cohesive idealisation of the group; that is not Foulkesian, it is better seen as basic assumption one-ness (Turquet) or massification/aggregation (Hopper), which are discussed later.

(b) Ecology refers to the ecological viewpoint brought to wide attention by Bateson (1972). It draws on principles of how human systems such as groups are formed and maintained by the communication of information, including the interaction of ideas. Durkin (1981), Blackwell (1994) and Agazarian and Gantt (2000) have developed these systemic ideas. Boundary issues are vital to any systemic approach, e.g. whether boundaries are permeable or impermeable. Interestingly Nitsun prefers the term ecological to systemic 'as it generates more directly a vision of the group in its multiple contexts as it struggles towards its destiny as a living system' (Nitsun 1996, p.289).

A well-functioning therapeutic group can become increasingly flexible and inclusive, so long as the pro-group predominates and comes to dialectical terms with the anti-group.

(c) Aesthetics relates to the way in which the group is experienced as a creation integrated from the fragments unfolding at the time into coherent patterns within the (dialectical) flux in the (ecological) holding environment. I think Nitsun is right when he suggests that both group members and therapists achieve aesthetic satisfaction from the transformational potential of the group which can lead to moments of insight, wisdom and beauty.

This creative view of group functioning, in which the group creates itself, contrasts with that of Anzieu (1984) whose work on training groups emphasises the *illusory* nature of groups but links naturally with Winnicott's idea about creative play within transitional space (Winnicott 1971). This is, as it were, the *Anlage* of the cultural products of society. It will be noted that this implies a centrifugal process, starting in the space between baby and mother, progressing outward to the space between wider and wider networks of people. It also implies that the individual comes first. This is directly challenged by Farhad Dalal, who emphasises the priority of the group, and the centripetal forces of influence. I turn now to Dalal's contribution without agreeing that either direction of influence can be seen as primary.

2. Farhad Dalal

Farhad Dalal's criticism of Foulkes is in some ways more radical than that of Nitsun. He makes a case for Foulkes having had a failure of nerve in the face of his own radicalness, anxious not to endanger his professional identity as a psychoanalyst. According to Dalal's reading of Freud and Foulkes, the latter drew back from the full recognition of his awareness of the social world penetrating and moulding not only the ego and superego, but also the id, the supposed seat of innate instinct (Dalal 1998, p.46). It is the deepest levels of communication that have the widest transpersonal influences which permeate groups and societies to a degree that comprises what he calls the social unconscious (Foulkes 1964, p.52). In contrast with psychoanalysts such as Winnicott, who considered healthy individuals make healthy groups, Foulkes said that whether or not individuals are healthy depends on the state of the group to which they belong; health and disturbance are a function of a 'balance in the total field of interaction...' (Foulkes and Anthony 1957, p.54). Anyone working with families or groups today would surely agree with this. Dalal however criticises Foulkes, and most group analysts, for sticking to Freud's theory and prioritising the mother–infant paradigm in formulating 'deep' interpretations.

What Dalal approvingly calls radical as opposed to orthodox Foulkes, breaking free from individualism, draws more on the work of the sociologist Norbert Elias (rather than Freud). But Foulkes was half-hearted about it, accepting Elias' idea that individual mind and personality are formed by the social nexus in which they develop, but ignoring the facts of social power relationships which Elias emphasised.

Dalal highlights the differences in our understanding of the relationship between the so-called internal world and the so-called external world, particularly in terms of which has priority. The philosophical and clinical arguments are perhaps endless and irresolvable. For example, Cohn (1996) has argued from a basis in existential phenomenology, that Foulkes recognised the intersubjective basis of mind, quoting his statement, 'I do not think that the mind is basically inside the person as an individual... The mind that is usually called intrapsychic is a property of the group' (Foulkes 1990, p.277). In the same issue of *Group Analysis*, Diamond (1996) attacks my interpretation of intersubjectivity (Brown 1994) as too restricted to a psychoanalytic viewpoint. Countering her criticisms of my interpretation of clinical material enabled me to clarify, at least for myself, that it was the cut-off 'autistic' elements, caused by intolerable pain and anxiety during individuals' development, that led to psychopathology (Brown 1996). This withdrawal is aided by the fact that people have their own bodies which become sanctuaries and projection screens, just as 'belonging groups' do in social life. (I refer to the body image further on). The situations of safety or suffering can become an infinite series in the unconscious (see references to bi-logic later on).

Foulkes's emphasis on communication, articulated increasingly in the therapeutic process, involves translating unthought and unspoken processes into symbols, including words, and extending them from the 'internal' awareness into dialogue with others – whether an individual therapist or a group; that is, from 'internal' into 'external' space. According to Elias, symbols (language, knowledge and thought) are directed towards control of the social and natural world in which a person is located (Elias 1991a, p.77). In place of narrowly sociological theories which view the individual as infinitely plastic, more sophisticated ones such as those of Elias (1991b), Vigotsky (1978), Mead (1934) and Burkitt (1991) present a picture of mutual engagement and transformation of the internal and external worlds, much nearer to the group-analytic view.

Dalal points out that even Winnicott, by placing the transitional space between mother and infant in which 'me' and 'not-me' are originally negotiated, cuts short a potentially wider perspective on self and other in the wider society by seeing the influence as one-way; i.e. avoiding seeing culture as penetrating the mother–infant relationship. One example of this is the effect of the infant's gender. Foulkes on the other hand, for example, saw the Oedipus complex not solely as a stage in the child's development, but as preceding even the birth of the baby, and as influenced by social attitudes towards gender and authority (Brown and Zinkin 1994: pp.3ff).

Dalal points to the radicalism of Fairbairn as being greater than Winnicott's, by giving the interpersonal, the 'external', priority over the intrapersonal, the 'internal'. He saw the libido as object-seeking rather than pleasure-seeking, with aims to relieve innate tensions, and the infant as constructing its internal object world – containing both libidinal and anti-libidinal objects – as a result of failures and frustrations in relation to external objects. Yet Fairbairn disappoints Dalal in his seeming disregard of the social world. In contrast Foulkes recognised that the social world permeates the individual, but Dalal criticises him for failing to extend his theory about what takes place *inside* a group (important for group therapy) to account for what takes place *between* groups (which would take us to a wider theory of the sort I am trying to adumbrate).

One of Dalal's master strokes is to recruit the thinking of the increasingly influential psychoanalyst Ignacio Matte-Blanco (Matte-Blanco 1975 and 1988: Rayner 1995). The theory of bi-logic describes two different systems of logic operating in the mind: *asymmetrical*, in which things are categorised as different from each other, either/or; and *symmetrical*, in which all objects are identical. The former is the world of rationality and 'secondary process thinking', the latter of poetry and dreams and 'primary process thinking', in which there is no necessity to split and differentiate, no negation. Asymmetrical logic differentiates, while symmetrical logic homogenises to an infinity in which all differentiation is lost. According to Matte-Blanco both forms of logic co-exist. Thus the psychoanalytic view that individuals exist in groups, and the view that groups exist inside individuals, are complementary. The complexity of this co-existence is clarified, Dalal asserts (1998 p.217), by comparing the flowering or unfolding model of development, with its roots in psychoanalysis, to the 'cybernetic' idea of fields of influence, of mirroring and coherence (Pines 1998), and corrective feedback loops to which Nitsun was also referring.

Dalal (1998 p.226) points to the fact that at different times Foulkes acknowledged that both the individual *and* the group are abstractions. But he did not join up these realisations. To have done so, in Dalal's opinion, would have led to a radical post-structuralist theory that is both exciting and frightening. To get a perspective we have progressively to stand outside the context we are inside in order to scan it, to enter another context, ad infinitum. He would rescue us by reminding us of the power structures in the world that decide who has power and who not, who is included in favoured categories and who excluded, in short, who is 'us' and who 'them'.

3. Yvonne Agazarian

Yvonne Agazarian has been developing her theory for nearly 40 years (Agazarian and Gantt 2000). One of her earliest published papers (Agazarian 1962) was on *role* as an isomorphic bridge in the relationship between the individual and the group. This links with G. H. Mead's earlier sociological work, but was systematically presented 20 years later in her theory of the 'visible and invisible group' (Agazarian and Peters 1981) in which she differentiated the several ways in which the individual and group systems interact as seen from different perspectives: (1) the *person perspective* 'explains individual behaviour in terms of genetic inheritance, developmental history and environmental influences'. (2) The *member role perspective* 'explains individual behaviour in terms of how the person unwittingly coaches the group to respond to him in ways that replicate and bind past conflicts'. (3) The *group-as-a-whole perspective* 'explains gross group behaviour in terms of group composition, developmental history and environmental influences'. (4) The *group role perspective* explains group behaviour in terms of the group as a whole delegating of one or more of its members to perform group roles that bind, contain or express group conflicts. 'Invisible group theory' explains individual dynamics in terms of a discrete individual system and separates it from the equally discrete group system which explains group dynamics. As Agazarian (1983) explicates, the individual system has two subsystems – person and member; and the group system has two subsystems – group role and group as a whole. 'All three systems are in hierarchical relationship. Their structure and function are, through their principle of isomorphy, related.'

This complex but careful description integrates systems theory and Lewinian field theory. Its clarity is far from most therapists' experience, unless perhaps they have been through Agazarian's vivid training seminars. However, her thinking sheds light on some of the problems highlighted by Dalal and links with some of Matte-Blanco's ideas mentioned above. For example, Agazarian distinguishes between *stereotype* and *functional* subgroups: the former forming around similarities and striking differences, the latter also forming around similarities but *integrating* differences. Unlike most group analysts, who characteristically lead from behind, she sees the task of the therapist to promote actively the 'right' sort of subgroup formation.

For Agazarian every system exists in the environment of the system above it, and is the environment for the system below it. This hierarchy is 'contexualised' as *the observing self-system* discriminates and integrates information, developing the ability to experience itself both as a person-as-a-whole with membership in many internal subgroups, but also as a member of the group as a whole and its subgroups (Agazarian and Gantt 2000, p.239).

Much of Agazarian's work is rigorously intellectual, as in the method she describes as SAVI (system for analysing verbal interaction), later her systems-centred practice. But concluding her recent book (Agazarian and Gantt 2000, p.254) she claims that her approach has contributed 'an understanding that it is not the human dynamics themselves that contribute to the success or failure in therapy, but the development of a context in which they can be addressed and explored rather than acted out. In this Agazarian is very group-analytic in the Foulkesian sense.

The active role that Agazarian takes in therapy to promote the 'right' sort of subgroup formation could be seen as similar to the promotion of enabling, as opposed to restrictive, group solutions to group focal conflicts, described by Whitaker and Lieberman (1964). Her awareness of the narcissistic trauma that can be inflicted by group-as-a-whole interpretations in training (T) groups conducted on the Tavistock model, led her to 'rescuing' individuals through eye contact, as though to affirm their continued existence for her. She proposed that Bion's basic assumptions are 'core emotional response states that serve the group much as ego defence mechanisms serve the individual' (Agazarian and Gantt 2000, p.83). She was influenced by the theory of group development in T group events described by Bennis and Shepherd (1956), involving two initial phases: (1) dominated by issues of power and control in which the group attempts to seduce the leader to a 'good protector role' to defend it against chaos (BaD); and (2) dominated by competitiveness, which when frustrated leads to a fight–flight Ba culture manifested in inter-member scapegoating, but finally coalesces into a 'barometric event' – a ritualised attack on the leader. When successful this leads to the location of 'evil' in the 'bad' leader and 'good' in the group, thus freeing the group from its struggle with the leader for power and control, and allowing it to turn to issues of intimacy. You will note the similarity of thinking to that of Winnicott when he described 'the-use-of an-object', mentioned below.

4. Fourth and fifth basic assumptions: Turquet, Lawrence and Hopper

In discussing the contributions of Nitsun and Dalal I have focused on the two-way relationship between the individual and group, extended to society, then with the help of Agazarian have begun to allow for the effect of intermediate groupings and subgroupings. This brings us to a body of knowledge and theory that have been mainly the preserve of specialists in group dynamics consulting to organisations in industry, commerce and public institutions. It has been promoted especially by the Tavistock Institute of Human Relationships and the Grubb Institute in the UK, and the A. K. Rice Institute in the USA. One method of working has been through group relations workshops, the so-called Leicester Conferences, in which the work task is the examination of relationships within and between groups of participants within the total situation of the conference. Another application is consultation to organisations in trouble. The fact that the interests of the organisation and those of the individuals in it can be in conflict, for example over methods and hours of work and levels of pay, is obvious, and so is the powerful effect on the functioning of the total organisation of whether or not workers at all levels are satisfied and motivated.

It is significant, I think, that this way of studying group processes can be very stressful for some individual company members. Agazarian's method of making eye contact described above differentiates her from the more detached style of some conductors who model themselves on Bion and the 'pure' Tavistock method. Kleinian psychoanalysts have contributed massively in this field (e.g. Jaques 1974, Menzies 1961) and the influence of Bion's work continues to predominate. This has resulted in a preoccupation with primitive 'psychotic' anxieties – fear of annihilation and persecutory attack – and defences against them. One could argue that, as with Bion's method of conducting small groups (Brown 1985, pp216–7) the way the staff of group relations workshops carry out their roles can also promote the anxieties they study. This is not to say that studying the worst possible outcome is not valuable in reaching towards healthy models of organisational life.

As Lawrence (2000, p.126) has pointed out, the theme of 'order' has always been present in the Tavistock conferences through emphasis on leadership, responsibility, authority, organisation and the 'politics of related-ness'. This is studied in the 'psychoanalytic' exploration of possible transfer-ence and countertransference feelings between the managerial and consultant staff of the conference and its membership. For example, the staff will often appear as a privileged subgroup in the conference, at the same time destruc-tive, persecuting, protecting and benign. The assumption is that such 'fanta-sies' are just that, but there is no doubt that such experiences occur in any conference when power is arrogated by staff. They could however be augmented by the style and method of leadership. Ideally, working through such transference feelings enables the membership to take responsibility for learning from such experiences.

These extensions to Bion's theory of basic assumption states, I believe, help to humanise it by recognising the complex ways by which individuals keep afloat in groups and find nourishment in them, even put roots down in them. Pierre Turquet introduced the basic assumption of oneness (BaO) in which 'members seek to join in a powerful union with an omnipotent force, unobtainably high, to surrender self for passive participation and thereby feel existence, well-being and wholeness' (Turquet 1974, p.357). In this state the individual is lost in oceanic feelings of unity – as in crowds of football supporters – or in oneness personified in a single person – as in 'salvationist inclusion' achieved by following a cult religious leader. Writing of his experi-ences in the large group in Leicester Conferences, Turquet (1975) traces the individual's 'conversion' from being a disconnected singleton to an individual member (IM) by establishing relationships with other singletons. He or she then has to struggle against being taken over as a membership individual (MI) in the large group in which group membership may be felt to counter self-definition and needs. This threat is greatest when membership of a large group is equated with the singleton's own destructive feelings. Turquet points to transitional states, between singleton, IM and MI and back again. Certainly this accords with my own experience in large groups held in the Group Analytic Society and Institute of Group Analysis, which some people find so threatening they drop out while others enjoy the exhilaration of the transformations. The latter are probably more secure personalities or, at least having survived such experiences before, feel less threatened.

Gordon Lawrence has introduced the complementary concept of a basic assumptions 'me-ness' (Lawrence, Bain and Gould 1966), starting with Turquet's idea of the singleton, and which Lawrence sees as increasingly dominant in a world of increasing individualism and consumerism. This precedes Turquet's analysis of the progression of the individual through the life of the group 'because the individual does not want to have relations'. Instead of moving towards intersubjectivity, in which the sentience of others is acknowledged in a mutual 'we-ness', the 'I' becomes an object to itself, a 'me'. BaM represents an attack on the possibility of learning from relating to others. The group is not allowed to exist and achieve its primary task.

BaO and BaM represent extreme states hindering the function of self-reflecting work groups that parallel the double nature of the individual as an ego and part of a 'we-go' (Klein 1976). They are integrated, seen as twin opponents of both unbearable suffering and of creative relating, in Earl Hopper's idea of a basic assumption of massification/aggregation (Hopper 1997, 2003). He developed this in the course of exploring, over many years, the interface between his first professional identity as a sociologist with his later practice as a group analyst and psychoanalyst, particularly with severely traumatised and/or personality disordered individuals.

Hopper's concept of a BaM/A seems particularly relevant in understanding what he calls 'the patterns of incohesion and traumatic experience in the unconscious life of groups'. Cohesion, Hopper states, refers to the *appearance* of unity of feeling and purpose enabling people to work together in harmony, and is not based only on patterns of communication (as it would be in a 'coherent' group). There is an optimal degree of cohesion for different phases of group development; too little interferes with decision and action, too much inhibits individual creativity and can lead to overidealisation of the group, scapegoating and denigration of other groups. The degree of cohesion is influenced by the therapist or leader. Pines (1981) has argued that a mature group aims for coherence rather than cohesion, the difference being the amount of diversity that can be creatively integrated within the group and its component members. I think the important thing is how people can co-operate and belong, along with others, to an identifiable group, while at the same time being true to themselves and their *own* component parts.

Whereas Turquet saw BaO as a regressive group response to multiple stimuli and response bombardment, Hopper sees Incohesion: Aggregation-/Massification (I:A/M) as occurring in a group of traumatised people who have encapsulated intrapsychic oscillations between fission and fragmentation, fusion and confusion. Those who developed contact-shunning 'crustacean' defences will tend to personify states of *aggregation*; those whose defences involve merger-hunger 'amoeboid' processes, will tend to personify states of *massification*. The former Hopper equates (Hopper 1997, p.459) with Turquet's singletons, the latter with his membership individuals, leaving Turquet's individual members (IM) as those with an optimal degree of cohesion for working in groups. (These two categories of Hopper are reflected in work I did on body image many decades ago, and to which I shall refer later.)

Hopper's thinking recognises the deep levels of pain and fragmentation that underlie such group phenomena, akin to Bion's ideas about basic assumptions and the Kleinian tendency to present the underlying anxieties as psychotic. Work in group relations workshops would indicate that they arise in 'average' groups of 'average professionals' and therefore, they arise from all levels of health and pathology. My own experience in therapy groups (Brown 1985) is that basic assumption phenomena are common transient features of well-functioning group-analytic groups with very mixed levels of pathology.

5. Group-analytic organisational consultancy

Following Robin Skynner (1989), in the last few years several colleagues have applied group analytic concepts to organisational consultancy. Rifkind (1995), working with staff groups dealing with HIV infection, has highlighted boundary and 'dynamic administration' issues in promoting staff's 'emotional literacy' and hence their ability to contain the huge emotional disturbance evoked by this work. She describes the staff group as a microcosm of the wider community setting, able to attend Janus-faced to their own internal processes and what is happening outside.

Nitsun (1998a and b) develops Foulkes's concept of *mirroring* in consultation, aiming to strengthen boundary differentiation by clarifying dysfunctional mirroring, in groups and individuals, to increase their capacity to adapt to the organisational task. He traces isomorphic mirroring through the concentric systems from the wider environment to what he calls 'the organisational psyche' with its shared fantasies and unconscious attributions [note, not the individual psyche]. Nitsun uses Foulkes's ideas of *levels* of group functioning (current, transference, projective and primordial), the group *matrix*, the inseparability of internal and external relationships, figure-and-ground, and the crucial role of *communication*; but he also introduces his own concept of the Anti-group in relation to organisational pathology (which we have already seen Nitsun equates with Bion's basic assumption states).

Wilke (1998) describes Oedipal and sibling dynamics in groups occurring especially at times of rapid change, and defending against the inability to mourn and feel remorse. Imposed organisational change, he holds, reproduces early infantile anxieties to do with 'separation of me and not-me' and the need to move into the early phase of Oedipal conflict; but at the same time puts it in terms of social psychology: 'An organisation of this type is characterised by high levels of anxiety about boundary issues, role strain and normative expectations.' (This double way of thinking implies isomorphism between the theoretical systems of individual and social psychology which may or may not be justifiable; we will need to think about this further).

Rance (1998) in keeping with Foulkes's emphasis on networks (nexus, 'plexus,' etc. at different points in his writing) uses systems theory and psychoanalytic theory, as well as Foulkes's basic idea of the social origins of personality. Rance develops the idea of staff consultation as a *conversation*, often extending over several months.

Like Wilke and Nitsun, Blackwell (1998) recognises the potential chaos in organisations undergoing change, but sees the creative potential of managing the anxiety stirred up by instability in the system. As he puts it, following Foulkes, a group analytic approach provides a model for counteracting regressive tendencies by promoting *communication* and *dialogue*. This helps to avoid the twin dangers of rigidity and chaos, especially when reflexivity in 'the bounded instability' of the matrix can include humour and playfulness.

However, Spero (1999), a group analyst who works with Harold Bridger (a colleague of both Bion and Foulkes at Northfield), quotes Foulkes's warning to those working in the organisational context not to go too far into underlying meaning or private personal motivation, i.e. to differentiate clinical and non-clinical work, therapy and consultation. For Spero an important function of the consultant is to keep the organisation in mind, along with its task and members' roles, reflecting at the same time on the tensions created by the task in both individuals and groups.

This *holding* and *containing* of very difficult countertransference feelings – also emphasised by Wilke in his way of working as a consultant – reflect Colin James' (1984, 1994) integration of Winnicott's and Bion's complementary but distinct concepts. Both can be seen to operate within the group-analytic matrix, and occur (or do not) in all group phenomena, from the mother–infant dyad to society.

Social construction (Campbell 2000) offers a unifying view of organisational consultancy and of the individual self which is consistent with Foulkesian group-analysis. The organisation is seen as socially constructed continuously, daily, even momentarily, by individuals interacting; it is continuously changing and re-inventing itself, like the dynamic matrix in group-analytic therapy (Campbell 2000, p.28). The individual self, likewise, is constructed in the interaction between the self and others (*ibid.*, p.16). This view is entirely consistent, for example, with Foulkes's basic law of group dynamics (Foulkes 1948, Brown 1998) that the group *constitutes* (i.e. creates) the norm from which individuals deviate. But it has to maintain its boundaries and contain its diversity despite difference and emergent tensions.

6. Transcultural work

I shall now draw on experiences studied by the European Association for Transcultural Group Analysis (EATGA), which relate to the sort of massive trauma and disruption to which Hopper refers. The history of Europe, especially in the last century, is one of oscillation between forced attempts at imperial massification and struggles to unpick larger masses into smaller groupings, both of which have involved destructive wars, wholesale dislocation and exile of populations, and mass exterminations, not to mention the continuation of social divides in power and discrimination. It would not be surprising then if rational co-operation between individuals and between groups and nations tends to be hampered by oscillation between the fears of massification and aggregation. Current disputes about European integration could be seen as a demonstration of Hopper's basic assumption.

The work of the intercultural workshops organised over the last two decades by the EATGA have demonstrated how, with good will and professional interest – often stemming from a personal history touched by past European trauma – much of the destructiveness can be contained and reflected on in ways that diminish scapegoating and stereotyping. Through alternating small and large groups, people from different cultures are confronted by how much they have in common. Intermediate-sized groups, between the size of a nuclear family and a large social group, have allowed exploration of issues to do with differences of language, religion, and nationality, and the effect of migration. Historical antagonists recognise the mutuality of their suffering inhumanity; 'You are the enemy I killed my friend' as the First World War poet Wilfred Owen wrote before he himself was killed.

The depth at which cultural and national identity and conflicts are incorporated in each individual's personality is part of what Foulkes (1975) meant by the foundation matrix, which included shared myths, values and standards. In the EATGA this is often referred to as the non-individualised part of the personality (Le Roy 1994). Kaës (1987) pointed to four major psychic functions of culture: 1. maintaining the individually undifferentiated basis of psychic structures needed to belong to a social whole, a 'we-go'; 2. ensuring a set of common defences; 3. providing points for identification and differentiation which guarantee the continuity of distinctions between the sexes and generations; 4. constituting an area of psychic transformation by providing signifiers, representations, and the means for organising psychic reality.

My own observations, during the first workshop in Maastricht (Brown 1987) is that there is a parallel in small and large group settings which can be related to movement between the (Kleinian) paranoid–schizoid and depressive positions. One way the small and large groups differed was in the relative linguistic homogeneity of the small groups, so that frustration, confusion and fear of annihilation, or at least non-recognition, were commonest in the large groups. (One manifestation was the non-provision of a German–speaking small group, and the apparent embargo on German in the large group.) Themes and developments reflected each other, though small groups were explicitly more personal, large groups more cultural. Issues of identity were prominent in both, but the former dealt more with the history of individual struggles with ambivalently cathected parental objects, while moving towards individuation and intimacy; the latter with cultural history, language and identity. The fear of non-recognition and annihilation gave way gradually in both settings as the paranoid–schizoid was succeeded by the depressive position, and basic assumption phenomena were replaced by differentiation, reconciliation and mutual concern. This was not without crisis and struggle, especially powerful in the large group, evident for example in the confrontation between Jews and Germans in the subsequent workshop in Heidelberg (Brown 1992). Such powerful and explosive phenomena are more likely in large groups, where it is much easier not to hear or see individuals, and to resonate to cultural history, myths and stereotypes. This is augmented by the 'psychic envelopes' (Anzieu 1984, 1990), illusory notions of nation and race, with their attendant mythology. These make it much more difficult to attain the empathic mutual identification that is necessary for reconciliation and mutual concern. This requires genuine encounters, real confrontation and encounter – not the pseudo-confrontation that is based on paranoid projection (Brown 1988).

Rouchy (1995) has contributed to our appreciation of 'secondary belonging groups' such as educational, occupational and recreational groups, beyond the primary family, as completing the cultural interiorisation begun in the family, perhaps permitting individuation and object relating that were not sufficiently attained there, and 'concretising the grasp on space and time'.

7. Boundaries and barriers – the analogy with the body image

As Louis Zinkin (1994) argued, boundaries between systems mediate a balance between centrifugal and centripetal processes. Exchange, vital in psychotherapy, economics and all living systems, implies permeable boundaries. One of our conclusions in *The Psyche and the Social World* (Brown and Zinkin 1994) was: 'Boundaries between individuals are to varying degrees permeable. The more rigid and seemingly impermeable the boundaries – that is, the more they become barriers – the greater the use of projection and projective identification to supplement them, and obtain an exclusive identification based on 'myths of purity and homogeneity, rather than plurality.'

The need for clear, even rigid and impermeable boundaries around oneself and 'one's own kind' is largely a measure of insecurity and fear of inner fragility. The analogy of the body image may be instructive. We all have an unconscious kinaesthetic and proprioceptive model of the body that influences the sense of ourselves in the world (Schilder 1935; Scott 1948) both in health and disease, and extend it beyond our physical boundaries, e.g. to our cars (Brown 1959). Fisher and Cleveland (1958) developed a way of studying the body image by means of the projective Rorschach ink blot test in a wide range of psychosomatic and psychiatric conditions, deriving barrier (B) and penetration (P) scores which can be rated as ranging from high to low. B scores were high in people suffering from 'body boundary disorders' (e.g. skin

and musculo-skeletal) compared with those suffering from internal (e.g. gas-
trointestinal) disorders. P scores were high in fragile schizophrenics. Many
years ago I used this test to study the susceptibility of chemical workers to
develop contact dermatitis (Brown and Young 1965). We discovered that psychological orientation towards either introversion or extraversion (differenti-
ating between social and thinking I/E, especially when these were
discordant) interacted statistically with other traits such as ego-strength,
anxiety threshold, hunger for tactile contact, and degree of rigidity and intolerance of ambiguity. Summarising these findings (Brown 1997) it appeared
that if subjects were social introverts but thinking extraverts (i.e. impulsive
rather than reflective) they had lower ego strengths and anxiety threshold and
more hunger for tactile contact; if they were social extraverts (but reflective
and perhaps ruminative) they tended to be emotionally constricted, rigid and
intolerant of ambiguity.

In his book *The Group and the Unconscious*, Didier Anzieu (1984) describes
groups as suffering from not having a body, and having to imagine one by
developing an imaginary 'envelope' or ego-skin (as do individuals).
Metaphors of the group as a 'body' with individual 'members' capable of
'esprit de corps' bear this out. Based on work in short-term training groups,
Anzieu describes the image of the group body as a 'pseudo-organised
principle' corresponding to a 'nostalgic dream of symbiosis between
members' (Anzieu 1984, p.241), echoing Turquet's BaO or Hopper's Ba. A
more dynamic approach could be offered by the application of Attachment
Theory (Marrone 1994, 1998) to the human need to belong from infancy to
the multiplicity of identifications and real belonging groups that make up a
human's life span. One can imagine a series of organising metaphors from
womb (Elliot 1994) to global universality.

8. Concluding questions and speculations

Is it meaningful to draw an analogy between the body image and models we
make concerning the inside and outside of the individual in relation to his or
her family, the family in relation to others, and the various secondary groups
with which we identify, and nations, etc.? I suspect it might help us to see the
complexity of developmental negotiations, for example, by enabling us to
allow for variations in basic security within each system, the degree to which
basic needs are met, and the predominant values and attitudes to others. These
would involve a capacity for centrifugal as well as centripetal empathy, for
flexibility and inclusiveness. There does seem to be a relationship between the

security and satisfaction experienced in a system and the values it develops towards others.

Do the apparent differences between 'optimistic' Foulkes and 'pessimistic' Bion relate first to the values of the conductor/therapist/chairman/leader, and second to 'where the group is at' in terms of the security, satisfaction of needs and the flexibility of the group and the individuals comprising it? I believe that a crucial differnce is Foulkes' view of persons and groups as open systems in dialectical relationship to one another.

A comprehensive 'metapsychosociology' would integrate the mutual interaction and interpenetration of psyches and social worlds, at all levels, conscious and unconscious. I suspect that a key role in this integration could be played by the concepts of bi-logic and mathematical set theory developed by the psychoanalyst Ignacio Matte-Blanco (1975, 1988), particularly in relation to what Foulkes (1964) called the Social Unconscious. These concepts involve the coexistence of two modes of thinking, asymmetrical and symmetrical, which on the one hand discriminate and classify, and follow the principles of 'secondary process' logic (things exist in specific time and space); and on the other hand follow the 'primary process' logic described by Freud (1915) as characteristic of the unconscious – without contradiction and negation and manifested in displacement, condensation and symbolisation. The unconscious is timeless and spatially infinite. Inside and outside coexist and are interchangeable – as we see in dreams and psychosis. Boundaries and barriers dissolve. A first step in applying Matte-Blanco's thinking to group-analysis has been taken by Wilson (1997), and Dalal, as mentioned earlier, has extended its use into social psychology and a deeper understanding of the social unconscious. He has used bi-logic to throw light on relationships between groups of 'us' and 'them'. These can have devastating consequences when feeling gets cut off from thinking, and stereotyping is associated with putting groups and/or populations into the same degraded or demonic category (Dalal 2002).

Matte-Blanco (1988) offers a new perspective on processes like projection and identification. He relates them to what he calls 'despatialisation'. Foulkes's thinking of the social world as simultaneously inside and outside us (here as well as there) would be described in bi-logic terms as a Simmasi – simultaneously asymmetrical/symmetrical structure. In relation to time, Volkan (2001) has described as 'time collapse' the process by which 'chosen traumas' are re-activated at times of conflict in the form of historical national myths, such as the 1389 AD Battle of Kosovo in the

Balkans, or the Sack of Jerusalem in 70AD, and the Crusades in the Middle East. In bi-logic this could be an Alassi – alternately asymmetrical/symmetrical structure.

It is well known that Foulkes emphasised communication in his theory and practice, and that he recognised it as occurring at several levels: 1. in every day communication; 2. through transference; 3. through projection and bodily processes, and 4. at the primordial level of the 'collective unconscious'. These levels, as they descend, are decreasingly individual and conscious. They move from the *personal*, as narrowly defined, to the *interpersonal*, to the *transpersonal*. But as Puget (1991) puts it, they interact in the dialectics of inner, interpersonal and social worlds.

Bion's concept of container–contained, the emergence of thought from primitive bodily sensations as a response to frustration, of conceptions and preconceptions, and the destructiveness of psychotic processes through attacks on linking and knowing can all be brought to bear on these dialectics. Basic assumption states in themselves reflect a one-way process, from the individually disavowed to the jointly enacted.

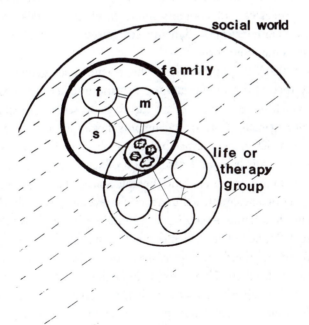

Figure 6.1 External and Internal Worlds. f = father, m = mother, s = siblings.

I shall return to the structures, processes and contexts required for a metapsychosociology mentioned at the beginning. In teaching I have used Figure 6.1 to illustrate the *structural* relationship of individuals and groups. It indicates that an individual is born into a family in a society, and carries both within him or herself, as well as being within them. The individual contains groups and therefore is, in a sense, a group; and takes these into the group and society in which it makes its home, or seeks therapy; these in turn, more or less contain the individuals constituting them. *Processes* by which people and groups develop involve 'psychoanalytic processes' such as introjection, identification and projection, but also interaction, intersubjectivity, dialogue, mutual construction and transformation, which are more the realm of group analysis, and of Winnicott (1971), Ogden (1994) and of self psychology (Harwood and Pines 1998). It is here that Foulkes's deeper level of communication and relationship are relevant, and Matte-Blanco's bi-logic is needed to understand the constant ready availability of pigeonholing, stereotyping and prejudice, but also their dissolution in waves of similarity (Rayner 1995). The *contents* of our cultures, values and ideologies *flow from* and *feed into* the processes which sustain the structures we create and have created for us. Structures, processes and contents interact. When we talk about mental structures, we are referring to dynamic structures: individuals and groups in complex dynamic interaction.

Stacey (2001), a group analyst who teaches management studies and complexity theory, has drawn attention to the interactional basis of social events in which unpredictable crises can develop seemingly spontaneously through self-organising patterns. As he puts it, we form the social in patterns of continuity which *at the same time*, paradoxically, give rise to transformations. At a micro-level this is a good description of what happens during spontaneous interaction in group-analytic therapy. Stacey states that mind requires that the maker of a gesture has the capacity to evoke, in the self, the response generated in the other(s). Accepting the attitude of others towards 'me' leads to a private dialogue between 'I' and 'me' (the subject and object). He claims that the individual mind involves conversation with self; the social mind a conversation with others. They coexist. You will see that complexity theory is consonant with Foulkes's idea of free-floating conversation, communication at all levels, resonance, condenser phenomena and universality. Making and apprehending similarities and connections – in bi-logic terms – involves symmetrisation. Reaching a limit and erecting a boundary involves asymmetrisation. Transformation in therapy entails redrawing boundaries.

The dynamic ebb and flow needs sufficient trust in the system for risks to be taken, and the necessary element of play in 'transitional space' (in Winnicott's terms) to allow transformation to occur.

How difficult and complex these processes can be has been highlighted by Nitsun and Dalal, and by Agazarian in her analysis of different ways in which individuals use and are used by groups. The intersubjective ground pointed out by existential phenomenologists such as Cohn and Diamond – nearer to the symmetrical relationships of bi-logic – is challenged by the sort of pseudo-individualism Foulkes described as 'autistic', and by groups (e.g. totalitarian societies) that constrain and oppress rather than contain and allow developmental transformation, and mistrust and hate others.

Behind this are the contents of the group, particularly the values of the group and social system, unconsciously active in what Foulkes called the 'foundation matrix'. Bion wrote about man being a group animal at war with his groupishness, and the struggle of the individual to relate to the group being as fraught as the infant's with the breast. In contrast Foulkes viewed the group as the matrix of individuality. These are two seemingly disparate views; unless one sees each as valid in certain circumstances – e.g. when the breast is experienced as predominantly bad or good, or we are talking about a 'good' or a 'bad' group. But the group-analytic view offers a set of values that I have described as in constant conflict with their opposites.

The Values of Group Analysis		
homo apertus	v.	homo clausus
inclusiveness	v.	exclusiveness
fairness	v.	entitlement
consensus norms	v.	imposed norms
ethics	v.	moralism[1]
democracy	v.	authoritarianism
religious dialogue	v.	fundamentalism
universalism	v.	nationalism
pro-group	v.	anti-group
—		—
etc.		etc.

Table 6.1 The Values of Group Analysis

These I believe are supported by much recent neurological, biological and sociological evidence (Brown 1998). They are part of a substantial philosophical stand represented by Axel Honnuth (1995), who emphasises the struggle for the establishment of relations of mutual recognition as a precondition for self-realisation. As he puts it, 'It is individuals' claim to the intersubjective recognition of their identity that is built into social life from the very beginning as a moral tension, transcends the level of social progress institutionalised thus far, and so gradually leads – via the negative part of recurring stages of conflict – to a state of communicatively lived freedom' (Honnuth 1995, p.5).

If we begin to discern meaningful patterns of dynamic structures, processes and values that influence the balance of creative and destructive processes within individuals and groups, and between individuals and groups – and thus influence psychological and social pathology and health – we shall have the makings of a useful metapsychosociology. Working with the contributions of Bion and Foulkes, and their discrepancies, will have helped us towards what will be a dynamic interactional model in which vicissitudes of relatedness play a key part (in contrast to the vicissitudes of instinctual drives in Freud's metapsychology). As implied by Figure 6.1, it will allow for the development from one-person to two-person psychology (as in the mother–infant and psychoanalytic dyads) to three-person psychology (a triangulation epitomised by the Oedipus complex), to four-body psychology (and thus sibling rivalry, as suggested by Rickman (1957), to multi-person psychology as in groups. It will at the same time allow for a contrary current, as social influences impinge on individual ontogeny. I have already proposed a spiral movement in good therapy groups from psychological confinement within individual and family ('the inner world') to a fuller intersubjectivity with others (Brown 1994); in a 'bad group' this could be reversed.

The model will reflect the establishment of identities, individual and social, and thus of differences and boundaries, which in some circumstances can be transcended in an ongoing creation and recreation of meaningful existence. The situation of power and authority, and the role of context in forming meaning will be acknowledged. So will the influence of group size – small, large or median (de Maré, Piper and Thompson 1991) – and whether dialogue and discourse are possible (Brown 1982, Schlapobersky 1994). Finally it will allow for the possibility of group function being based on defensive illusions (as in basic assumption states) or on coherent co-operation despite conflict, anxiety and pain. We might need a series of inter-related models and view points. These could include (echoing the structure of this chapter):

1. Nitsun's model of a dialectic between destructive and constructive forces in groups of individuals that can lead to transformation.

2. Dalal's rebalancing of individual and group to allow for the presence of the social 'even' in the mother–infant dyad, and his attempt to use bi-logic to explain intergroup dynamics e.g. stereotyping.

3. Agazarian's model of different types of relationship between individuals and groups, and how they use each other.

4. Extensions of basic assumption theory by Turquet, Lawrence and Hopper that relate to the deep anxieties aroused in some circumstances when people are combined in groups.

5. We need to account for the role of culture and personality, and for transcultural and intercultural phenomena, including social trauma. The social unconscious – Foulkes's deepest layers of transpersonal communication – could include the bi-logical symmetrisation of basic assumption states.

6. We need to develop clearer and more dynamic models for the formation and functions of boundaries – literal and metaphorical – within interacting systems, such as those sketched in Figure 6.1. Attachment theory might be useful in showing up the security-seeking need to belong, aided by complexity theory with its focus on emergent patterns that display both continuity and potential for transformation.

By taking equal account of positive and negative processes in groups, of association and dissociation, we might be clearer in our understanding of the view of Elias (1991b) – who influenced Foulkes – that the individual is a level of the group (even Homo Clausus, the 'we-less I') and of the way harmful group processes (e.g. Ba states) arise when the component individuals feel ignored or disenfranchised, or collectively want to avoid facing up to something. We are into the area of sociology. But what about the body, the area of biology? Can we develop a truly comprehensive bio-psycho-sociology? If so, we could begin to integrate social psychology – which Freud could only speculate about in essays such as 'Totem and Taboo', 'Group Psychology and the Analysis of the Ego', 'The Future of an Illusion', and 'Civilization and Its Discontents' – with deeper understanding of the struggle between social order

and chaos, between 'ego' and 'wego', and the individual physical consequences of stress and social trauma.

Freud's metapsychology (Freud 1915) was an attempt to provide a theory
of psychological processes in the absence – at that time – of an adequate
physical substrate. Now, the burgeoning of neuropsychology offers such a
substrate with its application to infant development within the mother–infant
dyad, attachment theory and affect-regulation via the right brain and limbic
system (e.g. Schore 1994, Taylor, Bagby and Parker 1997).

The neurobiological approach could complement a metapsychology, and
give it a bodily biological base. Indeed in a recent interview Schore (2001)
states his belief that groups and cultures offer affect-regulating self-object
functions – a self psychology concept – acting as external psychobiological
regulators of human internal states. Cultures, Schore holds, acting through
their prescribed child-rearing practices, imprint on the earliest members of
society those affects that can be socially expressed face-to-face. Almost
echoing Foulkes, he adds that this determines what affects are conscious and
what unconscious and/or expressed physically. Bion would say the latter
involves physical 'beta' rather than mental 'alpha' functions in individuals,
and predisposes to basic assumption states in groups. At this point, beyond
metapsychosociology, we could say that if Bion and Foulkes are not twinned
(thankfully), their thinking is intertwined.

References

Agazarian, Y. M. (1962) Unpublished paper referred to in Agazarian and Gantt (2000)

Agazarian, Y. M. (1983) 'Some advantages of applying multi-dimensional thinking to the
    teaching, practice and outcomes of group psychotherapy'. *International Journal of Group
    Psychotherapy 33*, 2, 243–247.

Agazarian, Y. M. and Gantt S.P. (2000). *Autobiography of a Theory: Developing a theory of living
    humans systems and of systems-centred practice.* London: Jessica Kingsley.

Agazarian, Y. M. and Peters R. (1981) *The Visible and Invisible Group.* London: Routledge and
    Kegan Paul.

Anzieu, D. (1984). *The Group and the Unconscious.* London: Routledge and Kegan Paul.

Anzieu, D. (ed) (1990) *Psychic Envelopes.* London: Karnac Books.

Bateson, G. (1972) *Steps to an Ecology of Mind.* New York: Chandler.

Bennis, W. G. and Shepherd H. A. (1956)' A theory of group development' *Human Relations 9:*
    415–457, abridged as Chap. 6 in G. S. Gibbard, J. J. Hartman and R. D. Mann (eds)
    Analysis of Groups. San Francisco: Jossey-Bass, 1974.

Bion, W. R. (1961) *Experiences in Groups.* London: Tavistock.

Bion, W. R. (1970) *Attention and Interpretation.* London: Tavistock.

Blackwell, D. (1994) 'The psyche and the system'. Chap. 3 in D. Brown and L. Zinkin (eds)
    The Psyche and the Social World.

Blackwell, D. (1998) 'Bounded instability, group analysis and the matrix: Organisations under stress'. *Group Analysis 31*, 4 532–546.

Brown, D. G. (1959) 'The relevance of body image to neurosis.' *British Journal of Medical Psychology. 32*, 249–260.

Brown, D. G. (1982) 'Text, context and texture: Free speech in the service of health and healing.' *Group Analysis. 15*, 207–218.

Brown, D. G. (1985) 'Bion and Foulkes: Basic assumptions and beyond.' Chap. 10 in M. Pines (ed) *Bion and Group Psychotherapy.* London: Routledge and Kegan Paul.

Brown, D. G. (1987) 'Context, content and process: Interrelationships between small and large groups in a transcultural workshop.' *Group Analysis 20*, 3 237–248.

Brown, D. G. (1988) 'Confrontation in the group analytic matrix: Towards a classification.' *Group 12* 191–197.

Brown, D. G. (1992) 'Transcultural group analysis I: Different views of Maastricht and Heidelberg.' *Group Analysis. 25*, 1 87–96.

Brown, D. G. (1994) 'Self-development through subjective interaction: A fresh look at "ego training in action"'. Chap. 6 in D. Brown and L. Zinkin (eds) *The Psyche and the Social World.*

Brown, D. G. (1996) Discussion on article by Nicola Diamond I. *Group Analysis 29* 3, 317–320.

Brown, D. G. (1997) 'The royal road to the mysterious leap: The psychosoma and the analytic process.' *Australian Journal of Psychotherapy 16*, 11–26.

Brown, D. G. (1998) 'Foulkes's basic law of group dynamics 50 years on: Abnormality, injustice and the renewal of ethics.' 22nd S H Foulkes Annual Lecture. *Group Analysis 31*, 4, 391–419.

Brown, D. G. and Young A. J. (1965) 'Body image and susceptibility to contact dermatitis.' *British Journal of Medical Psychology. 38*, 261–267.

Brown, D. G. and Zinkin, L. (eds) (1994) *The Psyche and the Social World: Developments in group-analytic theory.* London: Routledge.

Burkitt, I. (1991) *Social Selves: Theories of the social formation of personality.* London: Sage.

Campbell, D. (2000). *The Socially Constructed Organization.* London: Karnac Books.

Cohn, H. W. (1996) 'The philosophy of S H Foulkes: Existential–phenomenological aspects of group analysis.' *Group Analysis. 29*, 3, 287-302.

Dalal, F. (1998). *Taking the Group Seriously: Towards a post-Foulkesian group analytic theory.* London: Jessica Kingsley.

Dalal, F. (2002) *Race, Colour and the Processes of Racialization.* Hove and New York: Brunner-Routledge.

De Maré, P. (1972). *Perspectives in Group Psychotherapy.* London: Allen and Unwin.

De Maré, P., Piper, R. and Thompson, S. (1991) *Koinonia: From hate, through dialogue, to culture in the large group.* London: Karnac.

Diamond, N. (1996). 'Can we speak of internal and external reality?' *Group Analysis 29*, 3, 303-317.

Durkin, J. E. (1981) *Living Groups: Group psychotherapy and general systems theory.* New York: Brunner/Mazel.

Elias, N. (1991a) *The Symbol Theory.* London: Sage.

Elias, N. (1991b). *The Society of Individuals.* Oxford: Blackwell.

Elliott, B. (1994). 'The womb and gender identity.' Chap. 8 in D. Brown and L. Zinkin (eds) *The Psyche and the Social World.*

Fisher, S. and Cleveland S. E. (1958) *Body Image and Personality.* Princeton NJ: Van Norstrand.

Foulkes, S. H. (1948) *Introduction to Group-Analytic Psychotherapy: Studies in the Social Integration of Individuals and Groups.* London: Maresfield Reprints.

Foulkes, S. H. (1964) *Therapeutic Group Analysis.* London: Allen and Unwin.

Foulkes, S. H. (1973) 'The group as matrix of the individual's mental life.' Chap. 22 in *S. H. Foulkes: Selected Papers.* London: Karnac Books.

Foulkes, S. H (1975) *Group-Analytic Psychotherapy.* London: Gordon and Breach books.

Foulkes, S. H. (1990) *Selected Papers: Psychoanalysis and group analysis.* London: Karnac Books.

Foulkes, S. H. and Anthony, E. J. (1957) Group Psychotherapy: *The psycho-analytic approach.* Harmondsworth: Penguin.

Freud, S. (1915) *The Unconscious,* SE vol. XIV. London: The Hogarth Press.

Freud, S. (1923) *The Ego and the Id,* SE 19. London: The Hogarth Press.

Harwood, I. and Pines, M. (1998) *Intersubjectivity and Self-Psychological Pathways to Human Understanding.* London: Jessica Kingsley.

Honnuth, A. (1995) *The Struggle for Recognition: The moral grammar of social conflict.* Cambridge: Polity Press.

Hopper, E. (1997) 'Traumatic experience in the unconscious life of the group: A fourth basic assumption.' *Group Analysis 30,* 4, 439–470.

Hopper, E. (2003) *Traumatic Experience in the Unconscious Life of Groups.* London: Jessica Kingsley Publishers.

James, D. C. (1984) 'Bion's "containing" and Winnicott's "holding" in the context of the group matrix.' *International Journal of Group Psychotherapy 34,* 201–13.

James, D. C. (1994) 'Holding and containing in the group and society.' Chap. 5 in D. Brown and L. Zinkin (eds) *The Psyche and the Social World.*

Jaques, E. (1974) 'Social systems as a defence against persecutory and depressive anxiety.' Chap. 11 in G. S. Gibbons, J. J. Hartman and R. D. Mann (eds) *Analysis of Groups* San Francisco: Jossey-Bass.

Kaës, R. (1987) 'La troisième différence.' *Revue de Psychothérapie Psychanalytique de Groupe 9–10* 5–30.

Klein, G. S. (1976) *Psychoanalytic Theory: An exploration of essentials.* New York: International Universities Press.

Lawrence, W. G., (2000) *Tongued with Fire: Groups in experience.* London: Karnac Books.

Lawrence, W. G., Bain, A. and Gould, L. J. (1996). 'The fifth basic assumption.' *Free Associations 6,* 37, 28–55.

Le Roy, J. (1994) 'Group analysis and culture.' In D. Brown and L. Zinkin (eds) *The Psyche and The Social World.* London: Routledge. London: Jessica Kingsley Publishers, 2000.

Marrone, M. (1994) 'Attachment theory and group analysis.' In D. Brown and L. Zinkin (eds) *The Psyche and The Social World.* London: Routledge. London: Jessica Kingsley Publishers, 2000.

Marrone, M. (1998) *Attachment and Interaction.* London: Jessica Kingsley Publishers.

Matte-Blanco, I. (1975) *The Unconscious as Infinite Sets: An essay in bi-logic.* London: Duckworth.

Matte-Blanco, I. (1988) *Thinking, Feeling and Being: Clinical reflections on the fundamental antinomy of human beings and world.* London: Routledge.

Mead, G. H. (1934) *Mind, Self and Society.* Chicago: Chicago University Press.

Menzies, I. E. P. (1961) *The functioning of social systems as a defence against anxiety: A report on the study of the nursing service of a general hospital.* Tavistock Pamphlet No 3. London: Tavistock.

Nitsun, M. (1996) *The Anti-Group: Destructive forces in the group and their creative potential.* London: Routledge.

Nitsun, M. (1998a) 'The organizational mirror: A group-analytic approach to organizational consultancy, Part I - Theory' *Group Analysis 31,* 3, 245–267

Nitsun, M. (1998b) 'Part II - Application.' *Group Analysis 31,* 4, 505–518.

Ogden, T. H. (1994) *Subjects of Analysis.* London: Karnac Books.

Pines, M. (1981) 'The frame of reference of group psychotherapy.' *International Journal of Group Psychotherapy 31,* 3, 275–285.

Pines, M. (1994) 'The group-as-a-whole.' Chap. 4 in D. Brown and L. Zinkin (eds) *The Psyche and the Social World* . London: Routledge. London: Jessica Kingsley Publishers, 2000.

Pines, M. (1998) *Circular Reflections: Selected Papers on group analysis and psychoanalysis.* London: Jessica Kingsley Publishers.

Puget, J. (1991) 'The social context: Searching for a hypothesis.' *Free Associations. 21,* 21–33.

Rance, C. (1998) 'The art of conversation: The group-analytic paradigm and organizational consultancy.' *Group Analysis 31,* 4, 519–531.

Rayner, E. (1995) *Unconscious Logic.* London: Routledge.

Rickman, J. (1957) 'The factor of number in individual- and group-dynamics.' Chap. 19 in *Selected Contributions to Psycho-Analysis.* London: Hogarth Press.

Rifkind, G., (1995) 'Containing the containers: The staff consultation group.' *Group Analysis 28,* 2, 209–222.

Rouchy, J. C. (1995) Identification and groups of belonging. *Group Analysis 28,* 2, 129–141.

Schilder, P. (1935) *The Image and Appearance of the Human Body.* London: Kegan Paul.

Schlapobersky, J. (1994) 'The Language of the Group.' Chap. 14 in D. Brown and L. Zinkin (eds) *The Psyche and the Social World.* London/New York: Routledge.

Schore, A. N. (1994) *Affect Regulation and the Origin of the Self: The neurobiology of emotional development.* Hillsdale, NJ: Lawrence Erlbaum.

Schore, A. N. (2001) Interviewed by Roz Carroll in *The Psychotherapist issue 17,* 25–27 (UKCP journal)

Scott, W. C. M. (1948) 'Some embryological, neurological, psychiatric and psycho-analytic implications of the body scheme.' *International Journal of Psycho-Analysis 29,* 141–152.

Skynner, A. C. R. (1989) *Institutes and How to Survive Them: Mental health training and consultation.* London: Methuen.

Spero, M. (1999) *Comments on the Section 'Group Analysis and Organizations' in 'Group Analysis, 1998'.* Unpublished paper.

Stacey, R. D. (2001) *Complex Responsive Processes in Organizations.* London: Routledge.

Taylor, G. J., Bagby, R. M. and Parker, J. D. A. (1997). *Disorders of Affect Regulation: Alexithymia in medical and psychiatric illness.* Cambridge: Cambridge University Press.

Turquet, P. M. (1974) 'Leadership: the individual in the group.' Chap. 14 in G S Gibbs, J J Hartman and R D Mann (eds) *Analysis of Groups* San Francisco: Jossey-Bass.

Turquet, P. M. (1975) 'Threats to identity in the large group.' Chap. 3 in L Kreeger (ed) *The Large Group.* London: Constable.

Volkan, V. D. (2001) 'Transgenerational transmission and chosen trauma: An aspect of large-group identity.' *Group Analysis 34*, 1 79-97.

Vygotsky, L. S. (1978) *Mind in Society: The development of higher psychological processes.* Cambridge MA: Harvard University Press.

Whitaker, D. S. and Lieberman M (1964) *Psychotherapy Through the Group Process.* New York: Atherton.

Wilke, G. (1998) 'Oedipal and sibling dynamics in organizations.' *Group Analysis 31*, 3, 269–281.

Wilson, J. (1997) 'Matte-Blanco's theory of bi-logic and its relevance to group analysis.' *Journal of Melanie Klein and Object Relations 15*, 4, 585–593.

Winnicott, D. W. (1971) *Playing and Reality.* London: Tavistock

Zinkin, L. (1994) 'Exchange as a therapeutic factor in group analysis.' Chap. 7 in D. Brown and L. Zinkin (eds) *The Psyche and the Social World.*

Endnote

1. By this I mean the golden rule of 'Do to others what you would want done to you' versus self-righteous condemnation of others.

7

Group Mentality
and 'Having A Mind'

Robert Hinshelwood

Bion was fascinated that the experience of being in the presence of another person's mind is a difficult one. Having a mind is not easy, and his contributions add considerably to the debate about what is it to have a mind. In a late paper, he described the problem of having a mind that is aware of minds:

> When two characters or personalities meet, an emotional storm is created. If they make a sufficient contact to be aware of each other, or even to be *un*aware of each other, an emotional state is produced by the conjunction of these two individuals, these two personalities, and the resulting disturbance is hardly likely to be something which could be regarded as necessarily an improvement on the state of affairs had they never met at all. But since they have met, and since this emotional storm has occurred, then the two parties to this storm may decide to 'make the best of a bad job'. What this means in analysis is this.

The analysand comes into contact with the analyst by coming to the consulting room and engaging in what he thinks is a conversation which he hopes to benefit by in some way: likewise the analyst probably expects some benefit to occur – to both parties. The analysand or the analyst says something. The curious thing about this is that it has an effect, it disturbs two people. This would also be true if nothing was said, if they remained silent… The result of remaining silent, or the result of intervening with a remark, or even saying: 'Good morning' or: 'Good evening', again sets up what appears to me to be an emotional storm. What that emotional storm is one does not immediately know, but the problem is, how to make the best of it; this means a capacity to turn the circumstance – as I choose to call it for the moment – to good account. (Bion 1979, pp.1–2).

This encounter is often termed 'attachment' or 'bonding', adapted from Bowlby's psychoanalytic ethology. But those are quiet terms, and it seems to me Bion is describing something far from quiet – a storm, in fact. A mind not only craves an attachment to another mind but, having found one, is then disturbed by an emotional storm.[1] I think Bion is neutral about whether that is a storm of loving or of hating – or what the actual emotional tone is. But, his point is that an encounter is both craved and it is also resisted as a disturbance. It is 'minded'. And he attempted to dissect out that process of minding.

However, to not mind something interested Bion, too – how somebody manages not to do anything with their mind, both in the mindlessness of groups, and in the rubble of a destroyed mind of the schizophrenic. Because of the resistance to being 'stormed' by others, people take protective action. Psychotic patients can abolish their minds altogether rather than suffer those emotional storms. Those with personality disorders tend to exploit this kind of meeting by deliberately engaging with other minds to create such storms for specific purposes.[2] And those of us somewhat less disturbed manage to numb our minds in certain ways, and live in a psychic storm-shelter as it were, constructed of the familiar defence mechanisms, and live in socially prescribed rituals.

Psychoanalytic work with schizophrenic patients, in particular, goes to the heart of the question, what is a mind, since somehow schizophrenics seemed to lack a proper one. It is not that they have conflicts in their mind, as do neurotic patients, they seem instead to have a mind that fails to operate as a mind (Bion 1957). In this work, Bion, at his most creative during the 1950s, decided that the deficits in mental functioning can point the way to defining the essential function of 'having a mind'.

Meaning

The variety of different responses to the emotional storm of encounter leave us with the question of what constitute ordinary ways of dealing with such disturbances. In other words, what is involved in living within that perpetual storm, and how can one flourish there – rather than escape from it. Bion's answer was characteristically provocative. He described the ordinary process as 'alpha function'. He offered this as an empty term, one which further work would fill with further meaning. It is a supposed mental process which creates an individual mind out of this experience of encounter. He asked of us, his readers and successors, the task to fill in his empty term.

Bion's own work has led to what is now loosely called 'containment'. Alpha-function is the transformation of the storm into material that can be used for thinking, analogous to the metabolism of the body's digestive system. He referred to those products of alpha-function as the 'furniture of dreams'[3] which, arising from the conversion of raw experience of encountering another mind, are used to create structures we know as dreams, and of which we then have a further experience. The conversion of raw experience into dream-like creations is complex, and I will only take up one element that is central to how I understand Bion. As that conversion process takes the raw experience and creates thoughts, it creates a new quality. It is a quality which dream symbols have as their essence – that quality is 'meaning'.

I suggest that meaning is the inherent quality of the thoughts which our minds work upon; and without meaning such thoughts would be thoughts; and in some cases (psychotic people) the mind does not have meaningful objects with which to think. Thus, the human mind must deal in meanings, that is to say a 'substance' or a category which is not just information, as we might say of a computer. It is a specific experience we know as the quality of meaningfulness. A mind may register an event, but so can a computer, which creates a display on its screen. But a whole lot more happens in a mind than in a computer. What is registered in that mind acquires a collateral quality – the felt quality of something being meaningful.

This is the subjective 'addition' to the more mechanical recognition, and subjective qualities are described as 'qualia'. Whatever the ontological nature of qualia, that experience in which we say to ourselves 'that means something to me' is no doubt wired into the brain; it is something which then attaches to various experiences, memories and phantasies. The world of qualia is akin to the Kleinian notion of unconscious phantasy. An experience of a particular other person can have all kinds of associations, which derive from the accumulation of past experiences and memories of them; mother at the meal table may arouse very different meanings from mother typing at the keyboard of her computer, or mother in the bath. Various qualia accrue to registering the idea of mother, depending on all sorts of conditions. But generically qualia are what we call a meaningfulness.

To see something which looks blue, say the mug on my desk, I recognise the colour (the shape and purpose of the mug, too), and this is normally called the secondary characteristic, the subjective experience of blue. But I also have a sense in that subjectivity that blueness signifies something to me – it has meaning. For instance, when Heisenberg was asked to comment on the mathematical properties of space, he is said to have replied, 'Space is blue and birds fly through it' and he thus indicated that even a physicist finds powerful personal meanings in what he deals with.

In essence, 'to mind something' equates with 'meaning something to me'. In this view, it is the unique property of minds to give a meaning to experiences, and it produces them in the processing of those storms which mental interaction creates. Thus to have a mind implies dealing in meanings – not information. Nor does it deal in more material substances, as does the body, on which of course a mind must also depend. But despite depending on the body functioning with material substance, the mind functions (or alpha-functions) with meaning[4].

Representations: This suggests a further aspect of the conversion of raw experience to thinkable objects. The combination of registering an experience with, and the special quality of, meaningfulness creates an object of thought, and this is *represented* in a mind. To simple recognition is added meaning, and this combination produces what I believe we would call a 'representation'. In the immaterial world of the mind, a 'representation' has a felt existence, a thing that feels tangible and manipulable. Representation is not just a passive process. It indicates that something has been 'minded', and that goes beyond mechanical computing.

Having a mind: At the same time, there is another fall-out of alpha-function. This third component, to add to registering and meaningfulness, is the sense of having a 'place' where representations reside – and can be further manipulated, processed or transformed – with subsequent further meaningfulness, in the creation of new meanings. I suggest that this additional aspect of alpha-function is the sense of 'having a mind'. Thus Bion's transformation process (alpha-function) in creating a representation also creates the sense of a mind *in which* the products of the encounter exist. For Bion thoughts require a thinker, that is to say, a mind, a place where thinking can happen to thoughts. The experience of discovering a meaning, is linked to, or the other side of the coin to, having a mind. Both arise together.[5]

The space and time co-ordinates where that thinking occurs are then identified with a specific material place – the body on which the mind depends. A lot seems to explode into existence with alpha-function – recognition, meaning representations, a thinking mind; and even, one might say, the basis of a personal identity, a self which is irrevocably linked to that space (mental) and location (bodily).

Reversal of alpha-function: I suggest I have not distorted Bion too much in elaborating his views in this way. His aim initially was to find the contrast with what happened in a schizophrenic where mind, meaning and identity all seem to be corrupted. He started his investigation of alpha-function in effect with the results of some sort of 'reversal of alpha-function' (Meltzer 1978). The schizophrenic dismantles his own mind by making attacks on the meaningfulness of the representations in his mind. He destroys the links that make up the matrix of meaning – the configuration of space which is blue with birds flying, for instance. As a schizophrenic once told me, 'the sky is emptied, that's why birds can't fly' – meaningless deconstruction of his thoughts, which might have once been the bleakness of Keats' *La Belle Dame Sans Merci*, with its chilling refrain 'And no birds sing'. In that sense the reversal alpha-function disconnects meaning; and the result is the bleakness and depression that Keats experienced in his own life.

Group mentality

I now wish to move to phenomena in groups. The nature of a group is to be the place for the encounter between persons. And I shall claim a group is a particularly good arena to investigate minds that 'mind' encountering. I want especially to shed light on the to-and-fro process, between constructing meaning and mind, and the dissolution of it.

Bion started his small group work with the three concepts, 'group mentality, group culture and the individual' (Bion 1961, p.61). 'Group mentality' was the idea that the members of a group can pool a lot of contributions 'anonymously'. Neither explicit nor conscious, these contributions exist as a collective pool that is the group, rather than any individual.[6] He gives, as an example, an air of hostility in a group whilst each of the individual members denied feeling hostile.

However, these three concepts proved inadequate. In his third paper in his series on groups, Bion was forced to admit that his experience eventually 'knocked holes in my theories' (Bion 1961, p.61). He then had to rethink. He did not give up his idea of group mentality but developed it, bringing in then the idea of the basic assumptions – to which the individual contributes implicitly and anonymously. Implicitly, the purpose of the basic assumptions is to preserve the group – and to do so in one of the three forms (pairing, fight/flight and dependency).

Merely by relating to a group the individual regresses to this innate set of assumptions about being in a group. Bion could then define group mentality as 'a machinery of intercommunication that is designed to ensure that group life is in accordance with the basic assumptions' (Bion 1961, p.65). These assumptions seemed to him to be innate or instinctual, a set of three endowed 'valences' that embodied unthought assumptions about the nature and purpose of the group and which all human individuals have available for linking with each other. This kind of instinctual linking underlies, and can often override, the conscious communication system.

Later, around 1952, after he finished working with groups, he began to review his ideas again. At that time he was already working psychoanalytically with schizophrenic patients. As Eric Miller noticed, Bion moved away from the innateness of basic assumptions:

> ...early on [Bion] made references to the instinctiveness of the phenomena, but later he shifted to treating them as postnatal formations and linking them to Kleinian theory of the infant's very early development of defences to cope with distressing unconscious phantasies. (Miller 1988, p.40)

In that paper, in 1952, he made a hypothetical suggestion, that basic assumptions might be derived from something else – derived from psychological developments, rather than innate (Bion 1952). And he speculated that the basic assumptions were derived from the very thing he happened to be pre-occupied with in 1952, the analysis of psychosis. That speculative move was to suggest that the basic assumptions are based on the mechanisms central to schizophrenia. Matias Sanfuentes (2000, personal communication) has pointed out that the 1952 paper, published in the *International Journal of Psycho-Analysis* collection to celebrate Melanie Klein's 70th birthday, was revised for publication in Klein, Heimann and Money-Kyrle (1955). That 1955 version filled out this speculation.[7] Bion had by then begun to clarify his theories of schizophrenic thinking (Bion 1954, 1955) – the self-destructive dismantling of thought processes, the obliteration of time and of sophisticated cognitive function. These were 'attacks' made by schizophrenics upon linking, and remarkably they resemble his earlier descriptions of the state of mind of a group dominated by basic assumptions. So, Bion moved, first speculatively (1952), and then on the basis of his clinical work with schizophrenic patients (1955), from an innatist explanation of basic assumptions to an explanation in terms of psychotic mechanisms. Group mentality is thus a psychotic mentality. It is a mentality become mindless.

In these basic assumption states the group appears to have lost the non-psychotic, alpha-function of the individuals – there is no moral sense, a loss of mature judgement (all is exclusively good or bad), an absence of recognising consequences to actions, a lack of development in group thought and achievement, a failing of the sense of time, etc. What we witness is the reversion to a psychotic mental functioning – the reversal of alpha-function.

Bion's view of psychosis was that the individual mind dismantles itself with the loss of the 'furniture of dreams', and instead creates meaninglessness (nameless dread) and 'bizarre objects'. In a group, a similar process goes on in which mentalisation reverses. This is a reversal of alpha-function *as a group*. I shall give extracts from two groups to contrast states in which mentalisation – the awareness of other minds in the group – occurs, and states where it seems absent.

These are two rather ordinary pieces of clinical material from out-patient groups of non-psychotic patients. In the first, we can see how the individuals link together, not just in the *surface* content of what each one says, but also at an emotional level. The emotional storm of the encounters impels the course of the dialogue:

> Two men in a group were discussing a trivial detail about some maintenance work on a car that belonged to one of them. 'A' described his difficulty with a rusty bolt. 'B' talked about how he had once had the same problem and had solved it by hitting the bolt with a hammer; he seemed pleased with himself. Another man, 'C', gave a slight laugh and remarked on 'B's' hint of pride. 'A' looked startled and then a little angry, as he realised that he had given 'B' the opportunity to be pleased with himself. He told 'B' that it was no solution to hit the bolt with the hammer and explained why. Clearly he now wanted to put 'B' down. Two women in the group were looking on with some fascination at this male sparring. One said 'Men!' with mock exasperation. The other said her husband had returned from a football match recently with a bruise on his cheek which he had refused to talk about.

In this interchange five people were involved who seemed willing to tune in, in their own characteristic ways, to the male rivalry and psychological bruising which was going on. They tuned in to each other at an emotional level as well as a cognitive one. One person's comment seemed to stimulate the next through having an emotional colouring that linked to the previous person. And this was repeated through a number of links between all five. The emotional colour that one person was expressing was intuited and responded to, at that implicit level. This was not just exchanging information, meaning was passing from one to another. They were 'working' together on some feeling. Of course, in this case it was not particularly harmonious, respectful or friendly. But they were reading each other accurately and it is this quality of being 'in tune' which I emphasise here.[8] I contrast it with the second piece of clinical material:

> In another group a woman, 'X', described an event in which her husband had had a row with her mother. Another woman, 'Y', waited just until this story had finished, and immediately asked for the dates of a forthcoming break in the group sessions. They had been announced recently. The therapist pointed out how 'Y' had cut across the first woman's story. She had also cut out her own memory of the dates. 'Y' immediately turned to enquire of someone else. A man started to talk about his mother-in-law, seemingly following the first woman, though clearly absorbed only in his own tale – more to do with seeking out a mother for himself because in childhood he had spent long periods separated from his own mother.

In this group, the connections between the separate contributions are quite different. People cut across each other's contributions. They did not really encounter each other. There may be some connection in terms purely of content – for instance the man at the end returned to a discourse about his mother – but the connection was only superficially linked with the first woman, 'X'. Each seemed to remain cut off in an emotional sense from the one before. There was plenty of talk but no encounter; no-one worked on the emotional storm – rather the storm was obstructed. In the second group, that obstruction destroyed meaning, *at the group level*. Any coherent experience of being together was annulled.

Thus they did not register each other in the sense of another mind filled with emotional meanings, and the dialogue is constructed of fragments of unintegrated meanings. One could say that the group mentality is a mindless one.

These clinical examples of ordinary dialogue show a crucial difference. At first glance perhaps one could say it was a difference in the dominant basic assumption: in the first group, there is a tendency for a hostile fight/flight atmosphere; in the second, a dependency atmosphere (about mothers, the need to be told the dates again, etc.).

However, I have stressed another difference, one highlighted in Bion's latter work. In the first group, the individuals remain in contact with each other as individuals.[9] They appear to relate to each other's feelings with their own storms of feelings. There are repeated encounters that can be followed in sequence as one person is mobilised to respond in key with the emotional impact of the speaker before. But in the second group, a dismantling of links seems to dominate, so that the members are not individuals but members of a group in which linking has collapsed.[10] From a group point of view, the second group has come apart and fragmented. Coherent meaningfulness has disappeared, and internal representations cannot be communicated.

Despite the incoherence, a peculiar state of homogeneity pervades the second group. The homogeneity is a joint agreement, but it is the agreement to be in this incoherent, disconnected condition! Thus, a kind of unthinking, mindless co-operation occurs. Bion expressed his surprise at this paradox when he saw it in a group of patients:

> I have always been quite familiar with the idea of a patient as a person whose capacity for co-operation is very slight... I reflect that from the way in which the group is going on its motto might be: 'Vendors of quack nostrums unite.' No sooner have I said this to myself than I realise that I am expressing my feeling, not of the group's disharmony, but of its unity (Bion 1961, p.52).

The individual is co-operating in a kind of way – co-operating in forming a stable group in which co-operation is impossible! This implies a complex phenomenology of the person as both individual and group member, which Bion tried to articulate: 'Thus we have a situation in which the individuals behave as if they were conscious, as individuals, of the basic assumption, but unconscious of it as members of the group' (Bion 1961, p.94).

In other words, they are committed to the 'machinery of intercommunication that is designed to ensure that group life is in accordance with the basic assumptions'.[11]

Here Bion is struggling to conceptualise some radical inconsistency in the members of the group. The individual functions in two separate ways at the same time – he can function mentally in a coherent manner with meanings that he can fashion and express. But as a group member, he dismantles meanings in the creation of the mindless group mentality. Reverting for a moment to an individual context, Freud described the Ratman's thought insertion, in which words were put into the Ratman's mind which disrupted his ability to think and study. Jonathan Lear commented on this, 'the vehicles of meaning themselves [words] are used to disrupt meaning' (Lear 1996, personal communication). So it is with this group situation in which the individual, as an individual, handles meaning but operates quite differently from the individual as a group member who dismantles meaning. This paradox that Bion puzzled over in groups, is once again premonitory of an idea he rediscovered and formulated later in his work with psychosis:

> The non-psychotic personality was concerned with a neurotic problem, that is to say a problem that centred on the resolution of a conflict of ideas and emotions to which the operation of the ego had given rise. But the psychotic personality was concerned with the problem of repair of the ego. (Bion 1957, p.272)

The paper from which this quote is taken described a personality as having this contradictory form – being both psychotic and non-psychotic in different parts. His work with psychotic people enabled him to see these two kinds of functioning in which an individual can be in two different states of mind. It might of course mean that a psychotic is split up in such a way that in different relations he operates differently, or at different times, or under different internal conditions. But the example of the group shows the individual operating on the one hand as a creator of meaningful communications, and simultaneously destroying meaningful links. In fact the very act of expressing a meaningful symbolic contribution to the group disrupts the possibility of meaning in the group. When the woman, 'Y', turned to the group therapist to ask the dates of the break, she was making a meaningful communication, but she was at the same time destroying the meaning of the woman, 'X', who had just spoken.

The group shows these 'parts' of the person, if parts they be, in interaction with each other. 'Function' would seem to be a better term than a 'part' of the mind in this case – one function, the creation of meaning, being set to interfere with itself! The psychotic process of reversal of alpha-function is implicated in the specific linking via the basic assumptions.

Groups and psychosis

Clearly there is something amiss with Bion's idea that attacks on linking, and thus reversal of alpha-function, render the individual psychotic, in the straightforward way he described. And Jaques too thought that 'the relationship between the operation of basic assumptions and of depressive and persecutory phenomena remains to be worked out' (Jaques 1955, p.487). People in the group in which meaningful contact is being actively abolished are not necessarily psychotic. They abolish their encounters, but not their minds.

Bion tended to see the nature of psychosis as a structural problem, the intrusion into a sane personality of an increasingly large psychotic part. Thus one or other part – the sane or the psychotic – can take over, and be in charge of the overt personality, at different times. He did not pursue this anomaly of structure in the personality. However Rosenfeld (1971), O'Shaughnessy (1981) and many other contemporary Kleinians have put this kind of structuring of the personality under close examination.

But structural phenomena of this kind are only one possibility. In groups we can see an intricate phenomenology that weaves between the creation of meaning, and its dissolution. In the example of the second group, the individuals were not in a clinical sense psychotic. They remained quite able to formulate articulate, coherent statements about themselves and others' minds. Therefore their attack on linking was not a sufficient condition for a psychotic state of mind. It may be a necessary one – without which a mind cannot become psychotic and mindless. But other factors must come into play. When does the attack on links produce a psychotic person and when does it not?

A group highlights, and magnifies up to visible proportions, the divergence between the attacks on linking and the full psychotic state. The group mentality, which embodies a reversal of alpha-function, is not in fact a psychosis. At the level at which the problem starts – the level of encounter with other minds – the dismantling of mind is not complete. To understand this further needs a wider discussion about the group as the locus for symbolisation. But in passing we can note Kaës' view that a group supports 'an accreditation for an intra-psychic representation and a "re-run" in speech-form which gives it meaning within the context of interpersonal, group and societal relationships' (Kaës 1984, p.363).

Thus, meaning itself is enhanced and codified within a group which renders it into a transmittable form – using a symbolic system, language. Language seems to hold together with a kind of extra-personal system of meanings. Links cannot be broken between words and within the system of semantics. That survives even when personal meanings are under attack. In this sense, a group gives a second dimension to meaningfulness – the codified language. It exists as a separate dimension from the personal meanings conveyed in the emotional side of a communication. Those I described as the product of the individual alpha-function. Meaning is the product of individual mentalising based on encounter, but it has in the context of a group where those encounters happen, an external component, as well as the internal one. This sense of meaningfulness sustained by language seems to operate at a group level, and thus to sustain the meaningfulness which the individuals require to continue having a mind. It suggests that new developments might be made in the psychoanalytic theory of symbolism, and they might be informed, partly, by observations on groups.

Bion made a rather unwieldy synthesis of his views on groups and psychosis. This entailed trying to elaborate group basic assumptions with psychotic mechanisms of defence. But this first effort can be made more fluent, and has true relevance to the phenomena in groups if we consider the phenomenology of emotional linking between people. It gives us opportunities for thinking about therapeutic opportunities which I tried to show in my brief examples. This greater fluency comes from teasing out the implications of alpha-function as the core of what is now known as mentalising.

Conclusions

Psychoanalysis has a good record in contributing to the philosophy of mind and can potentially make an important contribution to the current interest in the philosophy of consciousness. And Bion's work on thinking and on groups is central to any such contribution.[12]

The new reality principle

When Freud talked of the reality principle, he talked as if it (reality) had the quality of a physical reality, stable, consistent and reliable and contrasted it with the psychic reality of the subject's inner world of impulses, dreams and feelings. Increasingly, psychoanalysis has come to recognise that reality, the really important reality for the human being, is the reality of other people. A person's external reality is the inner reality of someone else. The implications of this for the psychoanalytic theory of mind has been the development of object-relations – they are relations with other minds.

Recently the word 'mentalise' has been used to describe the ability to conceive a mind. Mitrani (1996) describes the autistic defect in those terms, and the relations and whole way of life of the autistic person appear to function mindlessly. Fonagy and Target (2000) have used the term to pinpoint the deficit which, in their view, characterises borderline personality disorders. There is clearly an inter-'mental' or interpersonal aspect to mentalisation, which Kaës (1984) has pointed out in groups. He described mentalisation as: 'first and foremost, a psychic work, that is work concerned with the formation and transformation of psychic qualities' (Kaës 1984, p.362). And he explicitly connected this with Bion's 'alpha-function'.

It would seem that the core feature of a mind is that it encounters other minds. A mind is, as it were, a mind-recognising apparatus, and this could supplement the Turing test.[13] The mind could in this way be distinguished from a machine that simulates mental functions. If one of the pre-occupations of philosophy is to construct a theory of mind, then it would seem that such a sophisticated philosophical field of endeavour is common to everyone who has a mind. We must all have a theory of mind in order to qualify as having a mind.

Mindblindness

The psychoanalysis of which Bion was an exponent takes it as central that the human mind recognises other minds. Failure to do so is a major psychopathological event. We might take either a psychopathological point of view of such a failure, or a developmental one. Frith (1994) makes it the central feature of the psychopathology of schizophrenia, following Bleuler's (1986) early recognition of this deficit in schizophrenic patients.

From the developmental point of view, failure to develop a mind in this way is now commonly regarded as a core of autism, a 'mindblindness' as Baron-Cohen (1999) calls it. The notion of 'mindblindness' starts from the premise that the core feature of a mind is that it can recognise the existence of another mind – that is to say, a mind, in order recognisably to be a mind, must have a theory of mind. Autistic children appear to miss that developmental step, and schizophrenics to have retreated from it. Hobson (1993) reviewed this core problem of autism from a psychoanalytic point of view. Originally, Klein (1930) described an autistic boy, in fact before Kanner (1943) first labelled the syndrome. Thereafter, the interest in autism has been pursued by Meltzer *et al.* (1975), Tustin (1981, 1986; see also Spensley 1994), and Alvarez (1992) who with others have extended this work considerably.

The new neuroscience

Such an object-relations theory of the mind can inform recent neuroscience and the philosophy of consciousness. To relate adequately to the external world means recognising the existence of a personal mind in others, an experience which presumably involves the sense of 'having a mind' oneself. This has led to a 'philosophy of consciousness'. Originally, the attempt to solve the question: What is it to have a mind? was addressed in an evolutionary way by asking: Who (or what) has a mind? In other words, what distinguishes the human mind from the 'minds' of other animals. For instance Lloyd-Morgan (1930) attempted a comparative appraisal of the 'minds' of animals, and Premack (1988, see also Premack and Woodruff 1978) was interested to compare the chimpanzee with man. These were somewhat speculative appraisals, but more recently there has been investigation of consciousness in terms of human psychology (Nagel 1986, Dennett 1991, Humphreys 1993, Damasio 2000, Papineau 2000). Little of this work takes account of psychoanalytic discoveries, although as Solms and Kaplan–Solms (2000) point out, psychoanalysis originally derived from neuroscience, and Freud's work in neurology and on aphasia.

Bion's views can fit with those emerging from the new neuroscience, and enhance them by contributing details of specific subjective experiences. Though they can specifically describe the causal 'subjective' matrix – recognition, meaning, representation, mental space and identity – within which mind occurs, they do not clarify the objective conditions under which these subjective phenomena erupt into being. For much of neuroscience, a theory of mind is an infantile achievement. However, work in psychoanalysis and in groups suggests that such an achievement is a wobbly one, and adult life, within our interpersonal context with others, is fluctuating experience of encountering others and 'having a mind'.

What is it to have a mind? How do the first flickering moments of a mind come into existence? How and under what conditions does it snuff out again? It is a research trail like that physicists are following back to the first moments of the universe itself. Following that trail is one of the current topics in psychoanalytic research. But we are not alone; psychiatrists, experimental psychologists, neuroscientists are on the trail with us. There is a potential in Bion's work and writings which is highly stimulating, despite running into contradictions, and which remains a source of ideas and evidence to be mined in the future long after him.

References

Alvarez, A. (1992) *Live Company.* London: Routledge.

Baron-Cohen, S. (1999) *Mindblindness.* Cambridge, MA: MIT Press.

Bion, W. R. (1952) 'Group dynamics: A review.' *International Journal of Psychoanalysis 35,* 235–247.

Bion, W. R. (1954) 'Notes on the theory of schizophrenic.' *International Journal of Psychoanalysis 35,* 113–118. Expanded as 'Language and the Schizophrenic' in M. Klein,

P. Heimann, and R. Money-Kyrle (1955) (eds) *New Directions in Psychoanalysis*. London: Tavistock. Republished (1967) in W. R. Bion *Second Thoughts*. London: Heinemann.

Bion, W. R. (1955) 'Group dynamics: A review.' In M. Klein, P. Heimann, and R. Money-Kyrle (eds) *New Directions in Psychoanalysis*. London: Tavistock. Republished in W. R. Bion (1961) *Experiences in Groups*. London: Tavistock.

Bion, W. R. (1956) Development of schizophrenic thought. *International Journal of Psychoanalysis 37*, 344–346. Republished (1967) in W. R. Bion *Second Thoughts*. London: Heinemann.

Bion, W. R. (1957) 'Differentiation of the psychotic from the non-psychotic personalities.' *International Journal of Psychoanalysis 38*, 266–275. Republished (1967) in W. R. Bion *Second Thoughts*. London: Heinemann, and in E. B. Spillius (1988) *Melanie Klein Today, Volume 1*. London: Tavistock.

Bion, W. R. (1959) Attacks on linking. *International Journal of Psychoanalysis 40* 308–315. Republished (1967) in W. R. Bion *Second Thoughts*. London: Heinemann. And in E. B. Spillius (1988) *Melanie Klein Today, Volume 1*. London: Tavistock.

Bion, W. R. (1961) *Experiences in Groups*. London: Tavistock

Bion, W. R. (1979) 'Making the best of a bad job.' In W. R. Bion (1987) *Clinical Seminars and Four Papers*. Abingdon: Fleetwood Press.

Bleger, J. (1972) *Sybiosis y Ambiguidad*. Buenos Aires: Paidos.

Bleger, J. (1980) 'Le groupe comme institution et le groupe dans le institution.' In R. Kaës (ed) *L'Institution et les Institutions*, Paris: Dunod. English translation (1989) 'The group as institution and within institutions.' *International Journal of Therapeutic Communities 10*, 109–115.

Bleuler, E. (1986) [1911] 'Dementia praecox or the group of schizophrenias.' In J. Cutting and M. Shepherd (1986) *The Clinical Rots of the Schizophrenia Concept*. Cambridge: Cambridge University Press.

Damasio, A. (2000) *The Feeling of What Happens*. London: Heinemann.

Da Silva, G. (1997) 'The emergence of thinking: Bion as the link between Freud and the neurosciences.' Available online at www.sicap.it/amercai/papers/silva.HTM

Dennett, D. (1991) *Consciousness Explained*. New York: Little Brown.

Frith, C. (1994) *The Cognitive Neuropshchology of Schizophrenia*. Hove: Lawrence Erlbaum.

Fonagy, P. and Target, M. (2000) 'Mentalization and personality disorder: A current perspective from the Anna Freud Centre.' IN T. Lubbe (ed) *The Borderline Psychotic Child*. London: Routledge.

Hinshelwood, R. D. (1994) 'Attacks on the reflective space.' In V. Shermer and M. Pines (eds) *Ring of Fire: Primitive Object Relations and Affects in Group Psychotherapy*. London: Routledge.

Hinshelwood, R. D. (1997) *Therapy or Coercion: Does psychoanalysis differ from brainwashing?* London: Karnac.

Hobson, P. (1993) *Autism and the Development of Mind*. Hove: Lawrence Erlbaum.

Humphreys, N. (1993) *A History of the Mind*. London: Chatto and Windus.

Jaques, E. (1955) 'The social system as a defence against persecutory and depressive anxiety.' In M. Klein and R. Money-Kyrle (eds) *New Directions in Psychoanalysis*. London: Tavistock.

Kaës, R. (1984) 'Representations and mentalization: From the represented group to the group process.' In R. Farr, S. Moscovici (eds) *Social Representations*. Cambridge: Cambridge University Press.

Kanner, L. (1943) 'Autistic disturbances of affective contact.' *Nervous Child 2*, 217–250.

Klein, M. (1930) 'The importance of symbol formation in the development of the ego.' *International Journal of Psychoanalysis 11*, 24–39. Reprinted in M. Klein (1995) *The Writings of Melanie Klein: Volume 1*. London: Hogarth.

Klein, M., Hyman, P. And Money-Kyrle, R. (1995) *New Directions in Psychoanalysis*. London: Tavistock.

Lloyd-Morgan, C. (1930) *The Animal Mind*. London: Edward Arnold.

Meltzer, D., Bremner, J., Hoxter, S., Weddell, D., and Wittenberg, I. (1975) *Explorations in Autism*. Perth: Clunie.

Metzinger, T. (1995) (ed) *Conscious Experience*. Paderborn: Schoningh.

Miller, E. (1998) 'Are basic assumptions instinctive?' In P. Bion Talamo, F. Borgogno and S. Mercai (eds) *Bion's Legacy in Groups*. London: Karnac.

Mitrani, J. (1996) *A Framework for the Imaginary*. New York: Jason Aronson.

Morris, C. (1938) 'Foundations of the theory of signs.' International Encyclopedia of Unified Science. Chicago: University of Chicago Press.

Nagel, T. (1974) 'What is it like to be a bat?' *Philosophical Review 83*, 435–450.

Nagel, T. (1986) *The View from Nowhere*. Oxford: Oxford University Press.

O'Shaughnessy, E. (1981) 'A clinical study of a defensive organisation.' *International Journal of Psychoanalysis 62*, 359–369.

Papineau, D. (2000) *Thinking about consciousness*. Oxford: Clarendon

Premack, D. (1988) '"Does the chimpanzee have a theory of mind?" revisited.' In R. Byrbe and A. Whiten (eds) *Machiavellian Intelligence*. Oxford: Oxford University Press.

Premack, D. And Woodruff, G. (1978) 'Does the chimpanzee have a theory of mind?' *Behaviour and Brain Sciences 4*, 515–526.

Rosenfeld, H. (1971) 'A clinical approach to the psychoanalytical theory of the life and death instincts: An investigation of the aggressive aspects of narcissism.' *International Journal of Psychoanalysis 52*, 169–178. Republished in E. B. Spillius (1988) *Melanie Klein Today, Volume 1*. London: Tavistock

Segal, H. (1957) 'Notes on symbol formation.' *International Journal of Psychoanalysis 38*, 391–97. Reprinted in H. Segal (1981) *The Work of Hanna Segal*. New York: Jason Aronson.

Solms, M. and Kaplan-Solms, K. (2000) *Clinical Studies in Neuro-Psychoanalysis*. London: Karnac Books.

Spensley, S. (1994) *Frances Tustin*. London: Routledge.

Stern, D. (1985) *The Interpersonal World of the Young Infant*. New York: Basic Books.

Turing, A. (1950) 'Computing machinery and Intelligence.' *Mind 59*, 433–460.

Tustin, F. (1981) *Autistic States in Children*. London: Routledge.

Tustin, F. (1986) *Autistic Barriers in Neurotic Patients*. London: Karnac.

Endnotes

1.   By making these storms of feelings central to the working, and even existence of the mind, I am resorting to what I believe to be a fundamental psychoanalytic premise. However, in the field of experimental psychology too there is a similar position which makes 'feelings be the primitives of consciousness... [T]he idea that human consciousness depends on feelings helps us confront the problem of creating conscious artefacts' (Damasio 2000, p. 314).

2.   People with severe personality disorders, pre-occupied as they are with abuse, can employ their sensitivity to such storms of encounter in order to express something of their terror of intrusions, violation and abuse, *into* others.

3.   Formally, he referred to the raw material, upon which alpha-function works, i.e. the storm, as 'beta-particles', and the products of alpha-function as 'alpha-particles', which are the elements with which the mind can begin to work, as in dreams.

4.   I am here adapting Bion who described the food of the mind as 'truth' – in my account it is meaning.

5.   It seems important to distinguish 'representations', which can be restricted to these 'things' in the mind, from symbols. Symbols are clearly related to representations. They are, perhaps, external 'representations'. But they are more than representations – symbols are the conversion of representations into something that is communicable to other minds. There is a difference. Symbols are created as a result of some activity, that is, worked up representations – symbols are representations put in the form that can be externally recognised. The term symbol-formation is used, and it has something to do with Freud's notion of dream-work – that work that has to be done on the dream itself to communicate it to the analyst. It is put into words, it is converted into a formal narrative as far as possible – secondary process gets going on it. Thus symbols have three components: the real thing, the internal representation and the symbol that gives expression to the internal. This is roughly in line with Segal's formulation which she takes from Morris (1938):

I find it helpful following C. Morris (1938), to consider symbolising as a *three*-term relation, i.e. a relation between the thing symbolized, the thing functioning as a symbol and a *person* for whom the one represents the other. In psychological terms, symbolism would be a relation between ego, the object, and the symbol (Segal 1957, p.161).

6.   This has significant similarities to Bleger's idea of the pooling of primary undifferentiated aspects of the individual, in the group, which Bleger was developing at the same time (Bleger 1972, 1980).

7.   The 1955 version was republished without further changes as the last chapter in his *Experiences in Groups*.

8.   This connects with the notion of 'attunement' stressed by Stern (1985) and others in the mother–baby interaction.

9.   This is an example of a group in a work mode which is coloured by (rather than dominated by) the basic assumption.

10.   Elsewhere I have examined these kinds of group states in greater detail, and speculated on their therapeutic benefits or otherwise (Hinshelwood 1997).

11.   In that case, it is the dependency assumption. I do not want to add complexity by going further into the conditions when a basic assumption dominates in this psychotic way; and the conditions when encounters do happen, but flavoured with a basic assumption.

12.   See also Guy da Silva (1997).

13.   That test in effect determines the possession of a mind, as opposed to information processing (Turing 1950).

8

Incohesion: Aggregation/ Massification

The Fourth Basic Assumption in the Unconscious Life of Groups and Group-like Social Systems

Earl Hopper

The cohesion of groups has been studied in a number of related fields: general systems theory, social biology, classical psychoanalysis, sociology, and social psychology, as well as in group dynamics or group relations, group psychotherapy and group analysis. In 1981, these perspectives and literature were reviewed in depth in *Group Cohesion* edited by Kellerman. In 1997, Marziali, Munroe-Blum and McCleary referred to cohesion as '...the most frequently studied group-process dimension'. (Marziali *et al.* 1997, p.476) However, they wrote that 'despite these developments, Bednar and Kaul (1994) believe that the construct of cohesion continues to defy definition...' It seems that '...there is little consensus about the dimensions that best describe the complex phenomena that comprise group cohesiveness' (*ibid* p.476).

It is, therefore, entirely appropriate to think more about the nature of cohesion in groups and group-like social systems. I will present here a highly condensed version of my theory of the effects of traumatic experience on the cohesion of groups and group-like social systems in terms of the fourth basic assumption, which I call 'Incohesion: Aggregation/Massification' or 'ba I: A/M'. I have outlined previous versions of my theory in a number of publications, which include detailed clinical illustrations and extensive bibliography (e.g. Hopper 1997, 2001c), but have developed and illustrated it further in *Traumatic Experience in the Unconscious Life of Groups* (2003).

A theory of cohesion proposed by Bion and Turquet and modified by Kernberg and Lawrence

1. Acknowledging the influence of Freud, Klein and Rickman, Bion provided the first coherent psychoanalytical theory of many group processes. *Experiences in Groups* (1961) and his earlier papers and articles (Bion 1948–1951) constitute a time marker in the psychoanalytical study of groups that should be known as zero, all previous studies to be dated 'BB', and all subsequent ones 'AB' Although he did not regard his theory of 'basic assumptions' in the unconscious life of groups as a theory of incohesion, it can be understood in this way.

Especially useful summaries of his theory are provided by Kernberg (1978) and Lawrence, Bain and Gould (1996). However, Bion's work is indeed complex, and his style is often cryptic. It may be helpful to emphasise a few of the points made by these authors, and add some of my own, which offer a slightly different way of understanding the original theory of basic assumptions:

> (i) The three basic assumptions have been understood from many points of view, for example, in terms of phallic/Oedipal, anal and oral levels of psychosexual development; instincts concerned with the perpetuation of the species, the control of territory and the food and sexual partners within it; and of seeking dependable 'attachments'. However, Bion's work developed from the perspectives expressed in his earlier papers into those expressed in *Experiences in Groups*. His psychoanalytical views became more and more Kleinian, although subsequently they evolved into what is now called 'post-Kleinian'. Bion argues that when people are in group situations, they regress to levels of psychic life of an infant at the mother's body and breast, to be understood in terms of very early Oedipal phenomena, or to what some would call pre-Oedipal or triangularisation phenomena, involving relationships of the mouth, breast and nipple or the mouth, eye and hand or the mouth, ear and anus, etc., rather than in terms of relationships between the person, mother and father. In groups these relationships are experienced in terms of the vicissitudes of the primal scene, depending on the prevailing anxieties and defences against them. As Bion puts it, more in terms of the sphinx than of Oedipus.

(ii) Bion emphasised that the three basic assumptions are best understood in terms of the 'interplay' between the paranoid/schizoid and depressive positions. Although he was not clear about this, he implied that, based on the death instinct, innate pathological envy is the source of irrational and destructive rage, and that primal processes of splitting, denial and projection facilitate processes of idealisation and denigration in order to help the ego rid itself of painful rage and protect its most important objects. Dependency develops from idealisation associated with the schizoid component of the paranoid/schizoid position, and fight/flight develops from denigration associated with the paranoid component. The basic assumption of dependency protects people from the experience of helplessness and fear that they will be unable to fulfil the requirements of those tasks the completion of which is essential to life, such as, in infancy, obtaining food. Feelings of unsafety, uncertainty, being lost, of not knowing what to expect and what is expected, etc., are also involved. Pairing is based on sexualisation or erotization as a manic defence against anxieties associated with the depressive position, involving the conviction that goodness and perfection exist nowhere, not within and not without. In other words, pairing is not a matter of genital sexuality.

(iii) All basic assumptions are containers for psychotic anxieties. Basic assumption processes can be used in the service of the activities of the work group, but they can become grotesque and distorted, and interfere with the activities of the work group. This is analogous to the way that neuroses and possibly psychoses in adults are grotesque versions of the mental life of normal children and infants. However, the existence of basic assumption processes in parallel with work group processes is also analogous to the existence of unconscious mental and emotional life characterised by primary process in parallel with the unconscious, rational, secondary processes of the ego.

(iv) Basic assumption processes can be delineated in terms of patterns of interaction, normation and communication as properties of social systems (Hopper 1994a, first published 1975). The following examples stress how each pattern is seen in any basic assumption: with respect to pairing, a typical interaction would be a flirtation between a male and a female, encouraged by the rest of the group; a typical pattern of norms would be the expression of values that favour personal sacrifice for collective goals; and a typical pattern of communication would be an enthusiastic, hopeful and perhaps unrealistic discussion of future projects and plans. With respect to fight/flight: an apparently unsolvable argument between two members on behalf of factions that have arisen virtually from 'out of the blue'; the expression of values that favour debate and the importance of being true to principles; and discussion of the possibilities of forming two groups and of the various major differences among the people within the group. And with respect to dependency: very little interaction and hesitant participation; the expression of values that favour humility, risk aversion, conservatism on behalf of all rather than on behalf of individuality, and respect for authority; and discussion about 'being stuck' yet confident that the leader will soon help 'get us going', punctuated by long periods of silence.

(v) In any group, all three basic assumptions and combinations of them emerge kaleidoscopically, as do the correlates of the paranoid/schizoid and depressive positions on which they are based. For example, when the basic assumption of pairing fails as a defence against depressive anxieties, certain kinds of paranoid/schizoid anxieties are likely to emerge, associated with denigration, which, in turn, generates the basic assumption of fight/flight. However, when other kinds of paranoid/schizoid anxieties emerge, associated with idealisation, the basic assumption of dependency is likely to follow. The converse of these processes may also occur. For example, when dependency fails as a defence against feelings of helplessness, envy is likely to occur, and, in turn, either denigration develops and leads to fight/flight, or further idealisation develops and leads to an amplification of dependency.

(vi) Bion also discussed the leadership of a group. Ambiguously, he referred to the leadership of the work group as well as of the basic assumption group. However, Bion implied that a 'real' leader is the leader of the work group, who is able to use basic assumption processes in the service of work, depending on the nature of the task at the time. In other words, the work group is like a cork floating on the Sea of Basic Assumptions, and the leader of the work group is in chronic danger of being capsized, and likely to be replaced by a leader of a basic assumption group. A leader of a work group and leaders of basic assumption groups may exist and function simultaneously, and usually the situation is transitory and in flux.

Bion argued that as a consequence of ubiquitous processes of projective identification, patterns of 'valence' arise, based on the attraction that particular basic assumption processes and their roles hold for people with certain kinds of personality. The so-called 'leader' of a basic assumption group is someone with a valence for the roles and processes associated with a particular basic assumption. The leadership of a basic assumption group is not necessarily an indication of pathology as much as it is of a type of personality and character.

2. Only twice did Bion (1970, 1978) mention the possibility of a fourth basic assumption concerning illusions of fusion and oneness in connection with an infant's need to protect against the anxieties associated with birth, or more precisely, with the transformation from being a unique object of mother-and-foetus combined with the body of the mother, to being a separate object outside the mother. This fourth basic assumption concerns incohesion specifically.

Pierre Turquet, focusing entirely on large groups within group relations conferences, developed Bion's cryptic comments about a fourth basic assumption in two papers: in 1967, to the Paris Society of Psychosomatic Medicine, which gave rise to the publication in 1974 of 'Leadership: the individual and the group'; and in 1969, as one of the Winter Lectures sponsored by the British Psychoanalytical Society, which was the basis of the original publication in 1975 of 'Threats to identity in the large group' (Turquet 1994). According to Turquet:

> (i) The fourth basic assumption should be called 'Oneness' (BaO). Under the sway of this basic assumption members of a group '…seek to join in a powerful union with an omnipotent force unobtainably high, to surrender self for passive participation, and thereby (to) feel existence, well-being, and wholeness' (Turquet 1974, p.357) '…The group member is there to be lost in oceanic feelings of unity…(i)f the oneness is personified…(the group member is there)…to be a part of a salvationist inclusion' (Turquet 1974, p.360).

This basic assumption of oneness results from a transformation or 'conversion' that people experience as a result of threats to their identity through their attempts to participate in the large group. It is argued that a person begins in what is called an 'I' or 'singleton' state, but in order to protect against the unbridled envy, fear of annihilation and loss of identity that follow from uncontrolled regression, provoked by the 'multiple stimuli' and 'response bombardment' that typify a large group, a singleton '(S)' either becomes a 'membership individual (MI)' or an 'isolate', rather than an 'individual member (IM)'. Membership individuals unconsciously create a state of social and cultural 'homogeneity', characterised by absolute equality, absolute sameness of belief, no role differentiation, no use of personal authority as the basis of the interpretation of the role, the use of language in order to convey identity as a membership individual rather than the content of ideas, and the use of 'speaking-in-tongues' in order magically to be at one with the unified group as a whole. Homogenisation is said to be the source of the basic assumption of oneness.

(ii) An alternative defensive process, through which alienated isolates and bizarre objects create unconsciously a state of chaos and multiple splittings characterised by 'errancy' and 'polarities', should be called 'dissaroy', which connotes that the king-father has been dispossessed of his power and authority. In itself, dissaroy is not a basic assumption, and not explicitly connected to oneness. The 'dissaroy' of the group is based on the states of mind of the individuals who comprise it.

(iii) A good work group is characterised by 'heterogeneity'. However, as for Bion, the concept of the work group is used primarily as a foil for the analysis of the destructive processes of unconscious basic assumption groups, and, thus, Turquet did not describe heterogeneity. In any case, it is implied that under conditions of oneness the work group would only be momentary and transitory, and under conditions of dissaroy, the work group would cease to exist, as, shortly thereafter, would the group itself.

(iv) Having suggested that homogenisation is typical of charismatic movements in which people wish to be at one with God, Turquet suggested that a leader of the basic assumption of oneness is likely to be 'charismatic'. The charismatic leadership of oneness groups is different from Bion's depiction of a God of dependency groups or a Christ of pairing groups, and certainly from a General of fight/flight groups.

3. An assessment of the strengths and weaknesses of this entire approach has been provided elsewhere, for example, by group analysts such as Brown (1985), group psychotherapists such as Yalom (1985) and many students of group dynamics such as Stock-Whitaker and Lieberman (1964). However, to the positive side of existing critiques I would add that rarely have we been able to identify and to explain so many diverse phenomena on the basis of so few concepts and propositions. Nonetheless, as to the negative side of existing critiques, I would emphasise several points:

(i) Bion and Turquet nominalised groups and group processes, and denied the reality of social facts. It is not generally remembered that although Bion studied groups as 'wholes', and stressed that people were social animals, he also expressed the view that groups do not really exist except in the minds of people who are regressed. He wrote that a 'group' is a fantasy that is shared by people who are in similar states of regression.

(ii) With respect to the fourth basic assumption specifically, it is impossible to integrate the hypothesis that oneness or fusion is connected with the experience of birth, with the underlying Kleinian hypothesis that fusion is only a defence against envy, which is at the foundation of the theory of three basic assumptions. Within the context of the Klein/Bion model, it is impossible to conceptualise anxieties more primitive than schizoid anxieties, and, therefore, to imagine basic assumptions more primitive than dependency. Whereas primal envy is said to lead, on the one hand, to denigration, and therefore, to fight/flight, and on the other to idealisation, and therefore to dependency, primal envy is also said to lead to the fear of annihilation, and therefore to the basic assumption of oneness. Clearly, this is a contradiction and an inconsistency.

In my judgement, Bion became aware of this problem, but in order to solve it, he would have had to adopt some of the views of Fairbairn, Guntrip, Winnicott and others, such as Kohut, not to mention Foulkes, and, thus, to alter the Kleinian model of development. He would have had to ask the question that many years later Khaleelee and Miller (1985) and I (Hopper 1985) working independently, have put: what happens when dependency fails? And a related question: what anxieties underpin feelings of envy associated with the putative 'death instinct'? Or, is it possible that envy arises as a defence against more basic anxieties? The answers to these questions require a truly interpersonal, intersubjective model of the mind, and a theory of trauma that is more complex than 'failed containment', which was Bion's only contribution to understanding the nature of trauma. Instead, Bion stopped theorising group processes, and began to focus on the relationship between the body and the mind. Although he began to consider the nature of 'normal' projective identification, he also began to grant less and less importance to the external world of other people.

(iii) It is understandable that Turquet assumed that the basic assumption of oneness is both ubiquitous and inevitable, because he also assumed that oneness is based on envy, which, in turn, is assumed to be ubiquitous and inevitable. Although he mentioned that the members of large groups introject both projected anxieties and defences, he took projective processes to be primary. He concentrated almost entirely on the ways in which persons who are extremely regressed and frightened about their loss of identity project these emotions into others, who are similarly frightened, and who become ever more frightened, and who, in turn, project their fears into those around them. Thus, for Turquet, as for Klein and Bion, the fear of annihilation is based on the fear of retaliation from objects into whom envious impulses to annihilate have been projected. In other words, the state of dissaroy is created from projections. Although Turquet mentioned that the participants in large groups are likely to feel overlooked and unheard, in effect to feel narcissistically injured, this was peripheral to his central argument. It was implied that such experience is important only in so far as it promotes regression, and not that it is traumatic, and precipitates a traumatogenic process.

In contradistinction, I would argue that although dissaroy and homogeneity are ubiquitous, they are not inevitable. Large groups do not always evince either dissaroy or homogenisation. In other words, oneness may be associated with the emergence of envy, but the emergence of envy is not inevitable. Envy is variable, and governed by variable conditions. In fact, dissaroy and homogenisation in large groups in training conferences, which were the source of Turquet's observations, are often based on failed dependency, perhaps because inappropriate and plunging interpretations (Foulkes 1968) or confusion in the management and administration of such events have insulted the integrity of the group. In training conferences large groups tend to be experienced by people who are used to small groups as an attack upon them by the staff, rather than as a developmental challenge that might be related, for example, to a shift from the family to the school, or to the integration of multiple facets of the internal world. Moreover, the development and persistence of basic assumptions depend in large part on the style of the conductor. It is easy to conduct a group of inexperienced students of the dynamics of groups in such a way that they are provoked into a state of fear and bewilderment. It is more difficult to facilitate the development of a work group who share a sense of community, characterised by optimal cohesion. In any case, what may often be true for large groups in training conferences is not true for large groups in other settings (Brown 2001). Perhaps envy is not the primal emotion, and projection not the primal action.

Most importantly, Bion confined his discussion of aggression within the context of basic assumption groups to the basic assumption of fight/flight, as though aggression did not occur and have particular patterns within the basic assumptions of pairing and dependency. Moreover, Turquet implied that aggression was non-existent within the context of the basic assumption of oneness, because oneness was a defence against the dissaroy that followed rampant envy. However, oneness is never perfect, and any threat to it precipitates aggression towards the people and sub-groups who are seen to be associated with the threat. This is not so much a matter of envy as one of attacks on perceived obstacles to merger.

(iv) Bion and Turquet neglected the phenomenon of leadership, especially with respect to the work group. Although Turquet suggested that 'leaders' of oneness groups are likely to be charismatic, he did not examine the nature of charismatic leadership.

4. Like Bion and Turquet before him, Otto Kernberg is a renowned psychoanalyst who has taken a serious and deep interest in group dynamics, primarily in complex organisations, particularly hospitals and training institutes of psychoanalysis. In a series of papers he introduced the theory of basic assumptions to psychoanalysts whose understanding of group dynamics was based almost entirely on Freud's *Totem and Taboo* (1950, first published 1913) and *Group Psychology and the Analysis of the Ego* (1955, first published 1921), and suggested several modifications to it. Drawing on the ideas of Bion (1961) and Turquet (1994, first published 1975), as well as those of Anzieu (1981), Menzies-Lyth (1981), Chasseguet-Smirgel (1985) and others, Kernberg argues that:

(i) Small and large groups promote regression because they '... lack an operational leadership and lack or lose clearly defined tasks to relate them to their environment.' (Kernberg 1998, p.45) Also, it is implied that dissaroy is primary, and that homogenisation is secondary, and based on the sexualisation of aggression associated with dissaroy.

(ii) On the basis of 'role suction' (Redl 1942), people with certain kinds of anxiety and patterns of defence will be attracted to the roles provided by particular basic assumptions, and become leaders of them. More specifically:

...(A) spectrum of different types of *symbolic leadership* [my italics: that is, of basic assumption processes, E.H.] reflect(s) the degree of regression in the group. [For example, the] dependency group tends to promote infantile narcissistic (and even psychopathic) leaders, in contrast to the fight/flight group that seeks a leader with paranoid characteristics. (Kernberg 1998, p.46)

Kernberg also implies that the pairing group seeks a leader who has a surfeit of hysterical features.

(iii) With certain exceptions psychoanalysts and students of group dynamics in general have neglected to study leaders and leadership of the work group as a pro-active process. Nonetheless, it can be said that:

[T]he mature superego [is] derived from the post-Oedipal parental couple – [involving] the rational, protective, moral functions of the parents, [which is the basis for] the symbolic meaning of the rational leadership of functional organisations... (Kernberg 1998, p.46)

...[Rational leadership] is characterised by (1) high intelligence; (2) personal honesty and noncorruptibility by the political process; (3)

capacity for establishing and maintaining object relations in depth; (4) a healthy narcissism; and (5) a healthy, justifiable anticipatory paranoid attitude in contrast to naivety... (Kernberg 1998, p.47)

5. Like Bion and Turquet, Kernberg assumes that the unconscious dynamics of large groups can also be seen in more complex social systems, such as organisations and societies. Nor is he clear about the aetiology of aggression, even in his delineation of borderline conditions and pathological narcissism: although he does not assume the existence of a death instinct, and does not explain all aggression in terms of envy, he continues to focus on projective processes. Kernberg also neglects the traumatogenic process: although he is aware of the constraints of social facts on unconscious life, his brief reference to the absence of the good father in the context of post-war German society is the exception that proves the rule. In other words, like Bion and Turquet, Kernberg neglects the problem of failed dependency.

It also seems judicious to cite Scheidlinger's (1980) comments that Kernberg's discussion of the leadership of extremely regressed groups should have taken account of additional work, for example, Scheidlinger's (1952) own analysis of mature and immature leaders, Freud's (1931) delineation of libidinal types and their tendency to assume leadership roles, Bychowski's (1948) study of dictators, Alexander's (1942) and Erikson's (1948) analysis of mature and immature leaders, and Kohut and Wolf's (1978) discussion of the 'narcissistic group self'. Most importantly Redl (1942) implied that whereas the work group has leaders, basic assumption groups have 'central persons', and, thus, a so-called 'leader' of a basic assumption group is likely to be a follower who is vulnerable to role-suction, especially the charismatic 'leader' of a oneness group.

6. Lawrence (1993) and Lawrence *et al.* (1996) propose a fifth basic assumption of 'me-ness', the opposite of what Turquet called 'oneness'. They argue that in the same way that isolates are defined as 'me's, not-you's', me-ness is defined as 'not-oneness'. This putative basic assumption of me-ness is said to function as a defence against the anxieties associated with being a membership individual in a oneness group, such as the fear of contamination. The basis for me-ness is a developmental moment in the early life of persons. The authors cite Winnicott's statement: 'The idea of a limiting membrane appears, and from this follows the idea of an inside and an outside. Then there develops the theme of a ME and a not-ME. There are now contents that develop partly on instinctual experience' (Winnicott 1988, p.68). Curiously, it is also suggested that schizoid anxieties and defences (I suspect in the sense

that Guntrip would describe them) are the basis of me-ness, which, in turn, is manifest in various forms of alienation, withdrawal and pathological narcissism. In other words, it is argued that me-ness is not only a defence against the 'we-ness' of homogenisation, but also an expression of aggression against the whole, and involves attacks on linking, based on unbridled envy. Yet, such phenomena are said to be 'socially induced', through the experience of 'failed dependency', and are typical of life in modern societies. It is suggested that as do other basic assumption states, me-ness has positive uses for a work group. It is also said that particular kinds of people are likely to lead me-ness groups.

7. The argument advanced by Lawrence *et al.* (1996) has certain inconsistencies. For example, these authors ignore the fact that Bion's theory of basic assumptions in general and Turquet's theory of oneness in particular are predicated on the assumption that the primary anxiety associated with innate malign envy is an expression of the putative death instinct. This is a contradiction to a theory of human development that emphasizes traumatic experience. Although the authors have nodded in the direction of Winnicott, they think within the tradition of Klein, Bion and Turquet. This is seen in their having adopted the fundamental Kleinian tenet that fusion is a defence against envy, and that 'me, not-you' is a retreat from fusion. However, they also argue that this retreat is motivated by the envy of oneness. Moreover, 'me-ness' is not conceptualised as a characteristic of the singleton, who is associated with dissaroy, of which me-ness is the central feature.

In the context of their argument, 'me-ness' actually refers to what Bion (1958) called 'secondary splitting', which I (Hopper 1991) have called 'secondary fission and fragmentation', the fourth step in the encapsulation process. I have written:

> ...as a consequence of processes of secondary envy and internal projections, the fusional and confusional introjected object is likely to be perceived as dangerous. As a defence against the anxieties associated with fusion and confusion with an object that is perceived to be dangerous, there is likely to occur a regressive shift back towards processes of fission and fragmentation. (Hopper 1991, p.610)

In other words these authors have described defensive shifts from homogenisation to what Turquet might have termed 'secondary dissaroy'.

It follows that in the same way that Turquet was unable quite to conceptualise a fourth basic assumption, Lawrence, Bain and Gould have not quite conceptualised a fifth, because basic assumptions must be related to basic psychotic anxieties within a context of a model of development. Although they refer to a process of 'social induction', they do not give this process much importance in the aetiology of psychic life. Unless the Klein/Bion/Turquet model is modified, it is impossible to integrate an emphasis on projective processes with an emphasis on social induction.

8. In sum, although the psychoanalytical point of view does not provide a complete explanation of the phenomenon of incohesion in groups, the psychoanalytical theory proposed by Bion and Turquet and developed by Kernberg and by Lawrence *et al.*, is especially illuminating. Nonetheless, the main problem with this particular theory is that aggression is explained in terms of envy and, by implication, the putative death instinct, and therefore, that threats to identity are explained in terms of the fear of retaliation from objects that have been invested with projected envy and aggressive impulses. From this perspective it is impossible to postulate more than three basic assumptions. Furthermore, the 'leadership' of basic assumption processes is not distinguished from the leadership of the work group, which limits the application of this theory to clinical work and to consultations with organisations. Although these contradictions are insurmountable, certain modifications to the underlying metapsychology leads to an alternative theory of a fourth basic assumption, which negates the need to conceptualise a fifth.

Incohesion: Aggregation/Massification or Ba I:A/M as the fourth basic assumption in the unconscious life of groups

In my theory I focus on incohesion rather than cohesion. My theory of incohesion is based on the work of the Group of Independent Psychoanalysts of the British Psychoanalytical Society, including Rickman, Fairbairn, Winnicott, Balint, King and Bowlby. It draws explicitly from the work of group analysts such as Anthony, Brown, de Maré, Hume, Kreeger, Main, Pines, Skynner and others. Group analysis is based on psychoanalysis, but also on sociology and general systems theory. The concepts and theories of the group matrix (Roberts and Pines 1991), the sociality of human nature (Hopper 1981a), the social unconscious (Hopper 1996, 2000 and 2001a) and open systems (Hopper 1994a, first published 1975) are essential to the study of incohesion.

In my theory of incohesion of groups and group-like social systems it is argued that incohesion is a manifestation within the external world of the fear of annihilation, which is explained in terms of traumatic experience. Processes of incohesion are personified by central persons whose identities can be described in terms of characterological protections against the fear of annihilation (Hopper 1991, 1994b and 1995). Thus, it is also argued that incohesion is recursive, based on the continuing interaction of inter-personal and intra-personal processes within a wider social context.

The fear of annihilation and traumatic experience

1. The primary fear of annihilation is a response to the experience of profound helplessness arising from loss, abandonment and damage within the context of the traumatogenic process, which spans generations and involves the relationships between victims and perpetrators, and the responses to the traumatised. The traumatic experience of profound helplessness in response to loss, abandonment and damage may be understood in terms of: the Chinese water-torture strains of daily life, the cumulative build-up of small incidents into an overpowering wave of oppression, and/or the catastrophic violation of expectations. This is always a matter of failed dependency in both personal and social domains. Traumatic experience is ubiquitous, as is the fear of annihilation. Were this not so, it would be wrong to argue that the fear of annihilation is the source of the fourth *basic* assumption. However, traumatic experience is determined by both the magnitude of the strain and/or catastrophe, and the maturity of the ego (which is only partly a function of chronological age). A comprehensive classification of events that might be traumatic is impossible. However, events that have been traumatic can be seen in terms of whether they were primarily personal, random and idiosyncratic, or more patterned for large numbers of people. They may have been primarily social and political in nature or primarily natural or a mixture of both.

2. 'In the beginning', the primal emotion in psychic life is not envy, based on the putative death instinct, but 'grenvy', which is a neologism that is intended to convey a mixture of greed and possessive desire (Coltart 1989). On the basis of traumatic experience, grenvy is split into greedy desire and malign envy of objects who are perceived as able but unwilling to help, and who are perceived as responsible for failed dependency, that is, failed containment and holding. In other words, according to this perspective malign envy is not innate, but develops as a defence against feelings of profound helplessness. On the basis of the emergence of defensive, malign envy, paranoid/schizoid splitting leads to idealisation and denigration. Objects of failed dependency are then subjected to annihilating attacks, usually but not always in fantasy. In turn, the objects are perceived to be retaliatory. Sometimes, on

the basis of projective identification, they actually do retaliate, and, thus, a secondary fear of annihilation is likely to develop.

I would hypothesise that virtually by definition helplessness is a consequence of traumatic experience, and that envy arises as a defence against helplessness, which means that helplessness precedes envy, which is regarded as a defensive response to narcissistic injury (Rutan and Stone 2000). Of course, fusion can be a defence against envy and helplessness, and helplessness can be a consequence of fusion, but these are secondary processes; furthermore, envy can itself be traumatic, because it leads to the destruction in fantasy of the *good* object, but this too is a secondary process.

The fear of annihilation is closely connected with the fear of separation, because separation from an object with whom one has fused is likely to be felt as losing a part of one's self. Also, one is likely to have fused with an object who has been lost prematurely and/or precipitately, especially at the phase of unintegration, when it is difficult, if not impossible, to hold in mind representations of the object. In effect, the loss of the breast is experienced as the loss of the mouth.

3. Primary and secondary fears of annihilation combined are expressed as intrapsychic fission and fragmentation, which are associated with typical psychotic anxieties, for example: fear of disintegration and of dissolution. The first response to the anxieties associated with fission and fragmentation is introjective fusion and confusion with the lost, abandoning and damaging object. However, fusion and confusion are also associated with typical psychotic anxieties, for example: fear of suffocation, swallowing and being swallowed, being crushed, being entrapped, becoming a puppet, and becoming petrified. In order to protect against the anxieties associated with fusion and confusion, a retreat occurs to the state of fission and fragmentation. The relationship between fission and fragmentation, and fusion and confusion, and, then, in a secondary way, between fusion and confusion and fission and fragmentation, and back again to fusion and confusion, is, therefore, one of pendulum-like, non-dialectical oscillation, involving incessant psychic activity but no change and no development.

4. In order for life to continue and psychic paralysis to be avoided, the entire intrapsychic experience is encysted or encapsulated, producing autistic islands of experience, characterised by all-encompassing silence and grotesque internal developments of aggregated objects. Encapsulation is associated with two autistic forms of self-protection: 'crustacean' and 'amoeboid' (Tustin 1981). A crustacean type may actually refer to himself in

terms of crustacean imagery, for example, as a lobster or a tortoise or covered by a shell; and an amoeboid type, as a jelly fish, feeling utterly vulnerable, and as someone whose skin functions merely to distinguish what is felt to be a 'self' from a 'not-self', or a 'me' from a 'not-me' (Winnicott 1988). Amoeboid people find protection in merger and accommodation based on fantasies of vacuole incorporation. This distinction is virtually identical to that of 'contact-shunning' and 'merger-hungry' disorders of the self (Kohut and Wolf 1978). Several psychoanalysts have made similar comparisons, although with slightly different nuances. For example, Balint's (1968) distinction between the philobat who loves empty spaces and avoids people, and the ocnophile who clings to people, is especially apposite. These character types are supported by disassociation (Klein and Schermer 2000), as is encapsulation itself.

Both crustacean and amoeboid characters tend to use projective and introjective identification of malignant kinds, involving the repetition compulsion and traumatophilia, in the service of expulsion, attack, control and communication of that which would otherwise be enacted. After all, people who have had a history of traumatic experience are likely to have no other way in which to communicate. They are, therefore, exceedingly vulnerable to role suction. However, they also tend to create those roles which, if enacted, offer a sense of containment and holding, in that they bestow an identity within a field of turmoil and chaos.

The interaction, normation and communication patterns of traumatised groups

On the basis of various kinds of externalisation and internalisation, especially projective and introjective identification, groups of traumatised people are likely to evince processes of 'incohesion'. These processes are likely to be characterised by what I call 'aggregation', in response to fission and fragmentation, and then by what I call 'massification', in response to fusion and confusion; and, in turn, by oscillations between massification and aggregation. These states and processes of aggregation and massification comprise the bipolar forms of incohesion. Therefore, I call the fourth basic assumption in the unconscious life of groups and all group-like social systems 'Incohesion: Aggregation/Massification' or 'I: A/M'. I will now develop these hypotheses, and delineate the main features of aggregation and massification as the bipolar states of incohesion.

1. Aggregates and masses are the two most simple, primitive social formations. They are not merely collections of people, but nor are they groups. These two social formations have been described by social scientists and social philosophers from many points of view, using a variety of terms and concepts, but 'aggregate' and 'mass' are technically correct.

An aggregate is characterised by a minimal degree of mutual attraction and involvement among three or more people who are neither interdependent nor in sympathy with one another, on the basis of shared beliefs, norms and values. In contrast, a mass is characterised by a maximal degree of mutual attraction and involvement among three or more people who are neither interdependent nor in sympathy with one another but who share the illusion of solidarity with respect to beliefs, norms and values, usually for a brief period of time.

Although the members of a mass may feel otherwise, a mass is no more a group than an aggregate is. An aggregate and a mass are each social formations with dynamics of their own. Whereas an aggregate has too much individuality to be a group, a mass has too little. An aggregate is highly incohesive. A mass seems to be very cohesive, but in reality it is as incohesive as an aggregate. In fact, a mass is like an aggregate masquerading as a group, like an aggregate in drag.

Metaphors for an aggregate are a handful of gravel, a piece of granite, a set of billiard balls, or even a plate of deep-fried whitebait; in contrast, metaphors for a mass are a slab of basalt, a handful of warm wet sponges, a chunk of faeces, or a nice piece of gefilte fish (chopped and stuffed fish). Another metaphor for a mass is a highly condensed bundle of burning candles, such that they melt into one, becoming a mass of hot wax, which is an image that is conveyed by the very etymology of the word 'fascist'.

A mass usually consists of a large number of people. However, as a criterion for the formation of a mass, density of population may be more important than size. A 'few' people in a small room may be sufficient for a massification process.

2. Aggregates and masses, like all social formations, are manifest in typical patterns of interaction, normation, and communication, and styles of thinking and feeling, and of leadership and followership. In effect, aggregates and masses can be described as bipolar syndromes of features of each of these dimensions of social formation. For example, with respect to interaction, the aggregate of disintegration contrasts with the mass of bureaucratisation or mechanisation; and with respect to normation, the aggregate of insolidarity

contrasts with the mass of fundamentalism. In other words, both disintegration and bureaucratisation or mechanisation contrast with the integration of
the well-functioning work group; similarly, both insolidarity and fundamentalism contrast with solidarity.

With respect to communication, it is important to consider two forms of
incoherence (Pines 1986). In social systems characterised by aggregation,
people wish to avoid the recognition of agency and responsibility, and
therefore they tend to communicate in euphemism and bureaucratise. In therapeutic groups aggregation is associated with profound silences, and with the
language of 'either/and' (Britton 1994). In contrast, in social systems characterised by massification, 'membership individuals' attempt to define their
identities by using cult-speak and by speaking in tongues; words and
catch-phrases have nuanced meaning only to the core-members of the group;
and communication is laden with references to their history, which must have
been shared in order for statements to be fully understood. In therapeutic
groups massification may also be associated with silence, but the members feel
that they are merged in such a way that mutual understanding does not require
words, and the ambiguity of non-verbal communication is preferred.
However, such silences are not so much non-verbal as anti-verbal, that is, the
non-verbal communication is used to attack and undermine verbal communication, which requires thought and shared rules of discourse.

3. A group of traumatised people and/or a traumatised group are likely to
oscillate between states of aggregation and of massification for several
reasons:

> (i) The state of aggregation is associated with a distinctive set of difficulties
> and aspects of annihilation anxiety. For example, aggregation generates
> ignorance and misunderstanding of norms, as well as inurement to them;
> and under extreme conditions, aggregation generates normlessness. When a
> group is characterised by ignorance and misunderstanding of the norms,
> inurement to the norms, and processes of normlessness, levels of normative
> expectations tend to rise higher than the levels of achievement with respect
> to objects that are valued as goals both compulsively and fetishistically. In
> other words, aggregation causes anomie, in which rankings and differences
> become a source of invidious comparison, power is not supported by
> authority, and administration becomes manipulative (Hopper 1981b).

> (ii) In an effort to escape from the problems associated with aggregation,
> people attempt to merge with a perfect group. They create an illusionary – if
> not hallucinatory – state of perfection, and they attempt to obliterate all
> flaws, impurities and differences. Unconsciously, the fundamental goal is

safety within the body of the group mother, and the group is experienced in terms of her. All aggression is sexualised, and the objects of aggression are projected into 'other' groups, who are then perceived as a source of pollution, and, therefore, repudiated. Massification is based on such processes as 'twinning' (Kohut and Wolf 1978), imitative identifications (Gaddini 1992), and pseudo-speciation (Erikson 1968). Group perfection requires either total submission to impersonal law and order or absolute equality and sameness. For people who cannot abide even one tall poppy, massification is very desirable.

(iii) The state of massification, however, is associated with its own distinctive set of difficulties and aspects of annihilation anxieties. For example, massification is always transitory and fragile. It is highly dependent on the maintenance of enchantment, and on the perfect fulfilment of its promise; yet, the larger the population of a massified social system, the more likely is it that a core group will become differentiated from peripheral groups, and that horizontal social distance will be transformed into hierarchy, which is inimical to the perpetuation of homogeneity. It is very difficult to accomplish complex tasks, which require flexible social organisation and the maintenance of enchantment, which, in turn, requires energy and the expenditure of scarce resources which do not violate the prevailing norms of distributive justice. It becomes virtually impossible to utilise the variety of skills and idiosyncrasies within the population in order to provide for the greater good of the whole. Helplessness within peripheral groups is likely to generate envy of core groups from whom the former feel excluded. Of course, people may also feel helpless with respect to the pseudo-cohesion of massification, and wish to prevent such 'coming together', but this is likely to be a secondary process. In any case, it cannot be understood only in terms of the unconscious impulse to spoil parental intercourse.

(iv) In order to protect against the difficulties and anxieties associated with massification, a social system shifts back towards the state of aggregation, and the original anxieties and difficulties re-emerge. And the entire process repeats itself. In the same way that traumatised people who are over-whelmed by their fear of annihilation are caught in incessant motion, without possibilities of resolution, incohesive social systems oscillate incessantly between states of aggregation and states of massification. These oscillations manifest motion and process, but no dynamic, dialectical movement. An incohesive social system is in a state of social paralysis or social stasis.

4. It is useful to think in terms of processes of social formation or development, and of social regression. For example, although a social mass can be transformed into an aggregate very quickly, and vice versa, it is a more difficult

and lengthy process for either an aggregate or a mass to become a group; nonetheless, a group can become like an aggregate or like a mass very easily and very quickly. Similarly, groups can become organisations, and organisations can become bureaucracies, and vice versa. However, a group that becomes an organisation is very different from a group that becomes like an organisation while remaining a group, in which case the group is likely to have regressed towards a state of aggregation, and not developed into a more complex social system.

It is important to understand the determinants and the consequences of social development and social regression. It is also important to remember that properties of persons should never be inferred to social systems, and vice versa. However, there is one exception to this golden rule of social science: when social systems are traumatised through the experience of failed dependency, which is associated with widespread and intense feelings of helplessness, and, to be precise, the fear of annihilation, social systems are likely to regress from the complex to the simple, that is, societies become like villages, villages become like families, organisations become like groups, and groups become like their members, and vice versa (Hopper 1994a, first published 1975). Thus, when traumatised, the properties of people may be inferred to their social systems, and vice versa.

5. As is the case with all basic assumptions, virtually by definition, incohesion prevents the development and the maintenance of the work group. Aggregation and massification are grotesque versions of processes of authentic diversity and unity that are necessary for the optimal cohesion of the work group. 'Heterogeneity' is sometimes used to refer to the optimal cohesion of the work group, but this concept is ambiguous, and stems from Turquet's brief discussion of the homogeneity of oneness in contrast to the heterogeneity of the optimal cohesion of the work group. For this reason, I refer to the 'cohesion' of the work group, and think in terms of high, low and optimal degrees of cohesion. Under conditions of optimal cohesion, the work group manifests a 'good' sense of humour, tolerance and respect for differences, including differences of opinion, a degree of disinterest that facilitates a scientific attitude towards data and techniques, etc. High morale and passionate commitment to the achievement of collective goals are possible, and not to be confused with the pseudo-morale of fundamentalism.

In small groups, especially in those who meet for the purpose of psychotherapy, it is possible to use interpretations of underlying anxieties and defences in order to facilitate the development of the work group. Obviously, in larger, more complex social systems, this is very difficult, if not impossible, although working with large groups within organisational settings can be very effective. It is beyond the scope of this inquiry to address the problem of work group development in complex social systems.

The personification of Incohesion: Aggregation/Massification

People who have been traumatised, have experienced the fear of annihilation, and who have developed protective encapsulations are likely not only to create processes of aggregation and massification, but also to be vulnerable to the constraints of roles associated with them. People who have experienced the fear of annihilation are desperate for the holding and containing provided by roles that offer an identity which can be substituted for the one that has been threatened, fragmented or even lost. Such roles are like new skin or new clothes; perhaps a costume and mask are an apposite metaphor. Neither personification nor personality is easily dichotomised, especially in connection with the variety of complex processes that comprise aggregation and massification.

1. It may be helpful to discuss the concept of personification of basic assumption processes, as opposed to the 'leadership' of work groups. 'Personification' is usually defined as a literary device in which an author uses in the course of his narrative the action and personality of a particular person in order to represent abstract qualities, principles and more general processes and problems in the sub-text of the work. However, the concept is apposite for the discussion of valence and role suction. After all, the 'narrative' mode is very important in group analysis and in some schools of psychoanalysis, in which maturation involves an increasingly accurate and truthful rendition of a life history, as well as an opening up of new and transcendent possibilities for the authorship of future chapters (Hopper 1998, 2001b). Personification emphasises the possibilities for the active interpretation of a role to which a person has a valence, or a heightened sensitivity to its suction. Personification implies that a role can be enacted with many individual idiosyncrasies, and that it permits a range of interpretations.

Personification is always a social and cultural process that involves the group as a whole, as well as the individual member of it. In fact, this is what we mean when we say that the individual and the group are two sides of the same coin, and that the individual is permeated through and through by social and cultural factors and forces, and vice versa.

Personification is largely unconscious. Although it is active, it is based on a complex mixture of projective and introjective identification, as well as other forms of externalisation and internalisation. Whether conscious or unconscious, active or passive, people with a particular pattern of anxiety and defence are most likely to personify those roles that are unconsciously constructed in association with particular basic assumption groups.

Related to personification are the concepts of 'figuration' and 'fractal'. Norbert Elias (1995) introduced the notion of figuration in order to describe the interlocking social, cultural and personal aspects of a particular pattern of action. A figuration can be analysed from various points of view and on many levels, ranging from the constraints of social facts, on the one hand, to the constraints of intra-psychic unconscious fantasy, on the other. This is especially important in the elucidation of the social unconscious (Gfaller 1996).

The concept of fractal is borrowed from the new information and computer sciences in which the discovery has been made that in many realms of the universe parts seem to manifest the same fundamental structures as their wholes, thus illustrating the old idea that the universe can be found in a grain of sand. When applied to the social and psychological domain, it is possible to think of a person and his intra-psychic life as being a fractal of his immediate group, which in turn can be seen as a fractal of the group's wider social context (Lawrence 1993; Scharff and Scharff 1998).

The focus on an individual person as a fractal or as a figuration is exactly that, a matter of focus. This is consistent with Bion's idea that binocular vision is necessary in attempts to understand group process, and with the emphasis given by Foulkes to maintaining the tension between figure and ground of the gestalt. Thus, in group analysis patients can be seen in terms of a figuration or a fractal of the group, on the basis of which it is not only entirely justifiable but also clinically appropriate to engage an individual patient within a group when the patient is regarded as personifying a particular process, which, in turn, may be a function of the matrix of the group or of the foundation matrix of the wider society in which the group exists (Foulkes 1968).

2. I will call attention to only a few aspects of the personification of aggregation and massification:

(i) In general, aggregation is personified by central persons who have developed crustacean, contact-shunning characters, and massification by those who have developed amoeboid, merger-hungry characters.

(ii) There are different kinds of charismatic leaders and of leadership, or, to be more precise, of personifiers and personification. Some types may be more stable than others, and some may even be able to take leadership roles. Other types may be especially vulnerable to the role suction of basic assumption processes. Some types may be split between a competent, rational self and an incompetent, irrational self, who may be depicted in terms of a particular combination of amoeboid, merger-hungry defences against autistic anxieties. I would also suggest that in complex situations both charismatic leaders and charismatic personifers may be prominent, and susceptible to particular patterns of collusion. In fact, it may be appropriate to identify 'charismatic followers' who are either primarily crustacean or primarily amoeboid in the ways that they protect themselves.

(iii) Aggregation and massification processes are also personified by people with particular kinds of perversions or perverse characters, based on the 'core complex', the distinguishing characteristic of which is the fear of annihilation (Glasser 1979). Although some kinds of perversions would seem to lend themselves to the personification of the cold and distant patterns of the alienated detachment of aggregation, other kinds of perversion are associated with the hot, clinging and virtually parasitical mergers of massification. These perversions are marked by the desire to subvert all 'natural' differences between the sexes and the generations, and the compulsion to confuse all that would 'ordinarily' be regarded as 'appropriately' separate (Chasseguet-Smirgel 1985), although 'natural' and 'appropriate' are matters for negotiation.

(iv) Some kinds of addicts can be seen to personify aggregation processes, and other types, massification processes. Partly this is related to the nature of the drug of choice and how it is used. For example, marijuana addicts tend to personify massification processes, but cocaine addicts, aggregation processes. It can be argued that heroin addicts also personify massification processes.

(v) The personification of aggregation and massification reflects a multi-generational cycle in which victims become perpetrators, and vice versa, and in which all of us collude as bystanders. Under such circumstances all 'innocence' is inauthentic. Those who have been treated as vermin become the persecutors of those whom they regard as vermin. The collusive creation of these roles, and the propensity to fill them, involves the recapitulation of early life experiences within the matrix of the family and its surrounding social groups, but it also reflects 'later' sources of the fear of annihilation, such as war, terrorist activities and high rates of unemployment, as does the entire traumatogenic process (Hopper 1995; de Zulueta 1993).

3. An exhaustive inventory of the roles and character types associated with the personification of Incohesion: Aggregation/Massification is yet to be made. Jungian analytical psychology offers many examples of the personification of basic assumption processes in terms of archetypes. More colloquially, the 'scientist' of aggregation might be compared with the 'magician' of massification. The characters of many great books and other works of art are especially illustrative. For example, in *Julius Caesar*, Cassius might be compared to Brutus, and both to Casca, who is the most easily overlooked of all of Shakespeare's characters; and in *The Tempest* Prospero, to his younger brother Alfredo. In the film *Viva Zapata*, Zapata was played by Marlon Brando as an amoeboid character who personified the massification process, and the Trotsky-like fellow traveller was played by Joseph Wiseman as a cold crustacean character who personified the aggregation process. In clinical group analysis, the alienated schizoid 'space cadets' and 'lone wolves' who personify states of aggregation can be contrasted with the 'cheerleaders' and 'morale boosters' of states of massification.

4. With regard to the leadership of the work group, I would argue, following the work of de Maré (1972), that the leaders of work groups are also able to take the role of 'citizen', and to give meaning to this role. (Hopper 1996, 2000). Of course, good followers, who are essential to the optimal cohesion of a work group, must also be good citizens. The group analyst must struggle to lead the work group, thereby giving patients the freedom to personify basic assumption groups and all their processes.

A summary of the theory of Incohesion: Aggregation/ Massification or Ba I:A/M as the fourth basic assumption in the unconscious life of groups and group-like social systems

I will now summarise my theory of the fourth basic assumption:

1. The fear of annihilation is rooted in traumatic experience, and envy arises as a defence against the shame and helplessness associated with it. The phenomenology of the fear of annihilation involves non-developmental oscillation between fission and fragmentation in the first instance, and fusion and confusion in the second. Each pole of the fear of annihilation is associated with its own distinctive anxieties, and the phenomenology of each pole functions as a defence against the anxieties associated with its opposite. The

main, overall defence against the fear of annihilation and its vicissitudes is encapsulation. The two main types of encapsulated character structure associated with the fear of annihilation and its phenomenology are crustacean and contact-shunning, on the one hand, and amoeboid and merger-hungry, on the other. Various kinds of addiction and perversion are also associated with these two kinds of encapsulated character structures.

2. As a defence against pain, the phenomenology of the fear of annihilation is projected into the external world, and manifest in patterns of interaction, normation and communication, as well as in styles of thinking and feeling and styles of leadership and followership. The manifestations within the external world of these projected processes comprise the fourth basic assumption in the unconscious life of groups and group-like social systems. I call the fourth basic assumption 'Incohesion: Aggregation/Massification' or 'I:A/M'. States of aggregation, on the one hand, and of massification, on the other, can be denoted in these terms. Incohesive social systems tend to oscillate between these bipolar states. Incohesion: aggregation/ massification (I:A/M) occurs in all groups of traumatised people, and in all traumatised groups and group-like social systems. Of course, ba I:A/M can be a transitory phenomenon, but its appearance always indicates that the group has been traumatised.

3. The roles associated with processes of Incohesion: Aggregation/ Massification are likely to be personified by traumatised, contact-shunning crustacean characters, and traumatised, merger-hungry amoeboid characters, the former being sucked into the roles that are typical of aggregation, and the latter, of massification. These patterns of personification are, therefore, typical of traumatised groups and group-like social systems. The personifiers of processes of incohesion should be distinguished from the leaders of work groups. However, some leaders are split in such a way that they may be both leaders and personifiers. Moreover, when groups are under the sway of basic assumption processes, both leaders and personifiers are likely to exist. With respect to processes of incohesion, a charismatic leader may evince amoeboid characteristics, but it is also possible that the charismatic leader will be associated with a number of crustacean and amoeboid personifiers. This is absolutely central to our clinical work with difficult patients, because they are likely to personify the roles that are generated by the processes of incohesion. This is also relevant to our understanding the problems of leadership and corruption in traumatised organisations and societies.

4. It is beyond the scope of this article to examine the fate of aggression within the context of I:A/M. However, it must be emphasised that aggression remains rampant, and is essential to both the instigation and the maintenance of massification processes. It is essential to purge all parts of the massification 'mother' that may prevent a merger with her, such as distracting smells, colours, textures and words, for example, the nipple rather the breast itself; especially important is the elimination of the father and any of his parts that are perceived to block access and merger, for example, his phallus, his rules and his manifestations in male siblings. Within the context of massification processes, the work group leader is especially vulnerable, as is anyone who is perceived to have maintained the idiosyncrasies of personal identity. Crustacean and amoeboid characters are likely to be both the perpetrators of aggression and the victims of aggression from others, partly because they remain unable to mourn their losses thoroughly and authentically. Thus, although traumatic experience is the source of the fourth basic assumption of incohesion: aggregation/massification, the fourth basic assumption is also a source of further traumatic experience, which is why the relationship is recursive.

Postscript

As a psychoanalyst and group analyst who was formerly a sociologist, I am pleased to acknowledge that my theory of Incohesion: Aggregation/ Massification as the fourth basic assumption in the unconscious life of groups and group-like social systems is based not only on the work of Bion, Turquet and Kernberg, but also on the work of S. H. Foulkes and his colleagues, including various members of the Group of Independent Psychoanalysts of the British Psychoanalytical Society and several European and American sociologists. I have tried to stand on the shoulders of giants, which is not merely a matter of intellectual acrobatics. However, it has not been easy to study and to appreciate the ideas associated with competing and rivalrous schools of thought, at least not within the context of the intellectual cultures of psychoanalysis within the Institute of Psycho-Analysis in London and of group analysis associated with the Institute of Group Analysis in London. Others must assess the strengths and weaknesses of my thesis, as can be seen in the discussions of the application of it to the treatment of difficult patients in group analysis (Hopper 2001c).

References

Alexander, F. (1942) *Our Age of Unreason.* Philadelphia: Lippincott.

Anzieu, D. (1981) *Le Groupe et l'Inconscient: L'Imaginaire Groupal.* Paris: Dunod.

Balint, M. (1968) *The Basic Fault: Therapeutic Aspects of Regression.* London: Tavistock.

Bednar, R. and Kaul, T. (1994) 'Experiential group research: Can the canon fire?' In A. Bergin and A. Garfield (eds) *Handbook of Psychotherapy and Behavior Change.* New York: Riley.

Bion , W. R. (1948–51) 'Experiences in groups: I-VII'. *Human Relations,* Vols. 1–4.

Bion, W. R. (1958) 'On hallucination'. *International Journal of Psycho-Analysis 39,* 144–146.

Bion, W. R. (1961) *Experiences in Groups and Other Papers.* London: Tavistock.

Bion, W. R. (1970) *Attention and Interpretation.* London: Tavistock.

Bion, W. R. (1977) 'Attention and interpretation.' In *Seven Servants.* New York: Jason Aronson. (Original work published 1970.)

Bion, W. R. (1978) *Bion in New York and Sao Paulo.* Perthshire: Clunie Press.

Britton, R. (1994) 'The blindness of the seeing eye: Inverse symmetry as a defence against reality.' *Psychoanalytical Inquiry 14,* 3, 365–78.

Brown, D. (1985) 'Bion and Foulkes: Basic assumptions and beyond.' In M. Pines (ed) *Bion and Group Psychotherapy.* London: Routledge and Kegan Paul.

Brown, D. (2001) 'A contribution to the understanding of the social unconscious'. *Group Analysis 34,* 1, 5–8.

Bychowski, G. (1948) *Dictators and Disciples from Caesar to Stalin.* New York: International Universities Press.

Chasseguet-Smirgel, J. (1985) *Creativity and the Perversions.* London: Free Association Books.

Coltart, N. (1989) 'Personal communication.' In J. Berke (ed) *The Tyranny of Malice Exploring the Dark Side of Character.* London: Simon and Schuster.

de Maré, P. (1972) *Perspectives in Group Psychotherapy.* London: Allen and Unwin.

de Zulueta, F. (1993) *From Pain to Violence: The Traumatic Roots of Destructiveness.* London: Whurr.

Elias, N. (1995) *The Civilizing Process.* Oxford: Blackwell.

Erikson, E. (1948) 'Hitler's imagery and German youth.' In C. Kluckhorn and H. Murray (eds) *Personality in Nature, Society and Culture.* New York: Knopf.

Erikson, E. (1968) *Identity, Youth and Crisis.* New York: Norton.

Foulkes, S.H. (1968) 'On interpretation in group analysis'. *International Journal of Group Psychotherapy 18,* 4, 432–44.

Freud, S. (1950) [1913] *Totem and Taboo.* Standard Edition 13. London: Hogarth Press. (Original work published 1913.)

Freud, S. (1955) [1921] *Group psychology and the analysis of the ego.* Standard Edition 18, 67–145. London: Hogarth Press. (Original work published 1921.)

Freud, S. (1961) [1931] *Libidinal types.* Standard Edition, 21: 215–220. London: Hogarth Press. (Original work published 1931.)

Gaddini, E. (1992) *A Psychoanalytic Theory of Infantile Experience.* A. Limentani (ed). London: Routledge.

Gfaller, G. R. (1996) 'Diskussion: Zum Aufsatz von Earl Hopper'. *Gruppenanalyse 6,* 1, 114–117.

Glasser, M. (1979) 'Some aspects of the role of aggression in the perversions.' In I. Rosen (ed), *Sexual Deviation*. Oxford: Oxford University Press.

Hopper, E. (1981a) 'A comment on Professor M. Jahoda's Individual and the Group.' In M. Pines and L. Rafaelsen (eds) *The Proceedings of the VII International Congress of Group Psychotherapy*. London: Plenum.

Hopper, E. (1981b) *Social Mobility: A Study of Social Control and Insatiability*. Oxford: Blackwell.

Hopper, E. (1985) 'The problem of context in group analytic psychotherapy: A clinical illustration and brief theoretical discussion.' In M. Pines (ed) *W. R. Bion and Group Psychotherapy*. London: Routledge and Kegan Paul. Reprinted in E. Hopper (2003) *The Social Unconscious: Selected papers*. London: Jessica Kingsley Publishers.

Hopper, E. (1991) 'Encapsulation as a defence against the fear of annihilation.' *The International Journal of Psycho-Analysis 72*, 4, 607–624.

Hopper, E. (1994a) 'A sociological view of large groups.' In L. Kreeger (ed) *The Large Group: Dynamics and Therapy*. London: Karnac Books. (Original work published 1975.) Reprinted in E. Hopper (2003) *The Social Unconscious: Selected papers*. London: Jessica Kingsley Publishers.

Hopper, E. (1994b) 'L'incapsulamento come difesa contro il timore di annientamento'. *Plexus... Lo spazio del gruppo*, September, 103–127.

Hopper, E. (1995) 'A psychoanalytical theory of drug addiction: Unconscious fantasies of homosexuality, compulsions and masturbation within the context of traumatogenic processes.' *International Journal of Psycho-Analysis, 76*, 6, 1121–1142.

Hopper, E. (1996) 'The social unconscious in clinical work.' *Group 20*, 1, 7–43, and in C. Oakley (ed) (2000) *What Is A Group?* London: Rebus Press. Reprinted in E. Hopper (2003) *The Social Unconscious: Selected papers*. London: Jessica Kingsley Publishers.

Hopper, E. (1997) 'Traumatic experience in the unconscious life of groups: A fourth basic assumption.' *Group Analysis 30*, 4, 439–470.

Hopper, E. (1998) 'On the nature of hope.' Keynote lecture at the Thirteenth Congress of Group Psychotherapy in London, available on cassette: QED Recording Services Ltd.

Hopper, E. (2000) 'From objects and subjects to citizens: Group analysis and the study of maturity.' *Group Analysis, 33*, 1, 29–34.

Hopper, E. (2001a) 'The social unconscious: Theoretical considerations.' *Group Analysis 34*, 1, 9–29.

Hopper, E. (2001b) 'On the nature of hope in psychoanalysis and group analysis.' *British Journal of Psychotherapy 18*, 2, 205–226. Reprinted in E. Hopper (2003) *The Social Unconscious: Selected papers*. London: Jessica Kingsley Publishers.

Hopper, E. (2001c) 'Difficult patients in group analysis: The personification of (ba) I:A/M'. *Group 25*, 3, 139–171.

Hopper, E. (2003) *Traumatic Experience in the Unconscious Life of Groups*. London: Jessica Kingsley Publishers.

Kellerman, H. (1981) *Group Cohesion*. New York: Grune & Stratton.

Kernberg, O. (1978) 'Leadership and organizational functioning: Organisational regression.' *International Journal of Group Psychotherapy, 28*, 1, 3–25.

Kernberg, O. (1998) *Ideology, Conflict, and Leadership in Groups and Organizations*. New Haven: Yale University Press.

Khaleelee, O., and Miller, E. (1985) 'Beyond the small group.' In M. Pines (ed) *Bion and Group Psychotherapy*. London: Routledge and Kegan Paul.

Klein, R. and Schermer, V. (2000) 'Introduction and overview: Creating a healing matrix.' In R. Klein and V. Schermer (eds) *Group Psychotherapy for Psychological Trauma*. New York: Guilford Publications, Inc.

Kohut, H. and Wolf, E. (1978) 'The disorders of the self and their treatment.' *International Journal of Psychoanalysis 59*, 414–425.

Lawrence, W. G. (1993) 'Signals of transcendence in large groups as systems.' *Group*, 17, 4, 254–266.

Lawrence, W. G., Bain, A. and Gould, L. (1996) 'The fifth basic assumption'. *Free Associations 6*, 1, 28–55.

Marziali, E., Munroe-Blum, H. and McLeary, L. (1997) 'The contribution of group cohesion and group alliance to the outcome of group psychotherapy.' *International Journal of Group Psychotherapy 47*, 4, 475–499.

Menzies-Lyth, I. E. P. (1981) 'Bion's contribution to thinking about groups.' In J. Grotstein (ed) *Do I Dare Disturb the Universe?* Beverley Hills: Caesura Press.

Pines, M. (1986) 'Coherency and disruption in the sense of the self.' *British Journal of Psychotherapy 2*, 3, 180–5.

Redl, F. (1942) 'Group emotion and leadership'. *Psychiatry*, 5, 573–596.

Roberts, J. and Pines, M. (eds) (1991) *The Practice of Group Analysis*. London: Tavistock/Routledge.

Rutan, S. and Stone, W. (2000) *Psychodynamic Group Psychotherapy*. Third edition. New York: Guilford.

Scharff, D. and Scharff, J. (1998) *Object Relations Individual Therapy*. London: Karnac Books.

Scheidlinger, S. (1952) *Psychoanalysis and Group Behavior*. New York: Norton.

Scheidlinger, S. (1980) *Psychoanalytic Group Dynamics*. Madison: International Universities Press.

Stock-Whitaker, D. and Lieberman, M. (1964) *Psychotherapy through the Group Process*. Chicago: Aldine.

Turquet, P. (1974) 'Leadership: The Individual and the Group.' In G. S. Gibbard *et al.* (eds) *Analysis of Group*. San Francisco: Jossey-Bass.

Turquet, P. (1994) 'Threats to identity in the large group.' In L. Kreeger (ed) *The Large Group: Dynamics and Therapy*. London: Karnac Books. (Original work published 1975.)

Tustin, F. (1981) *Autistic States in Children*. London: Routledge and Kegan Paul.

Winnicott, D. (1988) *The Maturational Process and the Facilitating Environment*. New York: International Universities Press.

Yalom, I. (1985) *The Theory and Practice of Group Psychotherapy*. New York: Basic Books.

9

Building on 'O'

Bion and Epistemology[1]

Victor L. Schermer

Psychoanalysis tells you nothing: it is an instrument, like the blind man's stick, that extends the power to gather information. (Bion, *Cogitations*, p.361)

We need to invent some form of articulate speech that could approximate to describing these realities, the phenomena that I cannot possibly describe. (Bion, *Cogitations*, p.369)

Introduction

I remember now that I reacted with puzzlement to my initial reading, (around 1980, at the suggestion of a revered teacher, Dr Gunther Abraham) of Bion's (1977) *Two Papers: The Grid and Caesura*. Frankly, I felt as if I had read an archaeological text written in another language. Now, when I look back, I see that Bion's seminal essays on the psychoanalytic process were difficult to decipher partly on account of the richness of his ideas and partly because Bion often wrote in myths and metaphors mixed with seemingly abstruse or esoteric remarks, and with a minimum of explanatory discourse. Nevertheless, it gradually became impressed on me – as on many others – that his was a brilliant mind striving to grasp the very foundations of psychoanalysis.

Bion frequently wrote and lectured in a form of discourse derived from free association, the modern theater,[2] and the literary and poetic use of metaphor and myth. The term 'primary process Socratic dialogue' is perhaps an apt description of some of Bion's writing and lecturing – he means for us to question our cherished beliefs without quite stating it that way, for example when, in one of his *Brazilian Lectures* (1990b, p.35), he has a cup in his hand, and says, 'What would be the interpretation of this cup?' (Of course, the audience response is silence!) In a previous paper (Schermer 1999), I suggested that unconscious processes cannot be described *per se*, but rather we 'point to them' with metaphors and myths, as Freud did with Oedipus. Such was often Bion's way.

If he had merely been an astute clinician and synthesizer, Bion's clinical conceptualizations alone (see Symington and Symington 1996, for a thorough discussion of the application of, for example, Bion's concepts of attacks on linking, bizarre objects, the use of the Grid, container/contained, and catastrophic transformation) would have earned him a place as a significant follower of Freud and Klein. However, many now consider Bion to be one of the great innovators in the history of psychoanalysis (cf. Meltzer 1978; Grotstein 1981; Bléandonu 1994). Since Bion was not a prolific writer and sired no 'Bionic' school of thought, and since his writing is sometimes suggestive and generative rather than lucid and clarifying, it is legitimate to ask what earned him his stature as a great psychoanalytic pioneer.

The answer, for me at least, is that Bion had an uncanny ability to return to the basics and thereby to open up the field to new possibilities. Bion's questions are more important than his answers. For him, this volume ought better be called, not *Building on Bion* (he might even ask us, who is this Bion? thus separating the thinker from the thoughts), but, borrowing from one of his favorite phrases of Milton, *Building on 'the void and formless infinite'*. Bion's quest for the roots of psychoanalytic knowing made him first and foremost an epistemologist, one who asks persistently, deeply, with an admixture of skepticism and faith, 'What is the nature of knowledge? What is its subject matter? How do we know what we know? What are the limits of our knowing?' Bion correctly perceived the central epistemological problem posed by psychoanalysis: 'How can we know the *un*-conscious, that is how can we know that which – paradoxically – we do not or cannot know?' Freud (1954; 1895) struggled profoundly with this problem early in his career. Melanie Klein took it for granted that Freud had solved it via the instinct theory, and her penetrating analyses of pre-verbal and psychotic experience implied – at least for the initiated – a ready accessibility to the deepest layers. Bion, both utilizing and reacting to Ms Klein, revived the centrality of the problem of unconscious knowing, and tackled it from a different angle than before.

As for his intellectual credentials for such a task, we know that Bion was Oxford educated and exceptionally well read, especially in mathematics and philosophy, which were among his lifelong interests. *Cogitations* (Bion 1992), a compilation of Bion's notes, is laced with references to philosophers, including, among others, from the ancient Greco-Roman period: Theocritus; from the Enlightenment: Berkeley, Hume, Descartes, Kant; from the late nineteenth century: Bradley (who also had a great impact on the poet T. S. Eliot), Pierce (who influenced the psychologist William James), Pritchard; among the positivists and neo-positivists: Quine, Whitehead, Russell; and an assorted array of others: Buber, Heisenberg, Niebuhr, Teilhard de Chardin, Toynbee. In his seminal essay *Attention and Interpretation* (1970, p.130), Bion provides a reference to the mathematician, Gottlob Frege, a founder of modern mathematical logic, and in other places to the mystics Meister Eckhart (pp.88, 115) and Isaac Luria (p.115). Thus, this remarkable work moves with fluidity between realms of thought usually considered alien to one another. His daughter, Nicola Bion, tells us (personal communication, Bion97 listserv, June 2000) that he frequently read the Hindu spiritual text, the *Mahabarata*. Thus, he was interested in both logical rigor and the mysterious 'Other' that is beyond logic. Bion had a thirst for knowing about knowing, whether from philosophical, scientific, literary, artistic, or esoteric spiritual sources.

In particular, Bion possessed a great interest in the work of the philosopher Immanuel Kant. Bion's wife and editor, Francesca Bion (personal communication, June 21 2000) states that Bion had contact while at Oxford with the Kantian scholar, H. J. Paton, owned several of Paton's books, and had conversations with him. The interaction with Paton and his work may have served as a stimulus for his interest in Kant.

The Kantian epistemological vertex which Bion chose for his conceptual underpinning was unique for a tumultuous twentieth century which questioned everything enduring and requiring faith. It was that of the 'thing-in-itself,' an extension and variant of Plato's 'ideal forms,' the objects in the famous cave analogy, illuminated by a candle, and whose shadows we see on the wall. For Bion to choose the Kantian premise of an unseen, non-sensory reality (which according to Sandler 2000 is implicit in Freud despite his allegiance to the anti-Kantian 'empiricist' stance of Helmholtz) was to go against the prevailing temper of his time. In most of the twentieth century, empiricism, in the form of behaviorism, was the prevailing approach in the social sciences. Beyond that, phenomenology (which emphasizes experience as such, not an underlying 'reality'), as incorporated in the study of perception and interpersonal meanings (Merleau-Ponty 1945) and later in intersubjective theory (Stolorow, Atwood and Brandchaft 1994), and structuralism (De George and De George1972) (which does imply pre-given schema, while not fully committing to a philosophical stance such as idealism) were significant outlooks. Bion, radical aristocrat that he was, went against the *Zeitgeist* and adopted a traditional, even noble, vantage point which in his own time was iconoclastic. This served to stir up the psychoanalytic establishment and raise a host of questions about the nature of the human mind and the way in which it is approached in both the psychoanalytic and group contexts.

However, no single epistemological stance, even that of Kant, could fully satisfy Bion's requirements. As I will try to show, certain limitations of a Kantian point of view led Bion to go beyond its confines. As previously mentioned, he was well read in and utilized the ideas of the 'logical positivists' such as Russell, Whitehead, Wittgenstein and Popper, even though they were sharply critical of Kant. Bion used their ideas more as a way of clarifying the psychoanalytic method and, so to speak, emptying the analytic container to make it accessible to new awareness, than as a philosophical position as such. The positivists also mirrored Bion's interest in mathematics, logic and language, which is manifest in the Grid and the concept of 'transformations', for example. At the other end of the spectrum, Bion used the great mystics – Eastern and Western – to link the notions of 'thing-in-itself' and inner trans-formation in a striking way whereby, for example, to know oneself and the patient is also to change, so much so that the two are virtually inseparable.

In what follows, I hope to suggest some of the roots of Bion's perspective in the three vertices of the 'thing in itself,' logical positivism, and mysticism. Next, I will discuss how such understanding applies to a) psychoanalytic listening; and b) groups. With respect to the latter, many do not realize that Bion had two related but distinct group theories: that of the basic assump-tions, put forth in *Experiences in Groups*, and that of the relationship between the 'messiah' (mystic, genius) and the establishment, developed in *Attention and Interpretation* (1970, pp.112–13). I will suggest that Bion's basic assumption theory comes into sharper focus when one considers his own epistemological assumptions. Finally, I will discuss how Bion incorporated, but also went well beyond, Freud and Klein conceptually, based on an epistemological under-standing.

The three epistemic vertices

The Kantian 'thing in itself' or 'noumenon'

What distinguishes Bion's theorizing from that of his predecessors is his explicit use of the Kantian 'thing-in-itself' or 'noumenon' as a way of speaking about unconscious processes. Freud was well-versed in Kantian thought, as were most students of his day, but, in keeping with the medical establishment of his time, as put forth by his mentor and laboratory instructor, Brucke (Amacher 1965), he adopted the stance of the great physicist and physiologist, Helmholtz, which was in turn based in the empiricist philosophy of Hume and others. To put it simply, the empiricist position states that science is interested in observable phenomena, particularly of repeated or replicable events, such as are seen in a scientific experiment, where, under certain conditions, certain results follow. Kant held, on the other hand, that our perception of events is profoundly conditioned by our cognitions, by certain of our intuited axioms, which he called synthetic a priori propositions, which could also be roughly translated to mean our convictions about ultimate reality. Thus, for example, Hume's repeated observable events or 'constant conjunctions' occur within, indeed require, a matrix of time and space, 'categories' which Kant held were inherent in our thought processes.[3] Thus Bion was not merely interested in observable regularities, but in the 'invariants' (Bléandonu 1994, p.196) that underlie transformation and change and which bring us closer to the underlying Platonic forms or Kant's noumena.

The 'thing-in-itself' is synonymous in Kant with the 'noumenon,' which Allison (1983, p.350, note 20) defines as 'the object of a nonsensible[4] cognition. Such an object, however, could be either one that cannot be represented sensibly at all, such as God, or an object that is identical with a sensible object (phenomenon) but is known in a nonsensible manner (as it is in itself).' Bion incorporated both of these types: (a) that which is essentially unknowable, in his notion of 'O', and (b) 'that which is known as it is in itself' he called 'beta elements' which are, in a certain respect, derivatives of the specific non-sensory 'things-in-themselves' that affect our subjectivity and our consciousness. Since the latter conceptualization evolved earlier in Bion's thinking than the former, I will discuss the notion of specific, non-sensory 'things-in-themselves' first, especially as there is a common confusion about it which I wish to clear up. It also will be appropriate in that context to discuss how Bion made use of logical positivist formulations, just as a discussion of 'O' necessitates referring to the mystical or religious 'vertex'.

BETA ELEMENTS: THOUGHTS WITHOUT A THINKER

Bion's application of a Kantian formulation of the 'thing-in-itself' began with his attempt to understand the most primitive mental processes. He noticed that while some experiences of patients in analysis had the qualities of dreams and dream-like states, which could be thought about and explored, others seemed to exist in unmetabolized form that could not be 'thought about.' Hallucinations, thought fragments, and 'bizarre objects' which result from the coming together of random elements following a mental catastrophe, are inaccessible to the 'thinker.' They are sensory elements without a cognitive, subjective, emotional net to contain and utilize them. Bion called them 'beta elements' and differentiated them from 'alpha elements,' already-contained images and representations which could be the subject of thought, elaboration, and discourse. Bion in this way subdivided Freud's 'primary process thinking' into subcategories, including alpha and beta elements, as well as, in addition, dreams, myths, and other combinations of alpha elements. In and of itself, this subclassification of primary process was a major addition to theory and has had great clinical utility in helping analysts to differentiate between psychotic and non-psychotic presentations. Hanna Segal (1981) is one who has had a special interest in this area.

Despite their import in understanding psychotic and borderline process, there is some confusion about beta elements stemming from Bion's own discussions, and partly from Bion's interpreters (cf. Bléandonu 1994 p.152; Symington and Symington 1996, pp.59–72). The problem is whether beta elements are perceptible phenomena or non-sensible 'noumena', things-in-themselves. In places (Bion 1992 p.181), Bion describes them as 'unassimilated sense impressions,' such as a twinge of stomach pain or an hallucinatory figure. Elsewhere, he refers to them as unknowable 'things-in-themselves' (Bion 1970, p.11). This latter depiction suggests that he believed they were non-sensory noumena.

Since beta elements are experienced in the sensory realm – and who can deny the sensory power of an hallucination, or of a burst of pain, for example? – they are not, as Bion implied, things-in-themselves, but rather sensory phenomena. They are not noumena, as Kant would define this term. Beta elements do, however, have a 'thing-like' quality, that is, they seem to be outside the influence of our subjectivity and mentation – they merely present themselves, just as chairs and tables do. In this respect, they are believable stand-ins for things-in-themselves, and we are easily, perhaps delusionally, convinced of their 'reality.'

As Sandler puts it:

> 'I think that it is very clear in Bion's texts that beta elements are sensory stimuli – inner and outer, including feelings. The dilemma according to Bion is that the person feels that he or she has "caught" the beta-elements as if they were things in themselves and now understands them wholly. The person feels as if he or she has attained absolute truth, and now "owns" noumena, knows them.' (Sandler, personal communication, 23 January 2001)

This convincing quality of beta leads us easily to assume that they are things-in-themselves, or noumena. Such a belief also arises from a semantic confusion which is well understood by Allison (1983) with respect to Kant's philosophy, namely, that, for Kant, things-in-themselves are not the objects of our perception, like a chair or a table, but represent that transcendent otherness which conditions and affects perceptions, but is never known to us.

Thus, while it could be said that beta elements are 'thoughts without a thinker,' (in contradistinction to dreams, which, as Grotstein (2000, pp.1–36) emphasizes, are the products of very deep cognitions), they are not 'things-in-themselves' in the Kantian sense of 'noumena.' Indeed, 'things-in-themselves' are not 'things' or objects at all, but that which we assert to be the non-sensory 'actuality' which is inferred through intuition or analysis. As I will try to suggest, it is not the sensory beta elements, but the non-sensory noumena which the psychoanalyst is trying to access, and this requires, as Bion (Bion 1970, pp.31–33, 41–54) has said, the suspension of memory and desire. Parenthetically it is precisely the difficulty distinguishing sense impressions from noumena which haunts the psychotic patient.

Bion did, however, recognize that beta elements are in some way 'very close to' the noumena which condition our sensory experience. Thus, for example, a twinge of stomach discomfort in the analyst might signal an important aspect of the transference–countertransference which is not yet accessible in any other way. A patient's hallucination of a dead parent, while in itself delusional, could represent an emotionally powerful, unresolved linkage or bond between them. The present author likes to think of beta elements as 'messengers' from things-in-themselves, albeit in a raw, unmetabolized form. What Bion called 'alpha function' or 'alphabetization' provides a mental container for these messages.

'O': THE ARCHETYPAL UNCONSCIOUS OR UNKNOWABLE OTHERNESS

Partly to address this problem, and partly because of basic changes in his thinking, Bion introduced an additional symbol to represent noumena. 'O' is the thing-in-itself in the second meaning of Kant: as that which is totally unknowable as it is in itself, but only 'known about.' When Bion discusses 'O' (Bion 1970, pp.26, 30), he is referring to a totally 'other' which differs in this way from 'K', cognitive knowledge. For example, the analyst might have a 'K link' with the patient as he develops a 'definitory hypothesis' about the patient's real and fantasied relationship to his parents. However, 'O' would be manifest in the shifting and evolving emotional state of the patient in the immediacy of the session. 'O' could impact upon the analyst, but is never fully assimilated in cognition. Bion came to believe that these 'transformations in O' were the real substance of psychoanalysis, the 'tiger' we might eventually encounter, so that, while today psychoanalysis is just one of the tiger's stripes, 'Ultimately it may meet the Tiger – The Thing Itself – O.' (Bion 1990a; Eigen 1998, opening quotes.)

Eventually, 'O' led Bion to a religious/mystical vertex which, however, must be carefully distinguished from any particular system and from mysticism and/or concepts of a higher Self which have supernatural connotations. Grotstein (2000, pp.219–304) has made this vertex as Bion saw it somewhat more explicit and elaborated it differently from Bion in terms of 'O' as a higher seat of awareness that he (Grotstein) calls the 'ineffable subject.' O is consistent with Kant's understanding of noumena and does not require a mystical vertex, but mysticism played such a significant role in Bion's later thinking, that we will discuss it further after exploring the role of logical positivism for him.

Modern philosophy of science: Logical positivism

Logical positivism is a modern movement in philosophy whose avowed goal has been to demonstrate that all meaningful propositions consist of nothing more than combinations of logic and sense data. It emerged as a coherent vantage point in early twentieth-century Vienna under the aegis of Moritz Schlick and others, and led to the work of Bertrand Russell, Ludwig Wittgenstein, Alfred North Whitehead, Karl Popper, and Rudolph Carnap, W.V.O. Quine, and many others.

It is of interest that Bion extensively studied the logical positivists and their successors and in fact had some personal contact with Bertrand Russell (Sandler, personal communication, 10 February 2001). He used their principles and ideas, and yet never, as far as the present writer can tell, addressed two of the major agendas of the positivists.

The first of these was their 'rallying cry' critique of Kant. The positivists held that metaphysical concepts, such as 'the thing-in-itself,' were neither logical nor empirical/sensory, hence could be assigned neither a meaning nor a 'truth value.' In particular, they made a devastating criticism of Kant's notion of 'synthetic a priori propositions.' These are statements which we know to be true not because they are logically provable or the result of experience, but because they reflect the nature of our cognitive nets; they must be true because we can't conceive of reality otherwise. The problem, of course, is that many such propositions, like the axioms of Euclidian geometry, have been shown to be arbitrary statements which could be easily replaced. The positivists correctly questioned Kant's implicit absolutism, but in doing so they rejected the entire notion of noumena, a notion which does not per se require an assumption of absolute metaphysical knowledge.

The second agenda which Bion seldom if ever discussed is the positivists' discovery of and attempts to resolve the problem of contradiction and paradox inherent in what might appear to be 'airtight' systems of thought. The famous paradox of Russell, 'Is the class of all possible classes which are not members of themselves a member of itself?' (if it is a member of itself, then it isn't, and vice-versa!), raised questions about Frege's attempt to show that mathematics was derivable from logic. Russell's resolution of the paradox by assigning different levels of classes, enabled him to extend Frege's thinking to help a symbolic logic that is today a part of the Western mathematico-scientific heritage. Godel's incompleteness theorem similarly proved that any logical system will have demonstrable contradictions. It is curious that Bion never came to grips with this problem, even though it raises serious questions about the validity of algebraic systems, which he sought with fervor to institute in psychoanalysis.

Bion chose to borrow from the positivists that which was useful without committing to their stance. Like them, he sought a clarity and universality of concepts. He was fascinated with the idea of logical and mathematical notation, and in his discussion of 'transformations' utilized Frege's concept of 'functions' which includes a constant and a variable (Bion 1990b, p.12). According to Bion, when the analyst identifies that which is constant in a session and that which has changed, he can begin to describe the type of transformation which has occurred in the patient, the analyst, and their inter-action (Bléandonu 1994, pp.196–202).

Bion, like the pioneering positivist, Ludwig Wittgenstein, had a preoccupation with the fallacies of language. He believed (Bion 1990b, p.13) that psychoanalysis had discovered a new language that would take centuries (!) to elucidate, and that everyday language merely masked this other level of communication. Like Wittgenstein (1953, 1961), he was acutely aware that language might take us down false paths and cul-de-sacs. Therefore, like some of the positivists, he sought to utilize an 'algebraic notation' (Bléandonu 1994, pp.160–162) to reduce the impact of language fallacies and illusions on psychoanalytic work. Thus, for example, human beings have many preconceived notions of what love is, but if we use the unsaturated letter 'L' instead of the word 'love', then we can use 'L' to refer to a generic bond or link, without pre-judging what that link might be. In this way, we can stay open to what we might learn, rather than project the preconceptions inherent in our language into the freshly arising emanations in the consulting room.

The culmination of Bion's search for a logico-mathematical base for psychoanalysis was the Grid.

	Definitory hypotheses 1	ψ 2	Notation 3	Attention 4	Inquiry 5	Action 6	...n.
A β-elements	A1	A2				A6	
B α-elements	B1	B2	B3	B4	B5	B6	...Bn
C Dream thoughts, dreams, myths	C1	C2	C3	C4	C5	C6	...Cn
D Pre-conception	D1	D2	D3	D4	D5	D6	...Dn
E Conception	E1	E2	E3	E4	E5	E6	...En
F Concept	F1	F2	F3	F4	F5	F6	...Fn
G Scientific deductive system		G2					
H Algebraic calculus							

Figure 9.1 Bion's Grid

He put forth the Grid as a way to classify and notate the events of a psychoanalytic session. However, the Grid also seems to have a deeper meaning, almost as if it is a symbol of an essence that Bion is seeking. The clues to this essence are (a) the organization of the Grid in the manner of the Cartesian system of coordinates; (b) the 'psi' function, denoted by Column II of the Grid, as the non-truth, which bears a resemblance to 'resistance/ counter-resistance;' and (c) the rows, each in a container/contained relation to the one above and below it, and representing the most primitive mental processes to the most abstract. Here is the 'mind's eye' as it were, in a contemporary grid-like and mathematical format.

The matrix of the Grid represents Bion's faith in the hypothetico-deductive system and the logical and mathematical nature of theory formation. A matrix also suggests infinite extensibility and divisibility of its categories, and Bion felt he was giving a bird's-eye view that could be further elaborated and detailed. For example, he says that each row is infinitely divisible (Bion 1990b, pp.41–42). This suggests that he eventually conceived of the Grid not just as a method for recording psychoanalytic sessions, but also as a way of operationalizing psychoanalytic process in a way consistent with modern science while retaining the Kantian emphasis on the noumenon and its cognitive 'net' in movement from beta elements on up to algebraic notation.

With *Attention and Interpretation*, Bion started out with a discussion of the scientific model, sensuous and non-sensory aspects of thinking, and the Grid, but quickly introduced a decidedly mystical element, explicitly referring to mystics with respect to self-transformation, and to 'messiah thoughts' in connection with the relationship between the genius and the establishment (Bion 1970, pp.112–114). One question that can be asked is whether the mysticism which pervaded his thinking thereafter is consistent with Bion's previous thinking, or whether it offers an entirely new perspective.

Mysticism

There came a point (perhaps, in real time, more like a 'line' of evolution, to use Bion's own geometrical terminology) where Bion's thinking underwent a shift away from logical and mathematical analysis, towards the opposite end of the spectrum: mysticism. On various occasions, he acknowledged that his project of operationalizing psychoanalysis in a scientific notation was premature and, at best, incomplete (Bléandonu 1994, pp.141–142). Then, in *Attention and Interpretation*, he explicitly used a mystical and religious vertex to develop his understanding of the listening process and of the group. While retaining the Kantian noumenon and algebraic notation as starting points, he redefined the noumenon from a different vertex, namely, the mystical tradition. He defines O, the 'thing-in-itself,' now not so much as reified entities or beta elements but as 'the ultimate reality represented by such terms as ultimate reality, absolute truth, the godhead, the infinite, the thing-in-itself' (Bion 1970, p.26). He emphasizes the unknowability of O, giving it a quality of mystery and indescribability, experienced, when encountered, with terror and awe. K links (knowledge, so central to both Kant and the postivists) are no longer the issue; one must *be* and *become* O, a process which creates an evolution in both analyst and patient. This is no longer the Enlightenment philosopher Kant speaking through Bion. It is now the mystics, such as Meister Eckhart and Isaac Luria, to whom Bion refers. It is even possible to argue, as Grotstein (1997) has hinted, that Bion here echoes the existential philosopher Martin Heidegger (1927) in now placing existence before essence, being before ideas.

Mysticism and philosophical idealism have been historically connected, beginning with Plato or before. Plato was influenced by the Eleusinian mystery rites (Kuhn 2001), in particular as regards the duality of mind and body, and Platonic philosophy much later influenced Christian mystics (Turner 1911). Idealists and mystics are both interested in 'essence', idealism in the essence of thoughts divested of misleading sensory distortions and connotations; and mysticism, with the essence of a soul and of a Higher Being. The Freud/Klein/British Independent legacy self-consciously avoided reference to the mystical dimension, partly on account of the agenda to explain the more complex in terms of the simple; later development as a consequence of the earlier; higher sublimations in terms of the primitive drives. Suddenly, Bion overturned all this by presenting himself as a mystic. Why?

It would seem that Bion had become aware of the aspect of the infinite, the spontaneous, the chaotic and the creative aspects of the unconscious. We can speculate that there were various influences that may have impacted upon him: Marion Milner's (1957, 1987) suggestion of a mystical aspect of creativity; Bion's own reading of mystical texts; his contacts with psychoanalysts in Los Angeles, Brazil, and elsewhere, where the cultural matrix was shifting towards spirituality; Matte Blanco's (1975) ideas about the unconscious as infinite sets.

Thus, while never relinquishing the logico-mathematical structure of the Grid, Bion came to address the dimension of the 'void and formless infinite' as an energy and a source of change. Unlike Matte-Blanco (1975), who tried to grasp the infinitude of the unconscious in terms of a multi-valued symmetrical logic, borrowing heavily from Bertrand Russell, Bion embraced a larger view in which O is not reducible to logic (K), and is experienced in transformation rather than cognition.

In so doing, Bion opened the door to psychoanalytic and group dynamic discussions and explorations that go well beyond Kant, Bion's own prior formulations, and the province of psychodynamic thinking up to that point. It wasn't that he moved into the realm of supernatural phenomena – nowhere in his writing does he advocate such a position. Rather, he expanded the capability of the 'container' to allow for rich creativity and spontaneity, infinitude, and deep complexity. In this respect, he was perceiving mystical and spiritual texts as depictions of infinite containment experiences, and encouraging the psychoanalytic and group communities to consider spirituality as a vertex from which to achieve a deeper awareness of the psyche and the community. Bion thus paved the way for clinicians such as Nina Coltart (1992), William Meissner (1995), Mark Epstein (1996, 1998), Michael Eigen (1998) and James Grotstein (2000), all with traditional backgrounds, to write daringly and in depth about the spiritual dimension of psychoanalysis. In that respect, he moved from being a philosopher/scientist to a 'messiah' who revitalized the sacredness of the 'I–Thou' relationship of analyst and patient (Schermer 2001).

The listening process

Bion had a unique view of the psychoanalytic (and by extension, group leader) listening process. He held that the analyst should listen 'in the absence of memory and desire.'[5] Many have found this to be a cryptic statement, and/or one suggesting that the analyst is a latter-day swami. While it does have a mystical significance, the notion of emptying the mind of interference is not new to psychoanalysis. In the psychoanalytic literature, there are three distinct concepts of how to listen to a patient's associations: hovering attention (Freud 1913, pp.109–120), empathy (Kohut 1977, pp.249–266), and Bion's. A comparison of these notions is both interesting and useful, and has not been thoroughly discussed, so far as I know.

'Hovering attention' was defined by Freud (1913, pp.109–120) as evenly suspended listening without particular focus and which gives equal notice to each and every verbal association and non-verbal communication from the patient, in order to pick up the intrusion of the unconscious into the linear surface flow of the ego. Slips of the tongue, pauses, imagery, and so on, which are ordinarily tuned out in an attempt to understand the surface flow of linear communication, can then be detected by the analyst. Reik (1948) extended the scope of hovering attention to the analyst's own fleeting thoughts, fantasies, and emotions. These, too, may provide useful data about what is going on in the patient in terms of how it impacts on the analyst. Reik was thus one of the first to see that countertransference could be clinically useful, not merely an interference. Bion's 'absence of memory, desire' appears to contradict both Freud and Reik. He seems to be saying 'have no mind,' which both Freud and Reik would have considered an impossibility. We will return to this difference later.

Kohut (1977) and Wolf (1988, pp.20–21) introduced a different emphasis to the listening process. While he did not contradict Freud, Kohut implied a particular kind of focus and processing of data geared to the treatment of narcissistic personality disorder. Like Bion, he was acutely aware of how analysts could introduce cognitive bias into sessions, thus making their interpretations 'experience distant,' out of reach of the patient. Kohut advocated 'empathy' as the therapeutic mode of listening, and defined it as a steadfast process of immersing oneself in the patient's state of mind. Stolorow (Stolorow, Atwood and Brandchaft 1994) agreed with Kohut's phenomenological orientation as implied by empathic introspection. By focusing on the patient's experience, Kohut strove not only to describe the patient's inner world more accurately , but also to convey healing factors of emotional availability and attunedness to the patient, which could help mend his or her narcissistic wounds (Wolf 1988, pp.94-123).

Hovering attention and empathy seem sufficiently useful ways of hearing and being present for the patient, so why would Bion suggest a more demanding and, at first glance, esoteric way of listening? And, indeed, is the absence of memory and desire really listening, in any sense of the term?

Again, the epistemological underpinnings of these analysts is useful in grasping their purpose. Freud, at least consciously, was a laboratory-trained empiricist. He saw the analyst as a neutral, detached observer. Hovering attention is akin to the process a microbiologist might apply to looking at a slide. Without prejudging, he waits to see what patterns form in his mind's eye. Thus, he may see a spot or a line that is not obvious from the surface features of the slide preparation. This is a process which is both creative – may lead to new data and understanding – and sharp – attuning the observer to subtleties not ordinarily noticed.

For Bion, such a process was, I think, necessary but not sufficient. For him the analyst must not only see sharply with the senses, but must seek to grasp the noumenon, that which is not perceptible by the sense organs. Since the noumenon is *beyond* the sensory realm, any sensory or empirical input blinds the analyst's intuition of the deep unconscious events unfolding in the session. To 'see' these transformations ('see' = recognition of the truth), it is necessary to use a higher intuitive faculty.

In the work of Kant, one finds references to the intuitive type of knowing. It would take several books and years of studies fully to elucidate what Kant was saying in these writings (which is one reason why the positivists so easily dismiss him as a 'metaphysician'!). In simple terms, one could think of it as that which one comes to when one has eliminated one's preconceptions and a new formulation emerges. Kant and Bion were in agreement that genuine knowledge is arrived at through intuition, not through the senses.

It should be remembered that Bion was especially interested in psychotic processes. Those who work with psychotics know that the real significance of psychotic communications is only remotely related to what is verbalized. The present author conducted an initial interview with a patient who presented as reasonably intact and communicated in a quasi-normal way. Halfway into the session, he realized that the patient was putting him in a trance, and some further inquiry revealed that the patient was hallucinating and delusional. Psychotic mechanisms often present themselves as 'presences' rather than ideas and words as such. The listening attitudes that might be sufficient for more integrated individuals, such as hovering attention and empathy, probably do little to access the meanings of events in the psychotic realm.

Bion's dictum of listening 'in the absence of memory, desire, and understanding' does, however, present problems. For instance, nowhere does he say how one accomplishes it. The mind is ordinarily bombarded by sensory and cognitive input. Should the student study meditation before becoming an analyst? Does the student utter an incantation to whisk away sensory interference? Whereas Kant sought very deliberately to elucidate how the noumenon could be known, and the limits of how it could be known, Bion did not go very far to explain how such radical listening could be done. Furthermore, Dr. Howard Kibel (personal communication, 19 February 2000) raised the interesting question of how one could effectively 'listen' to a patient while blotting out sense messages. Who or what is listening, and to what? We can only surmise that Bion meant that the analyst does receive sensory input from the patient, but his mental function temporarily blinds itself while intuiting the patient's O. And certainly, he meant that extraneous sensory and mnemonic input such as the ringing of a telephone, or the recollection of a business appointment would be significantly diminished as the analyst applied his full concentration on the patient's communication.

That he was aware that accessing O is problematical is evident from his contending that the analyst does not actually *know* the noumenon, but *becomes* it (Bion 1970, pp.26–27). So we have the idea that what he is talking about is a state of heightened *receptivity* as a container, resembling the mother's reverie which gives her increased access to what is going on in her infant. This perhaps brings him somewhat closer to Kohut's phenomenologically based empathy. When the analyst is listening to O, he is highly attuned to the patient's inner state, but for Bion such attunement serves not so much to reflect it back to the patient as to intuit something that up until that moment has been inaccessible to both of them. Bion's emphasis on becoming O also bears a resemblance to Heidegger's philosophy in which existence (being) precedes essence (noumena), a point which has been made by Grotstein with respect to Heidegger's 'transcendent function' of 'becoming one with our *aliveness*...or with our very *being-ness* (our Dasein...)' Grotstein 2000, p.300). In other words, it is not so much 'what we know' (knowledge) as 'how we are alive' (being) which is decisive. In actual practice, hovering attention, empathy, and the absence of memory, desire, and understanding are three aspects of maternal reverie, which of course also occurs in the creative process.

It is difficult to reconcile Bion's notion of listening in the absence of memory, desire and understanding, whereby the analyst himself undergoes a transformation in O with the patient, and his agenda of developing a rigorous scientific schema for psychoanalysis. In transformation, the analyst is no longer a detached, objective observer, but rather one who is immersed in a process which he may never understand. The only way that I can presently see to try to bring the two together is to consider that the in-the-moment trans-formation of being and the truth value as intuited might somehow later be reflected upon, and that systematically relating these experiences to observable data could provide a basis for formulating models and theories and making predictions at the more 'surface' level. This process could be compared with that of western researchers, such as Herbert Benson (1997), who study the blood pressure and brain waves of eastern ascetics. Such findings are useful, but obviously not the essence of mediation. Self-transformation is what makes psychoanalysis so difficult to convey to non-initiates, and the fear of an encounter with O is what makes the whole process vulnerable to dogmatic slumbers when the wish for certainty steps in at the point of unknowing and faith.

Bion's two theories of groups

After tours of duty at Northfield and Tavistock, Bion made a decided shift away from the practice of group psychotherapy to individual psychoanalysis. Nevertheless, he continued throughout his career to see the two disciplines as closely interrelated and referred to groups in his later writings, sometimes very caustically with an implicit critique of the crustacean resistances of groups, particularly the psychoanalytic establishment itself, to change. His skepticism about groups is an aristocratic one, and not unlike Plato's view that philosophers (Bion rather referred to 'geniuses' and 'messiahs') should run the city-state and are the best group leaders.

The group theory for which Bion is deservedly famous is that of the basic assumptions: dependency, fight/flight, and pairing (Bion 1974, pp.92–93). He considered that groups operate as if the members anonymously share certain beliefs which they then act upon. Furthermore, these assumptions are of a primitive, psychotic-like character, recapitulating the infant's relationship to the mother's breast (Bion 1959, p.127). Bion insightfully saw that group-as-a-whole phenomena have their own existence, irreducible to the psychology of the individuals who compose the group.

Later, in *Attention and Interpretation*, Bion proposed another vantage point which supplemented rather than contradicted the earlier one. This theory is about the relationship between the mystic and the group, or more generally about the group's difficulty assimilating genuinely new ideas. He relates this problem to the pairing assumption, in the sense that the group struggles with conception and birth and the hope it engenders, along with dread and an attempt to crush the feared development. Regarding the dynamic of hope mixed with fear, one is reminded both of Yeats' (1919) lines about the beast slouching towards Bethlehem, and T. S. Eliot's opening lines of *The Wasteland*, in which hope, memory, and desire are anticipated with anxiety. The archetypal instance of the group crushing a new idea and its representative (then assimilating them in a way that hardly resembles what was originally and uniquely stated) is, of course, Christ, and Bion suggestively uses the term 'messiah thoughts' for the new ideas that come into the group.

In what follows, I will try to show that Bion's epistemology influenced both theories, in a way that makes Bion's differences with other group theorists more comprehensible.

The basic assumption states

Bion's genius first showed itself in relationship to groups. Although, in *Experiences in Groups* (1959, p.21), he expressed skepticism about the curative power of groups, it was in fact Bion's exceptional ability to detach from the group which positioned him ideally to perceive its dynamics. When given the challenge of the Northfield experiment to conduct therapy groups of soldiers hospitalized for war neuroses, Bion manifested two unique abilities. One was the ability to intuit what Agazarian and Peters (1981) called the 'invisible group,' that is, the noumena of the group-as-a-whole as distinct from the visible manifestations of the individuals in the room. Bion (1959, pp.118–119) stated ironically that 'I attach no intrinsic importance to the coming together of the group', implying that the 'group' pre-exists as an idea and that its meeting only provides its manifestation as sense data. The second was his ability to detach sufficiently from both peer pressure and leadership countertransference, maintaining what Hinshelwood (1994) has called the reflective space, to perceive the maneuvers and strategies the group engaged in to avoid its task. Bion was thus able to establish agendas for group psychologists for decades to come, especially within the Tavistock and A. K. Rice traditions: namely, to study how groups and organizations work 'as a whole' with respect to their unconscious dynamics, and to interpret and work through resistances to carrying out the tasks of the group. In part, it may be that one of the reasons that Bion was able to identify group-as-a-whole processes was because, in keeping with Kant, he was not reifying the mind as something with a location 'in a body' as Freud and Klein had done. Klein had said, consistent with Freud's emphasis on biological drives, 'The infant is an intensely embodied person.' Bion might have said, by contrast, that 'The infant is an inchoate thing-in-itself seeking to be contained in a body *and* in a group.'

A brief comparison of Bion's approach with that of his contemporary, S. H. Foulkes, will suggest how epistemological assumptions affect and shed light upon group theory. The Tavistock approach sired by Bion and the others has existed side by side in England (and elsewhere) with the Group Analytic school of Foulkes for about half a century. (Their respective facilities are actually within walking distance of each other in London.) Some, like Malcolm Pines, Earl Hopper and Morris Nitsun have worked extensively within both approaches. Despite their common focus on group-qua-group dynamics, the differences between the two vantage points are striking. Pines (1982), for example, has pointed out the Foulkesian focus on the self and its place in the group, giving group analysis an affinity with Kohut's self psychology. Foulkes' school places much more emphasis than Bion on group development from a leader-centered to a democratically run process. Bion's sense of the group is that it is caught in a karmic cycle of regression and progression. (An excellent recent paper by Rubenfeld (2001) on 'complexity theory' suggests that Bion and Foulkes may each have seen but one part of the proverbial elephant: groups do evolve, but they don't evolve in a linear fashion, rather in unexpected jumps and 'cascades'.) Nitsun (1996) suggests that Bion's approach addresses the group's aggression and self-destructive impulses more thoroughly than Foulkes'. All these differences are based partly in the epistemological premises of the two approaches.

Foulkes was reared in the gestalt psychology school of Wertheimer in Germany (not to be confused with Fritz Perls' gestalt therapy.) Gestalt psychology emphasizes pattern perception and therefore has a link to the then emerging phenomenology of Edmund Husserl (Smith and Smith 1995). Phenomenology, in keeping with the Aristotelean as opposed to Platonic tradition, gives epistemic credence to experience as such, while applying rigorous 'corrections' to grasp the flow of experience independently of implicit assumptions and beliefs. Phenomenology-qua-method emphasizes the need to 'bracket' the cognitive and theoretical biases of the observer in order to get a 'pure' distillation of the experience itself. (De Maré 1972, p.154, and Foulkes and Anthony 1965, pp.157–185 describe the important role of phenomenology in Foulkes' approach.) Although Husserl was profoundly indebted to Kant, he dealt with the thing-in-itself or noumenon in an entirely different way from either Kant or the positivists. He assimilated it into the phenomenological world in ways that continue to interest and confound philosophers (Smith and Smith, 1995, pp.285–290).

The point here is that the phenomenological and gestalt perspectives tend to trust and encourage the self and its growth and development more than a perspective based on 'the thing-in-itself.' Carl Rogers (1961, 1992), for example, was a phenomenologically (and later, existentially) based psychotherapist who placed empathy and unconditional regard at the head of the list of therapist assets. Empathy is helpful in recognizing gestalt configurations occurring in the patient and the group. However, empathy can interfere with grasping the 'thoughts-without-a-thinker' which come into the group in a 'psychotic-like' way (beta elements) and that tend initially to interfere with group development.

Bion was never a nihilist, never – even in his most difficult life crises, of which he had several – a person without hope. However, neither was he an optimist about the human condition. Both the Kantian and mystical perspectives gave Bion an awareness of the great obstacles in the way of relinquishing memory and desire in order both to grasp the 'thing-in-itself' and to achieve the 'categorical imperative,' Kant's version of the golden rule in which one seeks to behave in such a way as to exemplify how all others should act. (Bion was never a relativist or an eclectic.) Basic assumption theory was his testament to the way groups are haunted by 'thoughts-without-a-thinker' and to the powerful resistances in the way of thought*ful*, morally concerned human dialogue and action in groups.

The relationship between the messiah and the establishment

In *Attention and Interpretation*, Bion proposed a second group theory which, however, has never been acknowledged as such. In this theory, he 'zooms in' on the pairing assumption, and finds within it a paradigmatic relationship between the individual and the group. Although he never explicitly refers to the story of Christ, the parallel is obvious. The hope of the group is actualized in the pair who produce a 'messiah,' whose role is to introduce a genuinely new idea into the group. Hartman and Gibbard (1974, pp.317–324) explored this aspect of the pairing assumption in terms of 'mystical fusion,' 'deification' and utopian fantasies. The new idea is then ambivalently received by the establishment (but of course often eventuates in a new, even more dogmatic establishment!). The subsequent development of the group is then a manifestation of the relationship between the new idea, its bearer, and the establishment, i.e. the group's traditional values and beliefs, as well as its basic assumption resistances to change.

The true messiah is, for Bion, the one who is able to exist in the absence of memory and desire long enough to have the genuinely new awareness. The establishment wants to avoid the dread and transformation implicit in this awesome proximity to O. Thus, the group dynamic evolves out of a dialectic between the noumena and the group's memory, desire, and understanding, between the fateful encounter with the 'O'ther versus the living and partly living of the Chorus of Eliot's (1980, p.214) *Murder in the Cathedral*.

Although Bion tends to place the burden of this transformation on the genius who is able to receive the new awareness, there is another way to view such a dialectic which is more consistent with Foulkes' notion of the group evolution to a democratic process. It is that the group members are also capable of transformation in O. We say that 'God is in our hearts,' which means we each have a touch of divine awareness, of mystical experience, so that members and the collective may be the bearers of new awareness as much as the leadership. Part of the group leader's task is to help the group to recognize and access these states (cf. Schermer 2001), so that Bion's view of 'messiah thoughts' is not incompatible with Foulkes' evolution of a democratic process, in that the group-as-a-whole can develop the capability to be the bearer of such insights.

Bion's relationship to Freud and Klein

Explicating Bion's relationship to Freud and Klein is a task that already has been undertaken by Meltzer (1978), the Symingtons (1996) and others. Here, I would like only to make a few comments relevant to the epistemological vertex.

Bion's work can be seen both as an extension of the work of Freud and Klein and a radical revolution in theory and practice. This 'binocular perspective' is not exclusively relevant to Bion's work. Lacan (1977), for example, re-cast Freud's writings in terms of the linguistics of Saussure. At the same time, he spearheaded the 'back to Freud' movement in France in that he tried to remain true to the most central tenets of the Freudian perspective. Kohut (1977) claimed a radical revision of Freud, but many of his ideas about narcissim were in fact richly anticipated by Freud (1914).

Bion was a student and analysand of Melanie Klein. He also lived over forty years of his life while Freud was alive. He was profoundly influenced by both, as well as their students at the British Psycho-Analytical Society. Eventually, he established himself as an independent thinker seeking a broader view that could encompass both but go well beyond them. With respect to Freud, Bion seemed more interested in the nature of a psychoanalytic session than in the particulars of Freud's theories. Bion rarely used Freudian concepts such as drives, repression, or psychic structure as such. Nevertheless, there are some striking parallels in Bion to Freud.

For example, Freud (1915) early suggested a notion of what he called 'primary repression.' These are instinctual contents that are built into the infant but are never accessible as such. The comparison of the primary repressed with noumena, O and beta elements, is inevitable. Freud's emphasis on dreams and psychoses as realms which infiltrate even 'normal' 'daytime' experience infuses everything Bion wrote. In Bion's Grid rows, preconception and conception, there are shades of Freud's notions, developed in his

pre-psychoanalytic work on aphasia (Greenberg 1997) of 'object presentations' and 'word presentations'. Bion seemed to allow himself to use what he
wanted from Freud and blissfully ignore the rest, a freedom of spirit that has
been pointed out by Hinshelwood (Bléandonu 1994, pp.ix–xii). He was
totally uninterested in Freudian dogma except perhaps as a social
phenomenon. He derived his rigor from the discipline of thought, not from a
point-by-point elaboration of his predecessors.

Paulo Sandler has recently written some important papers and a book
(2000) in which he takes a position contrary to the view that Freud was an
empiricist. He argues that, instead, Freud was steeped in Kantian philosophy
and that this is the basis of his discovery of the unconscious. Certainly, even
the distinction conscious/preconscious/unconscious echoes Kant's 'categories.' The radical hypothesis of Freud was that most of our mental life is inaccessible to our awareness, a view much more consistent with Kant's idea of the
mind as a filtering 'net' than Locke's notion of mind as a 'clean slate'. If
Sandler is right, then, in retrospect, Bion did not revise Freud, but rather
brought out what was already implicit in Freud. Bion, in a certain respect, gave
us a new reading of Freud.

Melanie Klein's ideas had a clear influence on Bion's early work, although
he later diverged from her, going on his own path, more as regards theory, I
suspect, than practice. Bion's notion of 'attacks on linking' clearly derives
from Klein's 'splitting.' Container/contained is a direct outgrowth of the
notion of projective identification. K-links is an extension of Klein's
'epistemophilic instinct.' $PS \leftrightarrow D$ is a different formulation of the
paranoid–schizoid and depressive positions, as oscillating states which persist
throughout life rather than the exclusive province of infantile development.
His focus on the individual patient, moving from group leadership to psychoanalysis, was probably influenced by Klein. He always held, with Klein, that
countertransference is an interference rather than a useful tool (1990b, p.122)
In effect, Bion's divergences from Klein are a prime example of his notion of
'projective' transformations (Bléandonu 1994, p.190). He took Kleinian
thought up one or two levels of abstraction and, by giving them increased
dimensionality and power, transformed them.

Melanie Klein's epistemology is obscure because, in principle at least, she
adopted Freud in entirety. However, she was a brilliant thinker in her own
right, and her frequent reference to Freud's notion of 'psychic reality' – an
inner world different from but related to the outer world – is not empirical,
but presumes a life, 'intensely embodied,' which is its own universe of

discourse. She was brought up in the heady intellectual atmosphere of *fin-de-siècle* Vienna, and must have been exposed to various philosophical trends that were developing then, for example, via her exposure to a group of intellectual friends of her brother, Emanuel (Grosskurth 1986, p.17). Her tendency to make direct interpretations of unconscious processes to both children and adults implies that she may have inutuitively felt these processes to be surprisingly transparent, the unconscious is everywhere, but we selectively inattend to it! In this respect, she could be regarded as a 'phenomenologist of the deep,' i.e., one who made explicit what our experience is/was like. This also seems to me to represent a feminist and a maternal perspective about knowing. A study of the philosophical premises implicit in Klein's work is much needed.

So we can see that Bion went back well before Freud, to Kant (and well before that to Plato and to Meister Eckhart and Isaac Luria, the mystics) to try to take psychoanalysis to a different place. He kept articulating, in effect, 'it looks like this (phenomena), but it isn't quite.' At one point (1990b, p.131), he noted that the ancient Greek astronomer, Aristarchus, presciently thought the earth revolved around the sun, despite the evidence of the senses, but that it took hundreds of years to develop the telescopes so that Galileo and Copernicus could prove it. He implied that psychoanalysis accesses events which we may only begin to understand decades or centuries hence, when we have the vocabulary and ideas to describe what we are today 'seeing' in the consulting room. Bion echoes, although from a vastly different vertex, Atwood and Stolorow's (1993) notion that psychoanalytic theories at present are not the result of objective science per se but rather intersubjective 'faces in a cloud' which reflect the theoreticians' own personalities. The debates about which school of psychoanalysis is correct must have seemed futile to Bion and more a reflection of the theorist's narcissism than the search for truth. At the same time, his broad vision of psychoanalysis is the highest praise one can give to Freud (and what Freud always said of himself) – that the founder courageously opened the door (and we have hardly begun to overcome our fear of walking inside!)

Summary, conclusions and a dream

What I have tried to suggest is that Bion's epistemological premises were the cornerstone of his clinical thinking, theorizing, and world view. He utilized philosophy in a systematic, coherent way, drawing on a serious interest in it. This opens him up to the criticism that, like the philosophers, he was speculating on shaky grounds, and that for scientists, it is better to 'stick with the facts.' However, it is my opinion that the most innovative scientists are philosophers at heart. Certainly this was true of the quantum physicists Mach and Heisenberg who explicitly wrote about philosophy. As for Einstein, he possessed the questioning attitude and logical rigor of philosophy, if not the knowledge of the field. An ur-philosopher, he used one or two pieces of data to reconceptualize all of physics. Similarly, there were a few 'selected facts,' not reams of data, which guided Bion in his reconceptualization of psycho-analysis.

The most important philosophical underpinning of Bion's thought is the Kantian notion of the noumenon, which he linked to the unconscious. However, he drew on other philosophers to elucidate specific points. It is interesting to consider whether he used Kant's philosophy as a 'model' for psychology, something which rankles most philosophers, or whether he was not just transposing Kantian ideas but rather elucidating them. We need a philosopher to read Bion and give us his or her answer to this question.

Most importantly, Bion firmly held to the position consistent with Kant that the 'noumenon,' the knowledge we are seeking, is ultimately unknowable. But he is clear that without pursuing the thing-in-itself we are treading on thin ice. Eventually, he came to believe that unknowability is a reflection of the infinitude, the spontaneous, the chaotic, and the catastrophic in the psyche. At that point, he needed the mystics more than the logicians to articulate his position.

While writing this chapter, I had a dream, which I realized upon awakening was related to what I was writing. In the dream:

> I am at a seaside resort in England with a colleague. The weather is inclement, and we are walking along a sandy beachfront. A huge riptide threatenens to engulf the beach and all who are on it. Somehow, everyone is spared. We go up on a walkway and head towards a wooden cabin at the end of the beach. The cabin has a porch and there is a bulletin board announcing lectures. We are going to hear a lecture on the basic assumptions and the Northfield Experiment by someone who worked there with Bion.

Although the dream could be called an 'anxiety dream' which has certain meanings for me in terms of my 'personal unconscious,' it also seems to me to be an allegory about this chapter. (Not incidentally, Brighton is a seaside town in England, and I grew up in Brighton Beach, in Brooklyn, NY, USA – and Brighton contains the letters B-I-O-N in proper order!) I associated to the beach something opposite to the stormy weather and the tide, namely Winnicott's serene quote from Rabindranath Tagore: 'On the seashores of endless worlds, children play.' Winnicott and Bion were both interested in the spontaneous emergence of creativity from the deep unconscious. For Winnicott, although he was quite aware of the relationship between creativity and destruction, maternal holding and the transitional object, gave this emergence manageability and joy. For Bion, the encounter with O can be stormy and dangerous, like a rip tide, a view which is profoundly articulated by Eigen (1998, pp.61–79). We can see too that O is somehow related to the primal mother, the 'O'cean, and of course both Winnicott and Bion were aware of the connection between the maternal object, the group, and the unconscious, O.

The lecture in the cabin reminded me of a time some years ago when Harold Bridger came to Philadelphia to give a talk on the Northfield Experiment, and, as was characteristic of Bridger's great civility, gave a balanced but realistic portrayal of the differences between Foulkes, Bion, and some of the others who conducted groups there. Here we see the potential for rational discourse versus the way of a direct encounter with O, the experience-in-itself. Here, Bion perhaps returns as the 'O'cean, reminding us about the 'void and formless infinite' that is at the root of our various cogitations.

References

Agazarian, Y. and Peters, R. (1981) *The Visible and Invisible Group*. London: Routledge and Kegan Paul.

Allison, H. E. (1983) *Kant's Transcendental Idealism: An Interpretation and Defense*. New Haven: Yale University Press.

Amacher, P. (1965) 'Freud's neurological education and its influence on psychoanalytic theory.' *Psychological Issues 4*, 4, Monograph 16. New York: International Universities Press.

Atwood, G. and Stolorow, G. (1993) *Faces in a Cloud: Intersubjectivity in Personality Theory*. Northvale: Jason Aronson.

Benson, H. (with Stark, M., contributor) (1997) *Timeless Healing : The Power and Biology of Belief*. Minneapolis: Fireside.

Bion, W. R. (1959) *Experiences in Groups*. London: Tavistock. (New York: Ballantine Books, 1974.)

Bion, W. R. (1970) *Attention and Interpretation*. London: Tavistock.

Bion, W. R. (1977) *Two Papers: The Grid and Caesura*. Rio de Janeiro: Imago Editora.

Bion, W. R. (1990a) *A Memoir of the Future*. London: Karnac Books.

Bion, W. R. (1990b) *Brazilian Lectures.* London: Karnac Books.

Bion, W. R. (1992) *Cogitations.* London: Karnac Books.

BION97@LISTSERVER.SICAP.IT: 'The W. R. Bion Past and Future Mailing List.'

Bléandonu, G. (1994) *Wilfred Bion: His Life and Work: 1897–1979.* London: Free Association Books; New York: Guilford Publications.

Coltart, N. (1992) *Slouching towards Bethlehem.* New York: The Guilford Press.

De George, R. and De George, F. (1972) *The Structuralists from Marx to Levi-Strauss.* Garden City: Anchor Books (Doubleday).

De Maré, P. B. (1972) *Perspectives in Group Psychotherapy: A Theoretical Background.* New York: Science House, Inc.

Eigen, M. (1998) *The Psychoanalytic Mystic.* London: Free Association Books.

Eliot, T. S. (1980) *The Complete Poems and Plays: 1909–1950.* New York: Harcourt Brace and Company.

Epstein, M. (1996) *Thoughts Without a Thinker : Psychotherapy from a Buddhist Perspective.* New York: HarperCollins.

Epstein, M. (1998) *Going to Pieces without Falling Apart.* New York: Broadway Books.

Foulkes, S. H. (1973) Group Psychotherapy: The Psychoanalytic Approach. Harmondsworth: Penguin.

Foulkes, S. H. and Anthony, E. J. (1965) *Group Psychotherapy: The Psychoanalytic Approach.* Harmondsworth: Penguin.

Freud, S. (1895) 'Project for a scientific psychology.' In S. Freud (1954) *The Origins of Psychoanalysis: Letters to Wilhelm Fleiss, Drafts, and Notes: 1887–1902.* New York: Basic Books.

Freud, S. (1913) 'Papers on technique: Recommendations to physicians practising psychoanalysis.' In J. Strachey (transl., ed) *The Standard Edition of the Complete Psychological Works of Sigmund Freud.*London: The Hogarth Press and the Institute of Psycho-Analysis, 1958, 12.

Freud, S. (1914) 'On narcissm: An introduction.' In J. Strachey (transl., ed.) *The Standard Edition of the Complete Psychological Works of Sigmund Freud.* London: The Hogarth Press and the Institute of Psycho-Analysis, 1958, 14.

Freud, S. (1915) 'Papers on metapsychology: repression.' In J. Strachey (transl. ed) *The Standard Edition of the Complete Psychological Works of Sigmund Freud.* London: The Hogarth Press and the Institute of Psycho-Analysis, 1958, 14.

Freud, S. (1954) *The Origins of Psychoanalysis: Letters to Wilhelm Fleiss, Drafts, and Notes: 1887–1902.* New York: Basic Books.

Greenberg, V. D. (1997) *Freud and his Aphasia Book: Language and the Sources of Psychoanalysis.* Ithaca, NY: Cornell University Press.

Grosskurth, P. (1986) *Melanie Klein: Her World and Her Work.* New York: Alfred A. Knopf.

Grotstein, J. S. (ed.) (1981) *Do I Dare Disturb the Universe?* Beverly Hills: Caesura Press.

Grotstein, J. S. (1997) 'Bion's "transformation in 'O'" and the concept of the "transcendent position".' Presented at W. R. Bion: Past, Present, and Future. Conference held at Torino, Italy. Draft of paper available on the worldwide web at: http://www.sicap.it/~merciai/papers/grots.htm (Accessed January 28, 2001).

Grotstein, J. S. (2000) *Who is the Dreamer Who Dreams the Dream?* Hillsdale, NJ: The Analytic Press.

Hartman, J. J. and Gibbard, J. S. (1974) 'A note on fantasy themes in the evolution of group culture.' In J. S. Gibbard, J. J. Hartman and R. D. Mann *Analysis of Groups*. San Francisco: Jossey-Bass.

Heidegger, M. (1962) (Originally published in 1927) *Being and Time*. Third edition. Translated by J. Macquarrie and E. Robinson. San Francisco: Harper Collins.

Hinshelwood, R. (1994) 'Attacks on the reflective space: Containing primitive emotional states.' In V. L. Schermer and M. Pines , (eds) *Ring of Fire*. London: Routledge.

Kohut, H. (1977) *The Restoration of the Self.* New York: International Universities Press.

Kuhn, A. B. (2001) 'Sex as symbol: The ancient light in modern psychology.' Available at http://downloads.members.tripod.com/pc93/sexzsmbl.htm (Accessed January 28, 2001).

Lacan, J. (1977) *Ecrits: A Selection*, transl. A. Sheridan. New York: Norton.

Matte-Blanco, I. (1975) *The Unconscious as Infinite Sets: An Essay in Bi-logic.* London: Duckworth.

Meissner, W. W. (1995) *Thy Kingdom Come: Psychoanalytic Perspectives on the Messiah and the Millennium.* Barnhart, MO: Theological Book Service.

Meltzer, D. (1978) *The Kleinian Development.* Perthshire, Scotland: The Clunie Press.

Merleau-Ponty, M. (1945) *Phénoménologie de la Perception.* Paris: NRF Gallimard.

Milner, M. (1957) *On Not Being Able to Paint.* New York: International Universities Press (Reprinted 1979).

Milner, M. (1987) *The Suppressed Madness of Sane Men.* London: Tavistock.

Nitsun, M. (1996) *The Anti-Group.* London: Routledge.

Pines, M. (1982) 'On mirroring in group psychotherapy.' *Group Therapy Monograph No. 9*, New York: Washington Square Institute.

Reik, T. (1948) *Listening with the Third Ear.* New York: Farrar, Straus & Co.

Rogers, C. R. (1961) *On Becoming a Person.* Boston: Houghton Mifflin.

Rogers, C. R. (1992) 'The necessary and sufficient conditions of therapeutic personality change.' *Journal of Consulting and Clinical Psychology 60*, 827–832.

Rubenfeld, S. (2001) 'On complexity theory in group psychotherapy.' In F. Wright (ed) Special issue on 'Contemporary Theoretical Developments and the Implications for Group Psychotherapy.' *International Journal of Group Psychotherapy 51*, 4, 449–72.

Sandler, P. (2000) *Origens da Psicanálise na Obra de Kant*, Rio de Janeiro: Imago Editora.

Schermer, V. L. (1999) 'To know a mind: Freud, Oedipus, and epistemology.' *Psychoanalytic Studies 1*, 2, pp.191–210.

Schermer, V. L. (2001) 'The group psychotherapist as contemporary mystic: A Bionic object relations perspective.' In F. Wright (ed) Special issue on 'Contemporary Theoretical Developments and the Implications for Group Psychotherapy.' *International Journal of Group Psychotherapy 51, 4*.

Segal, H. (1981) 'A psychoanalytic approach to the treatment of psychosis.' In Segal, H. *The Work of Hanna Segal: A Kleinian Approach to Clinical Practice.* New York: Jason Aronson.

Smith, B. and Smith, D. W. (eds) (1995) *The Cambridge Companion to Husserl.* Cambridge: Cambridge University Press.

Stolorow, R. D., Atwood, G. E., and Brandchaft, B. (eds.) (1994) *The Intersubjective Perspective.* Northvale: Aronson.

Symington, J. and Symington, N. (1996) *The Clinical Thinking of Wilfred Bion.* London: Routledge.

Turner, W. (1911) 'Plato and Platonism.' Available on the World Wide Web at: http://www.newadvent.org/cathen/12159a.htm (published 1999; accessed January 28, 2001).

Wittgenstein, L. (1953) *Philosophical Investigations*. eds. G. E. M. Anscome, and R. Rhees, transl. G. E. M. Anscome. Oxford: Blackwell.

Wittgenstein, L. (1961) *Tractatus Logico-Philosophicus*. (transl. D. F. Pears, and B. F. McGuinness). London: Routledge and Kegan Paul.

Wolf, E. S. (1988) *Treating the Self*. New York: Guilford.

Yeats, W. B. (1919) 'The Second Coming.' In *Collected Poems*. New York: Macmillan, 1950.

Endnotes

1. The author would like to thank Paolo Sandler MD for his erudite and detailed comment and critique of a draft of this chapter.

2. The existential playwright, Samuel Beckett, was one of Bion's early patients, and certainly *A Memoir of the Future*, if not some of Bion's other works, seem to parallel the 'theater of the absurd' for which Beckett was known.

3. The logical positivists understood Kant to mean that these propositions and categories were considered by him to be 'absolute' and uncontradictable. Modern physics, of course, led by Einstein, devastated the categories of space and time as they were understood by Kant and his contemporaries. Some Kantian scholars propose that Kant did not hold such a rigid position.

4. 'Non-sensible' means 'not described in terms of the perceptions of the senses.' Thus, for example, one 'sees' a 'triangle' that the teacher draws on the blackboard. What one 'sees' is a configuration of white marks on a black background which forms a discernible pattern. But to a mathematician, a triangle is defined in terms of logical axioms which are not 'visible' as such. Similarly, a 'screen memory' would include sensory images, but the repressed memory of which it is a derivative is 'known' by intuition and logic, not by sense memories. Thus, the deep unconscious consists of noumena, rather than phenomena. This was one of Bion's key points.

5. Bion (1992, p.315) includes 'understanding' as an additional obstacle to the listening process. Describing such interferences, he states 'These are memory, desire, and understanding. All are opacities obstructing "intuition."' 'Memory and desire' can thus be understood as a 'shorthand' for all mental processes which produce perturbations. This is remarkably similar to the Zen Buddhist notion of 'no mind.'

10

Bion and Foulkes on Empathy

Malcolm Pines

What therapeutic significance was placed on empathy by these two great pioneers of group analysis?

First: Foulkes' paper 'My Philosophy in Psychotherapy' (1974), written not long before his death in 1976. (I was present at his death which occurred while he was taking a group in a very hot summer when he clearly should have been resting: he died in the service of his art and science.)

> Undoubtedly we need to have the capacity for empathy with our fellow humans. We are involved far more than we usually know; too much so, perhaps. The idea of this empathy comes from a certain philosophical attitude, by seeing things in proportion, as part of the human problem in which we are all continuously involved. With that capacity and with maturity we can retain a certain necessary detachment, despite all empathy; these do not need to be in opposition to each other. The good therapist should, at the same time, be above the situation. Such an attitude will make it easier to see both the tragedy and the comedy of human existence, see the absurdity in certain respects. It allows a feeling for a sense of humour; if we have that, we are not merely better off ourselves, but also in our function as therapists. In this way our work becomes more interesting, more satisfactory and more effective for our patients. (Foulkes 1974, p.280)

In an earlier passage in that same paper he writes:

> the true therapist has, I believe, a creative function – in a way like an artist, in a way like a scientist, in a way like an educator... I have sometimes compared this function with that of a poet, especially in conducting a group. By this I mean the therapist's receptiveness, his ability to see a bit better, a bit deeper, a bit sooner than others, what his patients are really saying, or

wanting or fearing; to help them to express this and sometimes, though rarely, to express it for them. (Foulkes 1974, p.279)

Here Foulkes illustrates what I call the passive feminine aspect of empathy, the opening of self to other. There is much else in this paper, in which he brings together his 40 years of experience as a psychoanalyst and group analyst. To my mind some other passages converge with fundamental aspects of Bion's conceptions. 'I think that the real nature of mind lies in each individual's need for communication and reception, in every sense of the term.' He writes about language which in each individual is what goes on in his 'own' mind, but at the same time it is a shared property of the group; the individual is forced into language from the beginning by the surrounding culture. But as well as by the use of language, individuals communicate without knowing it, through unconscious processes that are between them, which permeate each individual, 'transpersonal processes'. 'Just as a mind is shared, so is what is social, not outside; but deep inside the person, as well' (*ibid.*).

Clearly we need a deep study of similarities and differences between the fundamental concepts of Foulkes and of Bion. Hopefully some of these may be explored in this book.

Now I turn to Bion. Interestingly, there are no entries in the indices for empathy, so I extended my search to include sympathy and compassion, which are different but related concepts. I found two very interesting contributions, both included in *Cogitations* (Bion 1992). On 11 February 1960 Bion writes on compassion and truth (Bion 1992, p.125):

1. Compassion and Truth are both senses of man.

2. Compassion is a feeling that he needs to express. It is an impulse he must experience in his feelings for others.

3. Compassion is likewise something that he needs to feel in the attitudes of others towards him.

4. Truth is something man needs to express; it is something he needs to seek and to find; it is essential for fulfilment of his curiosity.

5. Truth is something he needs to feel in the attitudes of others towards him.

6. Truth and compassion are also qualities pertaining to the relationship that the man establishes with people and things.

7. A man may feel he lacks the capacity for love.

8. A man may lack the capacity for love.

9. Similarly, he may feel he lacks a capacity for truth, either to hear it, or to seek it, or to find it, or to communicate it, or to desire it.

10. He may in fact lack such a capacity.

11. The lack may be primary or secondary, and may diminish truth or love, or both.

12. Primary lack is inborn and cannot be remedied; yet some of the consequences may be modified analytically.

13. Secondary lack may be due to fear or hate or envy or love. Even love can inhibit love.

14. Applying 8. and 10. to the Oedipus Myth, the death of the Sphinx is a consequence of such lack, as the question posed was not intended to elicit truth, and consideration for itself could not exist to erect a barrier against self-destruction. Tiresias may be said to lack compassion less than regard for truth. Oedipus lacked compassion for himself more than he lacked regard for truth.

Bion is invoking the essential qualities in human relations of reciprocity and intersubjectivity. I am moved by this passage, by the counterpoint between truth and compassion.

Though neither Foulkes nor Bion seems to have read much of each other's writings, I believe that Foulkes would have had no problem accepting this thesis. Incidentally, though we know that Foulkes had read *Experiences in Groups*, Sutherland (1985/2000) to whom I shall refer shortly, writes that he never heard Bion discuss Foulkes in his presence.

Bion writes of the essential presence of sympathy in human experience in a passage in *Cogitations*, a paragraph headed 'Concern for Truth and Life':

By 'Concern' I mean something that has innate feelings of consideration for the object, of sympathy with it, of value for it. The person who has concern for truth or for life is impelled to a positive, not merely passive, relationship with both... Concern for life does not mean only a wish not to kill, though it does mean that. It means concern for an object precisely because that object has the quality of being alive... It means being curious about the qualities that go to make up what we know as life, and to have a desire to understand them. Finally, concern for life means that a person must have respect for himself in his qualities as a living object. Lack of concern means lack of respect for himself, and a fortiori, of others, which is fundamental and of proportionately grave import for analysis. (Bion 1992 p.247)

These passages in which Bion writes about concern, compassion and sympathy, can be related to empathy.

So, now to empathy. The Norwegian philosopher Vetlesen (1994) writes: 'Empathy is anchored in a deep-seated human faculty, one disposing a subject to develop concern for others (vide Bion, footnote). Hence, empathy is reduceably *other*-regarding or -directed; whereas there is such a thing as self-pity or self-love, there is no self-empathy.[1] Vetlesen goes on:

> In empathy there is always a thou, never only a me. Empathy sets up, indeed helps produce and sustain, a relation, the *between* or *zwischen*, involving subjects relating to another; its locus is the interpersonal as distinct from the intrapersonal. It is by virtue of this faculty that I can put myself in the place of the other by way of a feeling-into and a feeling-with. (Vetlesen 1994, p.8)

Empathy not only turns on the ability to see, it also requires an ability to listen. Both seeing and listening mean paying attention to. They are characteristics of what might generally be called attentiveness. Perception always requires attentiveness, attentiveness is made possible by receptivity, by the capacity to view oneself as 'addressed' by some situational incident.

In writing about addressing or being addressed I am reminded of the Russian philosopher Bakhtin's emphasis on speech communication as being that which addresses the other or through which one is addressed. In a sense one is clothed by the attention, perception and words of the other.

I searched through James Grotstein's *Do I Dare Disturb the Universe?* (1981) for any mention of empathy. So far I have found it only in Grotstein's own chapter and that by Frances Tustin.

Grotstein writes:

> Bion emphasised the importance of the self, of the need for the self to have an empathic relationship by the self for itself, and believed that there must also be an object whose empathic containment of the self is of vital importance for the infant's welfare. Bion was therefore the first Kleinian to give metapsychological enfranchisement to the independent importance of an unempathic (non-containing) external reality. I shall never forget an interpretation he gave me once in my own analysis which began somewhat as follows, 'you are the most important person you are ever likely to meet; therefore it is of no small importance that you get on well with this important person'. (Grotstein 1981, p.33)

So here Grotstein is linking containment with empathy, which is an interesting subject to be explored. As this containment is not passive but active, responding sensitively and appropriately to the infant's needs, this is both empathy and sympathy, the action of being with the other.

To turn to Tustin: frequently she uses the term empathy in describing very early states of mind and with pathological states of mind present in autism. She states that Bion has added to her understanding of early infancy by drawing attention to the mother's capacity for empathic reflection, for which she uses the apt term of 'reverie'. Through reverie the newborn infant is sheltered in what might be termed the 'womb' (Tustin 1981, p.185) of the mother's mind just as much as, prior to her physical birth, she was sheltered within the womb of her body. Tustin uses the concept of 'flowing-over' as the process by which the illusion of 'primal unity' is maintained. Tustin distinguishes between the 'softness' of primal unity and the 'hardness' of two-ness if the loss of the state of primal oneness has been experienced too early, harshly, suddenly.

Tustin also evokes the empathic process when she describes what she calls 'ecstasy'. (Tustin 1981, p.191). Ecstasy arises from states of intense excitement which are beyond the infant's capacity to bear and process alone. 'If the mother cannot hold the infant together in these intense states of excitement and cannot seem to bear the "overflow", and process it by empathy and understanding, the infant experiences a precocious sense of "two-ness" which seems fraught with disaster.' Then the infant feels adrift and alone and seeks pathologically to reinstate the sense of oneness. This leads to states of confusion with the maternal object.

In working with psychotic children Tustin attempts to describe elemental depths and elemental terrors as parts of everyone's infantile experiences through which we are psychologically born through being 'borne', that is carried, by maternal reverie and sympathy.

I raised the question of Bion's attitude to empathy with my co-editor Robert Lipgar; his opinion is that 'Bion was keen on individuation, adaptation to reality, working towards learning and knowing which could approximate Truth and Reality and not very impressed with empathy. His interest was in how we think, how we learn, how we know'.

Again, what now of sympathy? (See Wispe 1986.) The scope of sympathy must be greater than that of love for the other; it rests on empathy which can be directed to persons who are not unique to us, not only our loved ones, but to those whom we do not love. Sympathy is facilitated by the basic faculty of relating to others, which is empathy. Sympathy has a larger audience than the narrow circle of family and friends. The chief challenge to sympathy is indifference, which has often been described as being the opposite of love.

Sympathy as an essential feature of social animals, such as mankind, is receiving much attention in evolutionary psychology, as exemplified by the study of chimpanzee groups by Franz de Waal. De Waal (1996), one of the world's leading primatologists, writes that it is hard to imagine human morality without the following tendencies and capacities found also in other species.

Sympathy is shown when animals give care to or provide relief to distressed or endangered individuals other than progeny: this is called 'succorance behaviour'. If we, or animals, are vicariously affected by someone else's feelings and situation, we are being sympathetic and this behaviour is shown in the individualised bonding, affection and fellowship of many mammals and birds. Animals are attached by emotional bonds, exhibit emotional contagion – they are affected by the emotions of others – and this leads to caring behaviour, to 'cognitive altruism', behaviour in the interests of others. 'Despite its fragility and selectivity, the capacity to care for others is a bedrock of our moral system, which functions to protect and nurture the caring capacity' (Sutherland 1985/2000, p.88).

The other biological essentials for the social life of primates and ourselves are: internalisation of social rules; reciprocity; the capacity for 'getting along together'. The capacity to care for others is manifested through empathic understanding and sympathetic actions.

Both Bion and Foulkes view the process of psychotherapy as ways of helping persons to discover the truth about themselves. When we look at the group situation, Bion's thrust is that the uncovering of primitive regressive defences, the basic assumptions, releases the individual's capacity to work towards higher levels of understanding, understanding-in-the-moment of truth. The therapist's task ends with establishing that capacity. His long-time friend and colleague J. D. Sutherland wrote that Bion was an extremely caring person, but that he was not sympathetic or empathic towards the person's struggle to maintain a sense of safety of the self, the self imperilled by exposure to the group situation. Sutherland does not make direct comparisons between the approaches of Bion and Foulkes, but what he does write is: 'Foulkes was convinced total group interactions had to be used in therapy, and I believe that Bion, had he done more group therapeutic work, would have accepted that position, though he would have insisted on what might be loosely put, as more rigour and more depth, more attention to the primitive relationships'. (Sutherland 1985/2000, p.83).

By 'total group interactions' I believe that Sutherland is referring to mirroring, resonance and the other factors which Foulkes described as group-specific. It is through such processes that persons come more deeply to recognise the truth about themselves through their work with others, through being seen, and seeing denied, split-off, unwanted parts of the self in others; accepting the vision of others about hidden aspects of the self which come to the fore in the interactions within the group situation.

Deception is usually quickly uncovered (de Waal 1996, p.75). We can see through the defences of others in ways in which we cannot see within ourselves. This has a direct impact upon defensive narcissism, the arrogance that Bion wrote about. Group therapy is in many ways a humbling experience, recognising how much we are made of common stuff, stuff that we hold in common with others, basic earthy material. Bion wrote about the importance of acquiring 'common sense', that is all the senses working together to create a sense of unity and integration of the self. The capacity for detecting cheating is again a biological given (de Waal 1982, 1996); cooperation in groups, from primates upwards, necessitates the capacity to detect cheating for otherwise the cheat would obtain unfair advantage from the labours of others. This form of detection is more intuitive than empathic; intuition leads to immediate grasp of the reality of a situation, whereas empathy is a much less immediate process. Kohut emphasized that prolonged empathic immersion in the experience of the other is the main tool of psychoanalytic understanding, which is why the analytic process is so lengthy. If intuition was all that we needed to understand the other person and to translate understanding into action, therapy could be almost instantaneous.

As group members begin to recognise the truthful similarities and differences between themselves and the others, they can begin to appreciate the complexity of personality, to see what is similar and what is different in the other person(s). This inevitably counters the primitive defences of splitting and projection which lead to other persons being perceived as similar to oneself or totally dissimilar. This occurs particularly in inter-group conflicts when groups draw together to create a common identity that gives them a sense of strength and righteousness, which inevitably leads to the other group being seen as dangerously dissimilar and a threat to security. This is a powerful force in ethnic, political and religious conflicts, but when persons can recognise similarities and dissimilarities within their own group, and break down stereotypes of what they see in other groups, then progress can be made in reducing inter-group conflict. Both Bion and Foulkes would have wanted their work to lead in that direction. In the sphere of international tensions the psychoanalyst Vamik Volkan (1997) has done very interesting work in the reduction of ethnic tension through group programmes that involve disputants, such as Greek and Turkish Cypriots, Israelis and Arabs, Russians and Estonians. My friend and colleague Patrick de Maré (1990) has led the way in the use of median groups which enable persons to progress towards a fuller sense of citizenship and an overcoming of primitive prejudices.

I am trying to show how we can make use of the insights of both Bion and Foulkes to create two vectors which have points of convergence and which help us to uncover the deeper truths which groups so often try to hide from themselves. The place of empathy, sympathy, compassion and pity continue to call for our attention. Human beings are capable of experiencing and acting upon those feelings; we also are capable of anihilating those feelings with the result that we become inhumane, arrogant, capable of horrific actions towards others whom we cease to regard as in any way being of the same common stuff as ourselves. Bion's experiences in WWI immersed him in the horrors of front-line warfare and he never ceased to draw on his experience in his exploration of primitive psychic processes. Foulkes did not undergo such trauma as he was behind the lines in his post as a telephonist.

I speculate that the differences in their war-time experiences are of significance for their contrasting explorations of individuals and groups. Farhad Dalal (1998) has also suggested that Foulkes had unconsciously to hide from himself the full impact of his flight from Nazi Germany in 1933 and the increasing psychic trauma of the increasing persecution of Jews which led to the Final Solution of the Shoah.

References

Bion W. M. (1992) *Cogitations*. London: Karnac Books.

Dalal, F. (1998) *Taking the Group Seriously*. London: Jessica Kingsley Publishers.

de Maré P., Piper R. and Thompson S. (1990) *Koinonia*. London. Karnac Books.

de Waal, F. (1982) *Chimpanzee Politics*. Baltimore: John Hoplain's University Press.

de Waal F. (1996) *Good Natured. The Origins of Right and Wrong in Humans and Other Animals*. Cambridge: Harvard University Press.

Foulkes S. H. (1974) 'My philosophy in psychotherapy.' In *Selected Papers. Psychoanalysis and Group Analysis*. London: Karnac Books.

Grotstein J. S. (1981) 'Wilfred Bion: The Man, the Psychoanalyst, the Mystic. A Perspective on his Life and Work.' In J. S. Grotstein (ed) *Do I Dare Disturb the Universe?* Beverley Hills: Caesura Press.

Sutherland J. D. (1985/2000) 'Bion revisited: Group dynamics and group psychotherapy.' In M. Pines (ed.) *Bion and Group Psychotherapy*. London: Routledge, republished. Jessica Kingsley Publishers.

Tustin F. (1981) 'Psychological birth and psychological catastrophe.' In J. S. Grotstein op.cit.

Vetlesen A. J. (1994) *Perception, Empathy, and Judgement*. Pennsylvania State University Press.

Volkan V. D. (1997) *Bloodlines: From Ethnic Pride to Ethnic Terrorism*. New York: Farrar, Strauss & Siroux.

Wispe L. (1986) 'The distinction between sympathy and empathy: To call forth a concept, word is needed.' *Journal of Personality and Social Psychology 50*, 2, 314–21.

Endnote

1.   James Grotstein (1981) would not agree with this as he has written on self-empathy, and in this I agree with him. Vetlesen does not take account of the world of inner objects.

The Contributors

Dennis Brown is a psychoanalyst and group analyst at the Institute of Group Analysis, London and formerly Consultant Psychotherapist at St. Mary's Hospital and Medical School, London. He is co-author of *Introduction to Psychotherapy* (1979, with Jonathan Pedder; 1981; 2000, with Anthony Bateman) and co-author of *Psyche and Social World* (with Louis Zinkin; published by Jessica Kingsley Publishers, 2000).

James S. Grotstein is Clinical Professor of Psychiatry at the UCLA School of Medicine and a training and supervising analyst at the Los Angeles Psychoanalytic Institute and the Psychoanalytic Center of California, Los Angeles. He is the author of over two hundred published articles and eight books. His most recently published book is *Who Is the Dreamer Who Dreams the Dream?: A Study of Psychic Presences* (Analytic Press, 2000).

Robert Hinshelwood is Professor at the Centre for Psychoanalytic Studies, University of Essex, UK. He was previously Clinical Director at The Cassel Hospital and past Chair at the Association of Therapeutic Communities. He is also a member of the British Psychoanalytical Society and a Fellow at the Royal College of Psychiatrists.

Earl Hopper is a psychoanalyst, group analyst and organizational consultant in private practice in London, where he is Honorary Tutor at the Tavistock NHS Portman Clinic. He is also on the Faculty of the Post-Doctoral Program in Group Psychotherapy at Adelphi University in the USA. He is a Past President of the International Association of Group Psychotherapy, Past Chairman of the Group of Independent Psychoanalysts of the British Psychoanalytical Society, and a Fellow of the American Group Psychotherapy Association. His most recently published books are *The Social Unconscious: Selected Papers* and *Traumatic Experience in the Unconscious Life of Groups* (Jessica Kingsley Publishers, 2003).

Robert M. Lipgar, Ph.D., ABPP, is a clinical psychologist in private practice and Clinical Professor in the Department of Psychiatry at The University of Chicago. He is a Fellow in the A.K. Rice Institute for the Study of Social Systems and a Life Fellow in the American Group Psychotherapy Association.

Claudio Neri, M.D., has been deeply involved in group psychotherapy from the beginning of his career. His meeting with Wilfred R. Bion and contacts with his work have been of paramount importance for him in the development of personal ideas which are synthesized in *Group* (Jessica Kingsley Publishers, 1998). He is also co-editor of *Dreams in Group Psychotherapy: Theory and Technique* (with Robi Friedman and Malcolm Pines; published by Jessica Kingsley Publishers, 2001).

Malcolm Pines is a Founder Member of the Institute of Group Analysis, London, Past President of the International Association of Group Psychotherapy and a former consultant at The Cassel, St George's and Maudsley Hospitals and the Tavistock Clinic. His is Past President of the Group-Analytic Society and Editor of the *International Library of Group Analysis*, author of *Circular Reflections: Selected Papers on Group Analysis and Psycho-analysis* (1998) and co-editor of *Dreams in Group Psychotherapy: Theory and Technique* (with Robi Friedman and Claudio Neri, 2001) both published by Jessica Kingsley Publishers.

Paulo Cesar Sandler, M.D., M.Sc (Med), is a psychiatrist (AMB) and a training analyst at the Sociedade Brasileira de Psicanálise de São Paulo. He is also Past Director of the Mental Health Program at the Faculdade de Saúde Pública, Professor at the Instituto de Psicologia da Universidade de São Paulo where he specializes in the work of Bion and psychoanalytic psychotherapy, and an Honorary Member of F.A.B. (Brazilian Air Force). He has translated Bion's later works, including the first foreign version (Portuguese) of *A Memoir of the Future, Bion in New York and São Paulo, Four Talks with W. R. Bion, Cogitations* (with his wife, Dr Ester Hadassa Sandler) and the short papers as well as a revised edition of Bion's four basic books. He has authored papers and books on extensions of Bion's theory of alpha-function, links and dreams, including *An Introduction to 'A Memoir of the Future'* and *A Apreensão da Realidade Psíquica* (Imago Editura, 1997–2003), a transdisciplinary work in ten volumes that researches the origins of psychoanalysts and its scientific foundations.

Matias Sanfuentes is a psychologist and psychotherapist for both individuals and groups. He is currently a PhD candidate at the Centre for Psychoanalytic Studies, University of Essex. He is Full Member of the Associación Chilena de Psicoterapia Analítica de Grupo and a Member of the Federación Latinoamericana de Psicoterapia Analítica de Grupo (FLAPAG).

Victor L. Schermer, M.A., C.A.C., C.G.P., is a psychologist and psychoanalytic therapist in private practice and clinic settings in Philadelphia. He is Director of the Study Group for Contemporary Psychoanalytic Process and a Clinical Member of the American Group Psychotherapy Association. He has published several books and numerous articles on group psychotherapy and other subjects. Since 1975, he has maintained a special interest in object relations theory, self psychology and, in particular, the work of Bion. He is the author of *Spirit and Psyche* (Jessica Kingsley Publishers).

Nuno Torres is a psychologist and Ph.D. student at the Centre for Psychoanalytic Studies, University of Essex, UK. He has been conducting research on Bion's concept of 'group diseases', applied to addictions, psychosomatics and suicide. He is a member in training of the International Society for Bonding Psychotherapy and a member of the Group-Analytic Society (London). In 2001 he co-edited with J. Paulo Ribeiro the book *A Pedra e o Charco* (Lisbon: Iman Editions), a biopsychosocial approach to substance abuse in Portugal.

Subject Index

Author Index